✔ KU-415-569

Also by Jilly Cooper

FICTION
  Riders
  Rivals
  Polo
  The Man Who Made Husbands Jealous
  Appassionata
  Score!

NON-FICTION
  Animals in War
  How to Survive Christmas
  Hotfoot to Zabriskie Point (with Patrick Lichfield)
  Intelligent and Loyal
  Jolly Marsupial
  Jolly Super
  Jolly Super Too
  Super Cooper
  Super Jilly
  Super Men and Super Women
  The Common Years
  Turn Right at the Spotted Dog
  Work and Wedlock
  Angels Rush In
  Araminta's Wedding

CHILDREN'S BOOKS
  Little Mabel
  Little Mabel's Great Escape
  Little Mabel Saves the Day
  Little Mabel Wins

ROMANCE
  Bella
  Emily
  Harriet
  Imogen
  Lisa & Co
  Octavia
  Prudence

ANTHOLOGIES
  The British in Love
  Violets and Vinegar

Class

A view from middle England

Jilly Cooper

with drawings by
TIMOTHY JAQUES

CORGI BOOKS

CLASS
A CORGI BOOK : 0 552 14662 5

Originally published in Great Britain by Eyre Methuen Ltd

PRINTING HISTORY
Eyre Methuen edition published 1979
Corgi revised edition published 1980
Mandarin edition published 1993
Corgi edition published 1999

3 5 7 9 10 8 6 4

Set in 10/11pt Century Schoolbook.

Corgi Books are published by Transworld Publishers,
61–63 Uxbridge Road, London W5 5SA,
a division of The Random House Group Ltd,
in Australia by Random House Australia (Pty) Ltd,
20 Alfred Street, Milsons Point, Sydney, NSW 2061, Australia,
in New Zealand by Random House New Zealand Ltd,
18 Poland Road, Glenfield, Auckland 10, New Zealand
and in South Africa by Random House (Pty) Ltd,
Endulini, 5a Jubilee Road, Parktown 2193, South Africa

Reproduced, printed and bound in Great Britain by
Cox & Wyman Ltd, Reading, Berkshire.

CONTENTS

My husband, a publisher, claims that it is excruciatingly bad form to dedicate a book to one's publisher. It is therefore entirely in character for me to dedicate this book to my publisher, Geoffrey Strachan, with love and gratitude.

ACKNOWLEDGEMENTS

I am extremely grateful to the people who have helped me with this book. They include Andrew Batute, formerly manager of the French Revolution Restaurant in London, John Challis, formerly manager of Lloyds Bank, Sloane Square, Michael Davey, funeral director, Mathias of Putney, Brian Edgington, headmaster of Roehampton Church School, Brian Holley, divisional careers officer of ILEA (Putney), Heather Jenner, Auriol Murray, of Nannies (Kensington), Renate Olins, of the Marriage Guidance Council, Charles Plouviez, chairman of Everetts Advertising.

I also owe an eternal debt to my friends, who have entered into the spirit of things, and come up with numerous suggestions, some serious, some less so. They include Brinsley Black, John Braine, Lucinda Bredin, Christopher Brown, Madeleine Carritt, Tony Carritt, Camilla Dempster, Val ffrench-Blake, Jonathan Gathorne-Hardy, Bertie Gratton-Belew, Caroline Gray, Laura Hesketh, George Humphreys, Sophie Irvin, Jennifer Justice, Susan Kyle, Ronald and Sylvia Lewin, Miles and Juliet McNair, Nicholas Monson, John Parvin, Humphrey Pullar, Elizabeth Steel, Michael Stourton, Antonia Thynne, Guelda Waller, Alexander Weymouth, David Wright, Michael Ward, and Caroline Yardley.

Five other people made it possible for me to complete the book. I would therefore particularly like to thank my agent, George Greenfield, who has always shown such enthusiasm for the project, Beryl Hill, who typed out the manuscript and who miraculously managed to decipher my appalling handwriting, and my resident major domo, Maxine Green, who retyped chunks of the manuscript when I couldn't read my own corrections and kept up my spirits throughout those dark, desperate weeks, before the book was finally handed in and Tom Hartman and Alan Earney, who helped so much with the editing. The lion's share of my gratitude, however, must go to my publisher, Geoffrey Strachan, who has been amazingly kind, patient, and encouraging over a long long period, when he must have despaired that the manuscript would ever see the light of day, and finally to my husband, Leo, whose humour and powers of observation have been a constant source of inspiration, and who remained good tempered, even when the whole house, including our bedroom, disappeared under a sea of papers and reference books.

Putney 1979

DRAMATIS PERSONAE

The people you will meet in this book are:

HARRY STOW-CRAT, a member of the aristocracy
CAROLINE STOW-CRAT, his wife
GEORGIE STOW-CRAT, his son
FIONA STOW-CRAT, his daughter
and numerous other children, both regularly and irregularly
conceived
SNIPE, a black Labrador

GIDEON UPWARD, a member of the upper middle classes
SAMANTHA UPWARD, his wife
ZACHARIAS UPWARD, his son
THALIA UPWARD, his daughter
COLONEL UPWARD, Gideon's father
MRS UPWARD, Gideon's mother

HOWARD WEYBRIDGE, a member of the middle middle classes
EILEEN WEYBRIDGE, his wife

BRYAN TEALE, a member of the lower middle classes
JEN TEALE, his wife
WAYNE TEALE, his son
CHRISTINE TEALE, his daughter

MR DEFINITELY-DISGUSTING, a member of the working classes
MRS DEFINITELY-DISGUSTING, his wife
DIVE DEFINITELY-DISGUSTING, his son

9

SHARON DEFINITELY-DISGUSTING, his daughter
and numerous other children

MR NOUVEAU-RICHARDS, a millionaire
MRS NOUVEAU-RICHARDS, his wife
JISON NOUVEAU-RICHARDS, his son
TRACEY-DIANE NOUVEAU-RICHARDS, his daughter

Introduction

In the middle of the seventies when I tentatively suggested writing a book about the English class system, people drew away from me in horror.

'But that's all finished,' they said nervously, 'no one gives a hoot any more. Look at the young.' They sounded as if I was intending to produce a standard work on coprophilia or child-molesting. It was plain that, since the egalitarian shake-up of the 'sixties and early 'seventies, class as a subject had become the ultimate obscenity.

What struck me, however, as soon as I started the book was the enormity of the task I had taken on. It was like trying to catalogue the sea. For the whole system, despite its stratification, is constantly forming and re-forming like coral. 'Even a small town like Swansea,' wrote Wynford Vaughan Thomas 'has as many layers as an onion, and each one of them reduces you to tears.' To me the system seemed more like a huge, striped rugger shirt that had run in the wash, with each layer blurring into the next and snobbery fiercest where one stripe merged with another.

I found, too, that people were incredibly difficult to pin down into classes. John went to a more famous boarding school than Thomas, who has a better job than Charles, who's got smarter friends than Harry, who lives in an older house with a bigger garden than David, who's got an uncle who's an earl, but whose children go to comprehensive school. Who is then the gentleman?

A social class can perhaps be rather cumbersomely described as a group of people with certain common traits: descent, education, accent, similarity of occupation, riches, moral attitude, friends, hobbies, accomodation; and with generally similar ideas and forms of behaviour, who meet each other on equal terms and regard themselves as belonging to one group. A single failure to conform would certainly not exclude you from membership. Your own class tend to be people you feel comfortable with – 'one of our sort' – as you do when you are wearing old flat shoes rather than teetering round on precarious five-inch heels. 'The nice thing about the House of Lords,' explained one peer, 'is that you can have incredibly snobbish conversations without feeling snobbish. Yesterday I admired a chap's wife's diamonds; he said they came from Napoleon's sword, and before that from Louis XIV.'

I was continually asked as I wrote the book what right had I to hold forth on the English class system. Most people who had tried in the past, Nancy Mitford, Christopher Sykes, Angus Maude, had been members of the upper classes. The answer was no right at all. All I could claim was a passionate interest in the subject and, being unashamedly middle class, I was perhaps more or less equidistant from bottom and top.

It might therefore be appropriate here to digress a little and explain what my origins are. My paternal grandfather was a wool-merchant, but my paternal grandmother's family were a bit grander. They owned newspapers and were distinguished Whig M.P.s for Leeds during the nineteenth century. My mother's side were mostly in the church, her father being Canon of Heaton, near Bradford. Both sides had lived in the West Riding of Yorkshire for generations and were very, very strait-laced.

My father went to Rugby, then to Cambridge, where he got a first in two years, and then into the army. After getting married, he found he wasn't making enough money and joined Fords and he and my mother moved, somewhat reluctantly, to Essex, where I was born. At the beginning of the Second World War he was called up and became one of the army's youngest brigadiers. After the war we moved back to Yorkshire, living first in a large Victorian house. I was eight and, I think for the first time, became aware of class distinction. Our next-door neighbour was a newly rich and very ostentatious wool-merchant, of whose sybaritic existence my parents disapproved. One morning he asked me over to his house. I had a heavenly time, spending all morning playing the pianola, of which my mother also disapproved—too much pleasure for too little effort—and eating a whole eight-ounce bar of black market milk chocolate, which, just after the war, seemed like stumbling on Aladdin's cave. When I got home I was sick. I was aware that it served me right both for slumming and for over-indulgence.

Soon after that we moved into the Hall at Ilkley, a splendid Georgian house with a long drive, seven acres of fields for my ponies, a swimming pool and tennis and squash courts. From then on we lived an élitist existence; tennis parties with cucumber sandwiches, large dances and fêtes in the garden. I enjoyed playing little Miss Muck tremendously. I had a photograph of the house taken from the bottom of the drive on my dressing table at school and all my little friends were very impressed.

My brother, however, still had doubts about our lifestyle. It was too bourgeois, too predictable and restricted, he thought. One wet afternoon I remember him striding up and down the drawing-room going on and on about our boring, middle-class existence.

Suddenly my mother, who'd been trying to read a detective story, looked over her spectacles and said with very gentle reproof 'Upper-middle class, darling.'

Occasionally we were taken down a peg by a socialist aunt who thought we'd all got too big for our boots. One day my mother was describing some people who lived near York as being a very 'old' family.

'Whadja mean old?' snorted my aunt. 'All families are old.'

There were very few eligible young men in Ilkley; the glamorous, hard-drinking wool-merchants' sons with their fast cars, teddy-bear coats and broad Yorkshire accents were as far above me sexually as they were

13

below me, I felt, socially. But when I was about eighteen two old Etonians came to live in the district for a year. They were learning farming before going to run their estates. They were both very attractive and easy-going, and were consequently asked everywhere, every mum with a marriageable daughter competing for their attention. I was terribly disconcerted when, after a couple of visits to our house, and one of them taking me out once, they both became complete habitués of the house of a jumped-up steel-merchant across the valley. Soon they were both fighting for the hand of his not particularly good-looking daughter. But she's so much commoner than me, I remember thinking in bewilderment, why don't they prefer my company and our house? I realize now that they far preferred the easy-going atmosphere of the steel-merchant's house, with its lush hospitality, ever-flowing drink and poker sessions far into the night, to one glass of sherry and deliberately intelligent conversation in ours. I had yet to learn, too, that people invariably dislike and shun the class just below them, and much prefer the class below that, or even the one below that.

I was further bewildered when, later in the year, I went to Oxford to learn to type and shared a room with an 'Hon' who said 'handbag'. This seemed like blasphemy. Nancy Mitford's *The Pursuit of Love* had been my bible as a teenager. I knew that peers' daughters, who she immortalized as 'Hons', said 'bag' rather than handbag. At that time, too, aware of a slowly emerging sexuality and away at last from parental or educational restraint, I evolved a new way of dressing: five-inch high-heeled shoes, tight straight skirts, very, very tight cheap sweaters and masses of make-up to cover a still rather bad skin. I looked just like a tart. People obviously took me for one too. For when my room-mate introduced me to all her smart friends at Christ Church, one young blood promptly bet another young blood a tenner that he couldn't get me into bed by the end of the week. Before he had had time to lay siege the story was repeated back to me. I was shattered. Shocked and

14

horrified to my virginal middle-class core, I cried for twenty-four hours. My would-be seducer, who had a good heart, on hearing of my misery turned up at my digs, apologized handsomely and suggested, by way of making amends rather than me, that he take me to the cinema. On the way there he stopped at a sweet shop and bought a bar of chocolate. Breaking it, he gave me half and started to eat the other half himself.

'But you can't eat sweets in the street,' I gasped, almost more shocked than I had been by his intended seduction.

'I,' he answered, with centuries of disdain in his voice, 'can do anything I like.'

Hons who talked about handbags, lords who ate chocolate in the street like the working classes, aristocrats who preferred the jumped-up to the solidly middle class: I was slowly learning that the class system was infinitely more complicated than I had ever dreamed.

'It takes many years,' writes Jonathan Gathorne-Hardy in *The Rise and Fall of the British Nanny*, for the outsider to master those complex, subtle distinctions, those nuances of accent, attitude and behaviour which went, indeed which go, into that living, changing thing—English upper-class snobbery. He might have added that this is true of any class's snobbery.

When *Class* was eventually published in 1979, it caused a fearful rumpus. Having written most of it hiding in the potting shed, to avoid our creditors, I was enchanted when it stayed on the best seller list for 20 weeks. Less fun was promoting it round the country. I was berated by tattooed and nose-studded radio presenters. I was shouted down by miners, egged on by Lord Montague of Beaulieu.

The Duke of Edinburgh attacked me at a Hatchard's party, snarling that the class system no longer existed.

'That's odd,' I said politely, 'According to the 1971 Census, which categorizes people's social class by their occupation, Princess Anne, as an event rider, is the same class: 111 (Non Manual) as a game keeper.'

'Rubbish,' thundered the Duke, 'Keepers are working class.'

I got the most flak for being beastly to the working classes, by calling the couple who portrayed them: Mr and Mrs Definitely Disgusting. This was not because I thought them remotely disgusting, but because, as I point out, in reply to questions on everything from encroaching gypsy encampments to rocketing gas bills, they would tend to snort:

'Disgusting! Definitely.'

The main difference today is that they would probably say:

'Disgusting! Definitely. "Social" wouldn't unblock our drains for nuffink, and they didn't offer us any counselling neither.'

Having suffered so much opprobrium when *Class* came out I have hardly glanced at the book since, only opening it with colossal trepidation, like Pandora's Box, because my publishers suggested in view of this beautiful new reprint, I might like to draw readers' attention to how the class system has changed.

My first reaction was how on earth had I been brave or crazy enough to write all these things. But settling down, I realized I had been looking at a different era. For in 1979, everything changed. Margaret Thatcher came to power, and suddenly the English became obsessed with making money, buying their own houses, and rising socially. The Yuppie was born. Throughout the same time, recession kicked in, the stock market crashed, the power of the unions was broken. More tragically a new cardboard boxed underclass, suffering appalling poverty, grew up, which had hardly existed when I was writing.

Another tragedy I hadn't anticipated was the demise of the miner. Back in 1979, he was the ultimate macho hero, king of the working classes. Mining, as I write on page 150, was regarded as much grander than building because it was a steady job. I also singled out miners, power workers, dockers, engineers and lorry drivers as the new élite, because by striking they had

16

the power to bring the country to its knees.

Their hour of glory was brief, as pit after pit closed down. Today with short-term contracts, loss of pension and no certainty of a job for life, or in the poor miners' case, no job at all, the majority of the working classes have suffered.

I also state on page 149 that becoming a shop steward was the easiest way for a working class boy to get on, but since the weakening of the unions, this no longer applies.

But not only the working classes lost clout. 'Lorses' at Lloyds decimated the upper classes more effectively than any revolution and the middle classes, who are light years behind the working classes when it comes to working social security and the black economy, have also been laid off in the most brutal way. There's no kudos in working at a desk if it has to be cleared in an afternoon.

Much of what I wrote on my chapter on education, I think, still stands, except that since 1979 drugs have invaded all schools, and girls most of the public schools.

Eton has been one of the few schools resisting the latter.

'If one is caught in bed with a girl,' grumbled a young Etonian, 'one gets chucked out, but if you're caught with a boy, you get two hours gardening.'

Other changes were more of detail. Only the poorest of the working classes no longer have refrigerators. Mrs Definitely Disgusting has a hair dryer now instead of wearing her curlers to the corner shop and working class streets are entwined with satellite dishes like columbines. Upper class girls flaunt tattoos and nose-studs like radio presenters. Upper class mothers no longer wear fur coats and only think babygros are common if they have logos on. Many of the regiments I wrote about have sadly been amalgamated or disbanded. Many men's clubs now allow in women and are particularly charming to them.

Generally though, I was surprised and pleased, despite these changes, how the archetypes I'd created behave in just the same way today, and can be found in Harry Enfield's working class couple, Wayne and Waynetta, in his chinless wonder, Tim Nice But Dim, and in the socially mountaineering Hyacinth Bucket—all characters we love as we laugh at them.

As a writer, one must stand by one's prejudices. I have therefore only made a dozen or so small changes to the text, where I felt I had been totally inaccurate or unnecessarily cruel or insensitive.

I realize the entire book is wildly politically incorrect. This is as it should be, because political correctness with its insistence on verbosity and the use of euphemisms, like 'lone parent', 'replacement mother', 'sibling', 'vertically challenged' for short, 'young woman' for girl, 'member of the homeless community' for tramp, the dreadful 'partner' for lover, is irredeemably genteel and lower middle class.

As *Class* is a study of twenty years ago, we have left people's titles, prices and figures as they were then. It was a happy day when you could get a temporary secretary for £50 a week.

Flipping through the pages, I felt a huge sadness that so many of the friends who'd helped me with the book or contributed marvellous anecdotes: Frankie Howerd, Frank Muir, Larry Grayson, Dick Emery, Reginald Bousanquet, Jean Rook, to name only a few, are now dead.

When I went on Yorkshire television with the splendidly redoutable Miss Rook in the early seventies, the interviewer began most embarrassingly by saying:

'Now here you are: two columnists from Yorkshire but from very different backgrounds. You're working class aren't you, Jean. And Jilly, you're upper class?'

We both shrieked with horror.

'I'm middle, not upper,' I muttered going scarlet.

'I'm upper-middle,' said Jean witheringly, 'I know lots of duchesses.'

Even people, who pretend class doesn't exist, are affected by it. I am reminded of a psychiatrist who was treating an aristocrat for depression. A month went by and they seemed to be making little progress.

'I want you to be completely honest,' said the psychiatrist at the next session, 'and tell me exactly what's in your mind at the moment.'

'I was thinking,' said the aristocrat apologetically, 'what a vulgar little man you are.'

It was their final session. The psychiatrist was unable to go on because he'd completely lost any feeling of ascendancy.

'And so,' wrote John Coleman in the *Sunday Times*, 'the old movements of social advance and recoil go on, just as much as they always did. It is the perpetual inaccuracy of imitation that makes up the English social comedy and tragedy.'

But there is plenty of comedy. As a small boy at my son's prep school once pointed out in an essay,

'All people should be gentlemen except ladies, but it puts a bit of variety into life if some are not.'

I am very aware of the inadequacies of this book. I have made many sweeping generalizations, which I hope people won't take too seriously, because other classes are not better or worse than one's own, they are merely different.

One need look no further for an example than Dame Barbara Cartland being interviewed, back in the seventies, by Sandra Harris on the *Today* programme and being asked whether she thought the class barriers had broken down.

'Of course they have,' said Dame Barbara, 'or I wouldn't be sitting here talking to someone like you.'

1 THE CLASSES

THE ARISTOCRACY

All the world loves a titled person

According to sociologists the aristocracy is such a tiny minority—about 0.2% of the population—as to be statistically negligible. The ones who do not work or who run their own estates are not even listed in the Census. They are like the scattering of herbs and garlic of top of a bowl of dripping, or more poetically, like water lilies that float, beautiful and, some would say, useless, on the surface of a pond. Being a peer, of course, doesn't make you an aristocrat. Only about half the nobility are aristocracy, the rest being life peers, and only about a third of the aristocracy are ennobled, the rest being families of younger sons, or country squires living in manor houses, some of whom have had money and influence for far longer and can trace their families much further back than many a Duke or Earl.

A good example of this is Mrs James, the aristocrat in Pamela Hansford Johnson's novel *The Unspeakable Skipton*. Mrs James had an air of undefinable authority and spoke in a direct and barking shorthand:

'Feel sorry for poor Alf Dorset, son's marrying some girl who sings on the wireless.' Unbound by convention, she made all her own rules, making a point of going everywhere out of season.

'That's why seasons are inevitably such a flop' says one of the other characters, 'because if they're out of season they're wrong anyway, and if they're in season, Mrs James had buzzed off to Gozo or somewhere extraordinary.'

As so many of the aristocracy don't have titles they regard Burke's, which covers the landed gentry as well as the peerage, as far more important source books than Debrett's. One peer told his secretary she must get up-to-date copies of Burke's 'so you'll know all the people I'm talking about'. The point about the aristocracy is that they all know each other.

Traditionally, as will be shown in later chapters, the aristocracy didn't work for their living and, although many of them have jobs today, they find difficulty in applying the same dedication to their work as the middle classes.

They used, of course, to be terribly rich. At the turn of the century, if you were asked to stay at Woburn one chauffeur and a footman would take you as far as Hendon, where another chauffeur and a footman would be waiting to take you to Woburn. As a gentleman never travelled with his luggage, another two cars were needed to carry that. So it meant two chauffeurs and two footmen to get you and your luggage as far as Hendon, and two more chauffeurs and footmen to take you to Woburn—eight men to transport one guest for heaven knows how large a house party, down to the country. The Marquess of Hertford had a house in Wales he'd never been to, but where, every night, a huge dinner was cooked by a fleet of servants in case he did turn up.

The Westminsters today own 300 acres in Belgravia and Oxford Street, 12,000 acres around Eaton, 14,000 acres in North Wales, 1,000 acres in Kent, 400 acres in Shropshire, 800 acres in New South Wales, 1,000 acres in British Columbia, Hawaii and Australia. The present Duke inherited £16 million on his 21st birthday. Hardly the bread line.

Today, as a result of death duties and capital transfer tax, most aristocrats are desperately poor in comparison with their grandfathers and are reduced to renting off wings as apartments, selling paintings, turning their gardens into zoos and amusement parks, and letting the public see over their houses. Anyone who has experienced the nightmare of showing a handful of people over their own house when they put it up for sale will understand the horror of having a million visitors a year peering into every nook and cranny.

Although they have considerable influence in the Tory party, the aristocracy no longer run the country as they did in the eighteenth and nineteenth centuries. But if their privileges have been eroded, their responsibilities remain the same: responsibilities to the tenants, to the community (the good aristocrat always has a strong sense of public duty) and to the house he lives in, often so beautiful as to be a national monument, but to the upkeep of which the nation pays no contribution.

One of the characteristics of the aristocrat is the extreme sentiment he feels towards his house and his inheritance. His wife is expected to feel the same. When the Marchioness of Tavistock recently expressed her boredom at running Woburn her father-in-law's sharp reaction was quoted in the *Daily Mail*:

'If you marry some guy with a title, you have a duty and a responsibility to carry on what his ancestors did in the past. She was perfectly aware of what she was getting into. Trouble is she's an only child.'

Because they believe in their inheritance, the upper classes set enormous store by keeping things in the family. They don't buy their houses like the middle classes, they inherit them. When the house gets too big for a grandfather and grandmother, they might move into a smaller house on the estate, to make way for their eldest son, but they leave all the furniture behind, as their ancestors have for generations. One definition of the middle classes is the sort of people who have to buy their own silver.

Because the aristocracy were so anxious to preserve their inheritance, they tended only to marry their own kind. The middle classes married for love. The upper classes married to preserve their rank. All twenty-six Dukes are, at present, related to one another. And as long as rank was protected, and money obtained in

23

sufficient quantities to support that rank, infidelity after marriage was taken for granted, as Vita Sackville-West points out in her novel *The Edwardians*:

'A painter,' screamed the Duchess, 'What painter? Sylvia Roehampton's daughter to marry a painter? But of course she won't. You marry Tony Wexford, and we'll see what can be done about the painter afterwards.'

As they weren't expected to be faithful, unlike the middle classes they didn't feel guilty if they wandered, which explains the over-active libido of the aristocrat. He expected to excercise *droit de seigneur* over his tenants but he also saw himself as a Knight Errant like Don Quixote living in a world of romantic adventure. 'When your ancestors have been fighting battles and seducing women for thousands of years,' said one German nobleman, 'it's terribly difficult to settle down to one wife and an office job.'

As a result of all this infidelity a high proportion of the aristocracy is irregularly conceived, but, as they tend to sleep with each other, they're still pretty dotty with inbreeding. When my uncle was Lord Spencer's agent, my aunt said she met all the local aristocracy, many of them as mad as hatters. When they talked about one of their friends 'coming out', you never knew if they were doing the season, or being discharged from a psychiatric clinic.

Colossal self-confidence is perhaps the hallmark of the aristocrat. Like the chevalier he goes through life unafraid; he doesn't question his motives or feel guilty about his actions. When I went shooting in Northumberland last summer I noticed a beautiful blonde young man in a red sweater at the next butt. Why didn't he have to wear green camouflage like the rest of us, I asked.

'Because he's a duke's son,' said my host. 'He can do what he likes.'

Not answerable to other people, the aristocrat is often unimaginative, spoilt, easily irritated and doesn't flinch from showing it. If he wants to eat his peas with his knife he does so.

24

'Dear Kate,' said Henry V, 'You and I cannot be confined within the weak list of a country's fashion; we are the makers of manners, Kate; and the liberty that follows our places stops the mouth of all find-faults.'

As the maker of manners, many of the aristocracy, while feeling they have a duty towards the community as Sheriffs and Lord-Lieutenants, are indifferent to public opinion.

'One doesn't care what the press say,' said the Marquess of Anglesey at a dinner party. 'One's friends know what one's like and that's all that matters.' The only thing he minded, he went on, was that the National Trust film on television had said he was very rich. The hostess then asked him if he'd like moussaka or cold turkey.

'I'd like both,' he said.

Not caring a stuff what people think also leads to a rich vein of eccentricity: the Marquess of Londonderry throwing soup at a fly that was irritating him in a restaurant, and Sir Anthony Eden's father hurling a barometer out of the window into the pouring rain, yelling, 'See for yourself, you bloody thing.'

Or there was the imperious peer who, when he missed a train, ordered the station-master to get him another one.

Professor Ross has said that above a certain level all U people are equal. With respect, I think few upper class people would agree with him. The ancient aristocracy consider it very vulgar to have been founded after the Tudors, which puts most of our present Dukes beyond the pale. In fact, in the nineteenth century many of them were so worried about the comparative youthfulness of their families that they employed genealogists to try and trace their ancestry back to the Conqueror.

When Oliver Lyttelton was made Viscount Chandos, his wife Lady Moira, who was the daughter of the 10th Duke of Leeds, was furious at becoming Lady Chandos, and having ostensibly to drop rank. Oliver Lyttelton was evidently so thrilled to be ennobled that he went round putting coronets on everything, including books of matches. Brian Masters in his book *The Dukes* tells a story of the Duchesses of Buccleuch and Westminster sidling through a door together in their determination not to cede precedence.

Between aristocrats and other classes there is certainly a barrier of rank. My mother and father used to live near Hampton Court Palace, where widows of distinguished men, some of them aristocrats, have apartments. My mother met a peer's widow at a drinks party and they got on so well that my mother wrote to her next day asking her to dine. Back came a letter of acceptance but with a P.S. 'I hope you don't mind my pointing out, Elaine dear, that the Palace should be the first to issue invitations.'

Brian Masters thinks this obsession with rank probably had something to do with boredom. Without a career, the aristocrat had to fill his days. He was not a great intellectual: Jane Austen's Sir Walter Elliot, whose reading consisted of his own entry in The Baronetage, is fairly near the mark. He preferred more exciting entertainment, hence his addiction to blood sports and to gambling. I shall never forget watching an aristocrat and a television newsreader playing backgammon one evening. The newsreader's wife, who was ravishingly beautiful and bored with the lack of attention, suddenly came in with no clothes on and danced round and round them. Neither of them took any notice.

The aristocrat, when he wants to, has very good manners. The Scottish upper classes in particular have that shell-shocked look that probably comes from banging their heads on low beams leaping to their feet whenever a woman comes into the room. Aristocrats are also deeply male chauvinist, and although you get left-wing extremists like Lord Weymouth who sends his children to a comprehensive school and has revolutionary ideas, on the whole they tend to be reactionary.

26

Harry Stow-Crat, Caroline and Snipe

While writing this book I found that there were very much two strands in the character of the aristocrat: first the wild, delinquent, arrogant, capricious, rather more glamorous strand; and second the stuffy, 'county', public-spirited, but publicity-shy strand, epitomized by the old baronet whose family were described 'as old as the hills and infinitely more respectable'.

Or, as a small boy writing in my son's school magazine pointed out: 'Gentleman are of two types: the nose-uppish and the secluded.'

In order to write this book I have dealt in archetypes. The aristocracy and upper classes are represented by The Hon HARRY STOW-CRAT. Son of the sixth Baron Egliston, educated at Eton, he served in the Coldstream Guards. He now runs his diminishing estate, selling the odd Van Dyck to make ends meet, but does more or less what he pleases. He lives in a large decaying house in the North Riding of Yorkshire and has a flat in Chelsea. He has a long-suffering wife, CAROLINE, who does a great deal for charity, an eldest son, GEORGIE, a daughter called FIONA, and several other children. He has numerous mistresses, but none to whom he is as devoted as to his black labrador, SNIPE. He has had many moments of frustration and boredom in his life, but never any of self-doubt.

THE MIDDLE CLASSES

> 'Would you come round the world next year in the France with me? I got a letter from Gerry Wellesley on a cruise saying he'd never met middle-class people before, and they are quite different from us. Isn't he awful?'
>
> Nancy Mitford

The middle classes are in fact *quite* different—being riddled with self-doubt, which is hardly surprising after

28

all the flak they've received over the years. The upper classes despised them for their preoccupation with money, and because they suspected it was middle-class malcontents rather than the rabble who had plotted and set alight the French Revolution. 'How beastly the bourgeois is,' mocked the working-class Lawrence, and in fact *épater le bourgeois* has always been a favourite sport of both high and low. Marx, of course, divided society into two classes—the splendid workers, and the wicked bourgeoisie who owned the means of production. Even members of their own class, like Hilaire Belloc, attack them:

> *The people in between*
> *Looked underdone and harassed,*
> *And out of place and mean,*
> *And horribly embarrassed.*

And they have even been blamed for the evils of the class system. It is the middle classes, wrote one sociologist, with their passion for order and reason, who have sought to impose a kind of stratification on what is in fact an eternally malleable and bubbling class system. Which is rubbish because, as we have already seen, the aristocracy is just as obsessed with rank.

Occasionally they have their defenders, 'I come from the middle classes,' said Neville Chamberlain, 'and I am proud of the ability, the shrewdness, the industry and providence, the thrift by which they are distinguished.'

In a way the middle classes seem to suffer as the middle child does. Everyone makes a huge fuss over the firstborn and everyone pets and coddles the baby, (who, like the working classes, is shored up by the great feather bed of the welfare state), but the child in the middle gets the most opprobrium, is often left to fend for itself and is ganged up on by the other two. It is doubly significant that in the Civil War, the rabble

The Upwards

joined up with the King against the Puritan middle classes. For if Marx was the champion of the working classes, Calvin was the prophet of the middle classes. They believed implicitly in the Puritan Ethic, in the cultivation of such virtues as diligence, frugality, propriety and fidelity. Work to keep sin at bay, feel guilty if you slack. Shame is a bourgeois notion.

Although there is a world of difference between the top of the middle classes and the bottom, between the great merchant banker and the small shopkeeper, they are united in their desire to get on, not just to survive. Unlike the upper classes and the working classes they think careers are important. They start little businesses, they work to pass exams after they leave school, they believe in the law of the jungle and not the Welfare State. If you get on in life good luck to you.

For this reason they believed in the importance of education long before the other classes. They believed in deferred satisfaction. They saved in order to send their children to private schools, or to buy their own houses. If the upper classes handed on estates to their children, the middle classes handed on small businesses. To the working classes the most important criterion of middle-class membership after money or income is owning a small business or being self-employed.

At the moment they are under increasing pressure, as the working classes get richer and more powerful. One of the great divides between the middle and lower classes used to be that the former used his brain and the latter his hands. Today, however, the miner and the car worker with their free housing and free education have far more spending money than a newly qualified doctor or barrister, and certainly than a policeman or a major in the army. According to my ex-bank manager, the middle classes are having increasing difficulty making ends meet. In 1976, they rather than the working classes became the chief candidates for the pawnbroker, bringing in watches, wedding rings, golf clubs, and binoculars.

Although they don't 'know everyone' like the upper classes, the upper-middles and many of the middles, having been to boarding school, and have a much wider circle of friends than the working classes. They are able to keep in touch with them by telephone, or by their ability to write letters. Many of them also have a spare room where friends can come and stay.

They therefore tend to entertain 'outsiders' much more than the working classes, and don't need to depend on their immediate neighbours for help or for their identity. They can afford to keep themselves to themselves. Aloofness, reserve and a certain self-righteousness are also middle-class qualities.

To illustrate the three main strands of the middle classes we again fall into archetypes, with GIDEON and SAMANTHA UPWARD as the upper-middle-class couple, HOWARD and EILEEN WEYBRIDGE as the middle-middles and BRYAN and JEN TEALE as the lower-middles.

GIDEON AND SAMANTHA UPWARD— THE MERRYTOCRACY

The upper-middle classes are the most intelligent and highly educated of all the classes, and therefore the silliest and the most receptive to every new trend: radical chic, health foods, ethnic clothes, bra-lessness, gifted children, *cuisine minceur*. Gideon Upward gave his mother-in-law a garlic crusher for Christmas. The upper-middles tend to read *The Guardian* and are proud of their liberal and enlightened attitudes. They are also the most role-reversed of the classes: Gideon does a great deal of cooking and housework: Samantha longs to be a good mother and have an 'int'risting job' at the same time. To save petrol she rides round on a sit-up-and-beg bicycle, with wholemeal bread in the front basket and a bawling child in the back. Sometimes her long dirndl skirt catches in the pedals. She has a second in history and a fourth in life.

Gideon and Samantha both went to 'good' schools, Gideon probably to Winchester or to Sherborne. He might be an architect or work in the City. He wears a signet ring with a crest on the little finger of his left hand, in an attempt to proclaim near aristocratic status, just as the middle-middles wear an old school tie to show they've been to boarding school, the lower-middles give their house a name instead of a number to prove it isn't council and the working classes bring back plastic bulls from Majorca to show they've travelled.

Gideon and Samantha have two children called Zacharias and Thalia, who they might start off sending to a state school, and trying not to wince at the first 'pardon', but would be more likely to send to a private school. They love their English setter, Blucher, and feel frightfully guilty about loving it almost more than their children. Harry Stow-Crat would have no such scruples. Gideon plays tennis and rugger at a club, but he wouldn't use the club to make friends, and he and Samantha wouldn't go near the Country Club which, to them, reeks of surburbia. They prefer to entertain in their own house, which is large and Victorian, and being restored to its original state rather faster than they'd like. Samantha is into good works with a slightly self-interested motive: pollution, conservation, the P.T.A.

As they can't be the most upper class in the land, Samantha is determined that they shall be the most 'cultured'. She and Gideon go to the theatre, the ballet and the movies, as they rather self-consciously call the cinema, and try and read at least two books a week.

In the last fifteen years, the upper-middles have aimed at a standard of living they can't afford, taking on many of the pastimes of the upper classes. Gideon goes shooting quite often; they have two cars, which are falling to pieces, and for which they have to pay a fortune every time they take their M.O.T.; they used to

33

have a country cottage, holidays abroad, and a boat. Now they have two children at boarding school. Since the advent of the permissive society Gideon is playing at adultery like Harry Stow-Crat. As a result he spends a fortune on lunches, and another fortune on guilt presents for Samantha afterwards. They are both so worried about trying to make ends meet, they're drinking themselves absolutely silly—hence the sub-title 'The Merrytocracy'.

Virginia Woolf once wrote an unfinished novel about an upper-middle-class family called the Pargeters. 'Parget' is an English dialect word meaning to smooth over cracks in plastered surfaces: the Pargeters gloss over the deep sexual and emotional fissures of life. In the same way Samantha doesn't particularly like her mother-in-law, or several of her neighbours; but she tries to get on with them because she feels guilty about her dislike. In the same way she feels guilty about telling someone she employs that they are not doing the job properly. Caroline Stow-Crat would never have that problem. If she hired a gardener even for two hours, she wouldn't flaunt him as a status symbol, she'd keep quiet about him, because she feels it's more creative to do the garden herself.

She and Gideon call each other 'darling' rather than 'dear', and try to remember to say 'orf'. Gideon's parents, Colonel and Mrs Upward, living on a rapidly dwindling fixed income, are much more thrifty than Samantha and Gideon. As they're not drinking themselves silly, they don't smash everything and still have the same glasses and china as they did when they were married.

HOWARD AND EILEEN WEYBRIDGE— THE MIDDLE-MIDDLES

Howard Weybridge lives in Surrey or some smart dormitory town. He works as an accountant, stockbroker,

Bryan and Jen Teale

surveyor or higher technician. He probably went to a minor public school or a grammar school. He never misses the nine o'clock news and says 'Cheerio'. He wears paisley scarves with scarf rings and has no bottoms to his spectacles. He calls his wife, Eileen, 'dear' and when you ask him how he is says, 'Very fit, thank you'. He is very straight and very patriotic, his haw-haw voice is a synthetic approximation to the uppers; he talks about 'Ham-shar'. His children join the young *Con*-servatives and the tennis club to meet people. He buys a modern house and ages it up. It has a big garden with a perfect lawn and lots of shrubs. He despises anyone who hasn't been to 'public school', and often goes into local government or politics for social advancement. He is a first-generation pony buyer, and would also use the Pony Club to meet the right sort of people. Eileen shops at Bentalls and thinks the upper-middles are terribly scruffy. They are both keen golfers, and pull strings to get their road made private. Their favourite radio programmes are *Any Answers, These You Have Loved* and *Disgusted Tunbridge Wells*. They are much smugger than the upper-middles.

Howard Weybridge's father hasn't a bill in the world and is on the golf club committee. He found bridge to be one of the most wonderful things in life; it's a very easy way of entertaining. He has a sneaking liking for Enoch Powell: 'We should have stopped the sambos coming here in the first place.'

BRYAN AND JEN TEALE— THE LOWER-MIDDLES

The Teales are probably the most pushy, the most frugal and the most respectable of all the classes, because they are so anxious to escape from the working class. The successful ones iron out their accents and become middle like Mr Heath and Mrs Thatcher. The rest stay put as bank and insurance clerks, door-to-door salesmen, toast-masters, lower management, police ser-

The Weybridges

geants and sergeant-majors. In the old days the lower-middles rose with the small business or the little shop, but the rise in rates, social security benefits and postage has scuppered all that.

The lower-middles never had any servants, but as they are obsessed with cleanliness, and like everything nice, they buy a small modern house and fill it with modern units which are easy to keep clean. Jen and Bryan have two children, Wayne and Christine, and a very clean car.

As Jen and Bryan didn't go to boarding school, didn't make friends outside the district, and don't mix with the street, they have very few friends and keep themselves to themselves. They tend to be very inner-directed, doing everything together, decorating the house, furnishing the car, and coaching and playing football with the children. Jen reads knitting patterns, *Woman's Own* and *Reader's Digest* condensed books. To avoid any working-class stigma she puts up defensive barriers— privet hedges, net curtains—talks in a 'refained' accent, raising her little finger when she drinks. Her aim is to be dainty and wear six pairs of knickers. She admires Mary Whitehouse enormously, disapproves of long hair and puts money in the Woolwich every week. She sees herself as the 'Woolwich girl'. The Teales don't entertain much, only Bryan's colleagues who might be useful, and occasionally Bryan's boss.

THE WORKING CLASSES

One of the great class divides has always been 'them' and 'us' which, as a result of the egalitarian, working-class-is-beautiful revolution of the 'sixties, and early 'seventies, has polarized into the Guilty and the Cross. On the one side are the middle and upper classes, feeling guilty and riddled with social concern, although they often earn far less money than the workers, and on the other are the working classes who, having been totally brain-washed by television and images of the good life, feel cross because they aren't getting a big enough slice of the cake.

In a time of economic prosperity everyone tends to do well. Wages rise; the middle classes can afford a new car, or central heating; the working-class man buys a fridge for the missus. Man's envy and rivalry is turned towards his neighbour—keeping up with the Joneses—rather than towards the classes above and below. But in times of economic stress, when people suddenly can't get the things they want and prices and the cost of living outstrip wages, they start turning their envy against other classes. Antagonism against a neighbour feathering his nest tends to be replaced by an awareness of class inequalities.

In a time of economic security, society therefore tends to look fairly cohesive, which is probably why in the early 'seventies a lot of people genuinely believed that class barriers had finally broken down; but, as the decade advanced, the working-class people who'd bought their own houses and were up to their necks in mortgage and hire-purchase payments suddenly found they couldn't keep up. Their expectations had been raised, and now their security was being threatened by the additional possibility of mass unemployment. This discontent, fanned by the militants, resulted in the rash of strikes in the winter of 1978/79.

Although the middle classes often think of the working-class man as earning huge sums on overtime, the rewards of his job in fact are much less. The manual worker seldom has job satisfaction or a proper pension; he doesn't have any fringe benefits such as a car, trips abroad, expense account lunches and longer holidays; he has to clock in and out and his earning span is much shorter. Once his physical strength goes, he can look forward to an old age of comparative poverty and deprivation. This all results in workers avoiding any kind

39

of moral commitment to the management. 'We cheat the foreman,' is the attitude, 'he cheats the manager, and the manager cheats the customer.'

Richard Hoggart in *The Uses of Literacy* brilliantly summed up the workers' attitude to them:

'They are the people at the top, the highers up, the people who give you your dole, call you up, tell you to go to work, fine you, make you split up the family in the 'thirties (to avoid a reduction in the means test allowance) get yer in the end, aren't really to be trusted, talk posh, are all twisters really, never tell yer owt (e.g. about a relative in hospital) clap yer in the clink, will do y'down if they can, summons yer, are all in a click together, treat y'like muck.'

Because they dislike the management, the working classes don't like people saving their money or getting on through hard work. They put a premium on enjoying pleasure now, drinking their wages, for example, or blowing the whole lot on a new colour telly. The only legitimate way to make money is to win it. Hence the addiction to football pools, racing, bingo and the dogs.

Living from hand to mouth, they can't manage their money like the lower-middles. When the army started paying guardsmen by cheque recently, my bank manager said they got into the most frightful muddles. If he wrote and told one of them he was overdrawn by £30, he promptly received a cheque for that amount.

Traditionally working-class virtues are friendliness, co-operation, warmth, spontaneity, a ready sense of humour and neighbourliness. 'We're all in the same boat' is the attitude. That 'love', still the most common form of address, really means something. They have been defined as people who belong to the same Christmas Club, characteristicly saving up not for something solid, like the deposit on a house, but for a good blowout. They have a great capacity for enjoyment.

Because they didn't have cars or telephones and couldn't afford train fares, and the men tended to walk to work nearby, life centred around the street and neighbourhood. 'Everyone knew your business,' said one working-class man, so it was no good putting on airs because you earned more. The neighbours remembered you as a boy, knew your Aunt Lil, who was no better than she should be, and took you down a peg. The network acts as a constant check!

Girls seldom moved away from their mothers when they married; sons often came home for lunch every day, or lived at home, even after marriage. The working-class family is much closer and more possessive. They seldom invite friends into the house.

'I've never had a stranger (meaning non-family) in here since the day I moved in,' said one woman. 'I don't hold with that sort of thing.'

Being so dependent on the locality, the working classes are lost and desperately lonely, if the council moves them to housing estates, or shuts them up in little boxes in some high-rise block. The men have also lost much of the satisfacton that came from the old skills and crafts. Many of these have been taken away from them and their traditional occupations replaced by machines. In the old days the husband gained respect as a working man in the community.

Women's Lib hasn't helped his self-respect much either. The working classes are the most reactionary of all the classes. (You only have to look at those Brylcreemed short back and sides, and wide trousers flapping like sails in the breeze at the T.U.C. Conference.) But despite this, the working-class housewife now reads about Women's Lib in the paper and soon she's fretting to go back to work and make some extra cash, rather than act as a servant to the family and have her husband's dinner on the table at mid-day when he gets home. She starts questioning his authority and, having less autonomy at home, and never having had any at work, he feels even more insecure. Battering often starts if the woman is brighter than the man and the poorly educated husband sees his security threatened.

Leaving school at sixteen, he feels inadequate be-

The Definitely-Disgustings

The Nouveau-Richards

cause he is inarticulate. He is thought of as being bloody-minded and rude by the middle classes because he can't express himself and to snort 'Definitely, disgusting', in answer to any question put to him, is the only way he can show his disapproval.

The working classes divide themselves firmly into the Rough and the Respectable. The Rough get drunk fairly often, make a lot of noise at night, often engage in prostitution, have public fights, sometimes neglect their children, swear in front of women and children, and don't give a stuff about anything—just like the upper classes, in fact. The Respectables chunter over such behaviour, and in Wales sing in Male Voice Choirs; they are pretty near the Teales. They also look down on people on the dole, the criminal classes and the blacks, who they refer to as 'soap dodgers'.

MR AND MRS DEFINITELY-DISGUSTING

Our archetypal working-class couple are Mr and Mrs DEFINITELY-DISGUSTING. They have two children, SHARON and DIVE, and live in a council house with walls so thin you can hear the budgie pecking its seed next door. Mr Definitely-Disgusting is your manual worker. He might be a miner in the North, a car worker in the Midlands, or a casual labourer in the South. He married young and lived for a while with his wife's parents. After a year or two he went back to going to the pub, football and the dogs with the blokes. He detests his mother-in-law. But, despite his propensity to foul language, he is extremely modest, often undressing with his back to Mrs D-D and even peeing in a different way than the other classes, splaying out his fingers in a fan, so they conceal his member. He might do something mildly illegal, receiving a car or knocking-off a telly. He is terrified of the police, who, being lower-middle and the class just above, reserve their special venom for him. Mrs Definitely-Disgusting wears her curlers and pinny to the local shop and

44

spends a lot of the day with a cigarette hanging from her bottom lip gossiping and grumbling.

MR AND MRS NOUVEAU-RICHARDS

The other couple you will meet are the NOUVEAU-RICHARDS, of working-class origin but have made a colossal amount of money. Boasting and ostentation are their salient characteristics. At coffee mornings Mrs Nouveau-Richards, who lives in lurex, asks any-one if they've got any idea 'whether gold plate will spoil in the dishwasher'. She has a huge house and lots of servants, who she bullies unmercifully. She is very rude to waiters and very pushy with her children, TRA-CEY-DIANE and JISON, who have several hours after-school coaching every day. Mr Nouveau-Richards gets on the committee of every charity ball in London. The upper classes call him by his Christian name and appreciate his salty humour, but don't invite him to their houses. Jison goes to Stowe and Oxford and ends up a member of the Telly-stocracy, who are the real powers in the land—the people in communication who appear on television. They always talk about 'my show'.

2 CHILDREN

The kiddy is the dad of the guy

At the beginning of the 'seventies the small-is-beautiful brigade mounted a campaign to bring down the birthrate. Family Planning Association supporters brandished condoms outside the House of Commons and at parties sidled up bossily to women who'd just had babies saying, 'Two's yer ration'. Middle-class lefties were rumoured to be concealing third babies in attics rather than display evidence of such social irresponsibility. Disapproving ads appeared in the cinemas showing defeated slatterns in curlers trailing herds of whining children along the street. 'Superdad or Scrounger?' demanded the *Daily Mirror* when a man on Social Security proudly produced his twenty-first child.

In the face of economic gloom, a rocketing dole queue and mothers wanting to get back to work, people probably thought twice about bringing more children into the world. Whatever the cause, the campaign worked. The birthrate in the United Kingdom dropped by 30 per cent. The working classes in particular, having discovered the pill, curbed production dramatically and at the last count were only producing 2.16 children per family, while the upper-middles were down to 1.7. Indeed, the higher you go up the social scale, the smaller the family, although the aristocracy tend to run unpatriotically riot, probably because, as Evelyn Waugh pointed out,

'Impotence and sodomy are socially O.K., but birth control is flagrantly middle-class.' One can't imagine an aristocrat having a vasectomy.

47

With the working classes on the pill, the middle classes, particularly the wholemeal-bread brigade, started panicking about long term effects and switched to the coil or sterilization. The respectable working class still favour the sheath, described by Mrs Definitely-Disgusting as 'my hubby always using something'.

THE BIRTH

If she has a job, which is unlikely, Caroline Stow-Crat gives it up the moment she discovers she's having a baby. The office is relieved too; they're fed up with the endless telephone calls, the Thursday to Tuesday weekends, and falling over the labrador every time they go to the filing cabinet. Samantha Upward tends to work until the last possible minute, ticking away like a time bomb and terrifying all the men in the office.

Our Queen was born by Caesarian, feet first. When Prince Charles was born the Duke of Edinburgh was playing squash. Today he would probably have been squashed into the maternity ward of St Mary's Paddington. The higher socio-economic classes now tend to favour epidural injections which make the whole thing less harrowing and allow the husband, albeit reluctantly, to be present at the birth. 'They do rather get in the way,' said my G.P. 'It's best if they stand at the head of the bed to give their wife moral support, but they keep creeping down the bed to have a look'.

Despite working-class prudishness this trend will no doubt also creep down the social scale, since that sacred cow Esther Rantzen recently calved with husband Desmond Wilcox in attendance, beaming with besotted middle-aged joy afterwards. The labour wards will soon be as crowded out with nail-biting males as Twickenham during an England-Wales International.

When the wife of Super-dad-or-Scrounger produced their twenty-first child, four of the children were allowed to watch. Perhaps the television had broken down. 'It was very exciting,' said the eight year-old afterwards.

The upper classes are not wild about new-born babies. Nancy Mitford once described one as a 'howling orange in a black wig'. But they are delighted to have their double-barrelled names carried on by male issue.

A few years ago *Harper's* published a brilliant piece on the 'Sloane Ranger', the girl who has a flat in Kensington and parents in the country, who lives in headscarves and went to a 'good' girls' boarding school. She epitomizes the level at which the traditional upper-middles merge into the lower ranks of the upper classes. The Sloane Ranger husband is very chuffed whatever sex child he has. If it is a boy he goes to his club and writes two letters, one to 'my housemaster at Eton, and one to Mrs Ingham at Easton House'. Then he opens a bottle of champagne.

Harry Stow-Crat, who certainly wasn't present at the birth of any of his children, might ring up his mother or his old nanny, have a large whisky and soda, then go off and see his mistress.

Poor Gideon Upward is having a horrid time. He now knows exactly why it's called a 'confinement', that he's being conned rotten forking out for a private room, and it's not very *fine* the way Samantha who, disapproving of epidurals, insisted on natural childbirth and is now yelling her head off. Still he's delighted when little Zacharias appears. (Samantha went right through the Bible to find a name no one else had used.) It's so nice to have a boy first, so he can take little 0.7 to dances when they grow up.

While Samantha is in hospital Gideon plans to have a crack at his secretary, but ever-thoughtful Samantha arranges for married friends to ask him out every night. Gideon gets drunk, partly out of frustration and partly at the prospect of his mother-in-law coming to stay next week, and makes sodden passes at the wives while their role-reversed husbands are doing the washing up. The passes are tactfully forgotten about afterwards.

Mr Definitely-Disgusting finds it difficult to visit his wife in hospital because of shift work and National Health visiting hours. When he does, the conversations are usually monosyllabic and inhibited by groans from the labour ward next door.

Aristocrats often get married just before the birth to legitimize the child in case it's a boy. I attended one such wedding where the bride was actually in the last stages of labour. The hospital had thoughtfully provided an altar with a brass cross and two plastic orchids in a mauve vase. The bridegroom hadn't bothered to brush his hair but looked so impossibly handsome that the screaming queen of a hospital chaplain got thoroughly over-excited and spent so long holding his hand he almost forgot to join it to the bride's, who was manfully carrying on with:

'To have . . . (*groan*) . . . and to hold, from this . . . (*groan*).'

THE ANNOUNCEMENT

If you are very grand *The Times* reports the birth on the social pages free of charge. The rest of the upper classes put it in the birth column as briefly as possible:

'To Caroline, wife of Harry Stow-Crat—a son.'

Harry wouldn't have bothered, but Caroline thinks Mummy's friends would like to know. The Upwards' announcement would include the name of the baby (Zacharias Daniel) and a 'née Garland-Watson' to remind people of Samantha's up-market connections. Jen and Bryan Teale might include the name of the hospital and mention earlier children: 'a brother for Christine and Wayne.' Less smart but more reactionary members of the middle classes use the *Daily Telegraph*. The left-wing middles, conveniently combining parsimony with a flouting of convention, don't bother, which explains why the *Guardian* seldom has any birth announcements.

Mrs Definitely-Disgusting, who gets her children's names from the *TV Times*, tends to put the announcement of Sharon Esther, a sister for Dive Darren, in the local paper, with special thanks to the midwifery department at the hospital. It is a working-class characteristic to be touchingly grateful for any kind of hospital treatment, enjoying the rare treat of a rest and three free meals a day cooked by someone else.

Sometimes the Teales, who like a dainty word for everything, and the Definitely-Disgustings, who have difficulty in expressing themselves, will send out cards to friends and relations entitled 'Baby's Announcement' with a picture of a stork on the front. Inside they fill in:

'My name is Sharon Esther. I weigh 10 lbs. My happy Mum and Dad are ...'

Receiving one of these cards, Auntie might send off a nylon, quilted pram-set in canary yellow with the words 'A gift for baby from ...' printed on the box. Other alternatives might be a fluffy, brushed-nylon stuffed rabbit or a teddy bear, referred to by the lower-middle classes and below as a cŭddly (to rhyme with goodly) toy.

The upper classes, particularly the slightly retarded Sloane Ranger belt, have a tendency to add 'y' onto everything. In the 'twenties they did it with names: Bertie, Diney, Jakey, Piggy. Today they have 'choccy cake', 'pressies', 'cheesey things' which children like so much better, don't you agree, 'araby' which the private wards are getting awfully, and their 'gyny', whom they always fall in love with. The Queen's gynæcologist is called Mr Pinker, perhaps the colour he goes when he examines the royal person.

The upper classes don't mix socially with their doctors, but Caroline Stow-Crat makes an exception by asking her 'gyny' to her first dinner party after the birth. (Esther Rantzen did the same, so no doubt the

51

entire working classes will start giving dinner parties in order to follow suit.) Fantasizing about one's 'gyny' is the only thing that makes those agonising post-natal screwings possible. (Samantha Upward knows Gideon must not be denied sex longer than six weeks after the birth.) The crush on the 'gyny' usually lasts about six months.

On return from hospital the upper classes often get their old nanny out of mothballs to come and help with the baby. She usually leaves after a few days in high dudgeon because things are being done the wrong way. With the middle classes, Granny often forks out for a monthly nurse, or else the wife's mother comes to stay and husbands have to remember to put on a dressing gown when they go to the loo in the middle of the night. The working classes are often living with, or near, their parents anyway, or haven't got a spare room for anyone to stay in. The middle-class career mother, avid to get back to work, is praying that the new *au pair*, who isn't being very good about waking up in the night, is going to work out all right.

CLOTHES

The wages of synthetic fibres is social death.

The upper classes, who traditionally have servants to run things, think Baby-Gros are common. Thus, Caroline Stow-Crat prefers to dress babies of both sexes in long white dresses of wool or cotton. Which probably explains little Lord Fondle-Roy and the strong strain of sexual ambiguity about the aristocracy. 'Leggings and cardigans nubbly from being knitted by old Nannies,' say *Harper's*, are also all right; so is the matinee jacket, which always sounds like some moulting musquash cape worn by old ladies to afternoon performances of *The Mousetrap*. Anything nylon, polyester or made from any kind of synthetic fibre is definitely out.

Convenience, however, is a great leveller. Ironing long smocked dresses and washing eight Harrington squares and nappy liners a day was fine in the old days when there was Nanny to do it. Today, when there aren't any servants and upper-class mothers often have to cook dinner for returning husbands, they may resort to Baby-Gros and disposable nappies when no one is looking, their babies only going into regulation white dresses for tea parties or when grandparents come to stay.

Zacharias Upward lives in Baby-Gros, in whatever colour *Vogue* is promoting for grown-ups. He only goes into pink and yellow nubbly cardigans knitted by Samantha's mother when the family go and stay with her.

'Oh do stop being so neurotic—you look like a guttersnipe'

The Nouveau-Richards, having denuded the Toddler's Layette at Harrods, have also acquired the biggest, shiniest Silver Cross Pram for Tracey-Diane. They have furnished it like their cars, with nodding Snoopies, hanging dolls, parasols and frilled canopies to keep off the sun. Tracey-Diane rises from a foam of nylon frills and lace like Venus from the waves. Mrs Nouveau-Richards and the *Daily Mirror* think the word 'pram' is common and refer to it as a 'baby carriage'.

Samantha Upward, conscious of how important it is for children to be brought up with animals, nevertheless invests in a cat net. She also knows how jealous husbands get with new babies around and is paying particular attention to Gideon. In many Stow-Crat houses the only member of the family who suffers from post-natal depression is Snipe the labrador. One monthly nurse said half her day in upper-class houses was spent boosting the morale of the dogs.

Breast-feeding is also coming back into fashion. In the old days the upper classes had their babies suckled by wet nurses, or fed from bottles at once. Jonathan Gathorne-Hardy, in *The Rise and Fall of the British Nanny*, quotes one nanny as saying her mistress was 'remarkable, in fact as far as breast-feeding goes was well nigh incredible'. It turned out she'd fed the baby for one month. Today, as a backlash against working mothers abandoning their babies to the bottle and rushing back to the office, Caroline Stow-Crat and certainly Samantha Upward are tending to breast-feed for several months.

Breast-feeding in public is indulged in by left-wing trendies, and surprisingly by Jen Teale who, probably thinking it's uninhibited upper-class behaviour, will even whip out a tit in the middle of a christening, sending uncles, grandfathers and male godparents fainting into the garden. Mrs Definitely-Disgusting feeds little Dive whenever he's hungry. One remembers Mum in *The Larkins* plugging little Oscar into her massive bosom in hotel lobbies, dining-rooms and on the beach. The left wing middle-class mother also feeds her baby on demand, and it's been demanding ever since.

Old-fashioned nannies, who came from the working classes, tended to get their children on the pot and out of nappies very early—quite understandable as they had no washing machines or Napisan in those days. Geoffrey Gorer in his book *Exploring English Character*, suggests that the obsessive desire for privacy of the upper-class male is the result of being watched over on the pot:

'Immersed in clubs, behind ramparts of newspapers, silent in the corner of first-class carriages, at last he is free of Nanny.'

Caroline Stow-Crat talks about 'toilet-trining' with a cockney accent to excuse the word toilet.

It is very Jen Teale to use the word diapers. Caroline says 'nappies'.

Let us now digress slightly to nomenclature. While the upper classes say 'having a baby', Samantha Upward says 'pregnant', the lower-middle classes say 'expecting a baby' or 'starting a family'. The working-class mother, however, will say 'Three months after I had Dive, I fell for Sharon,' which doesn't mean that, due to post-natal gloom, she developed Lesbian tendencies, merely that she got pregnant again.

Upper and middle-class children call their parents 'Mummy' and 'Daddy', although the boy might call his father 'Dad' as he gets older, or refer to him as 'my father'. The lower-middles call them 'Mum' and 'Dad', and the working classes 'Moom' and 'Dud'. Socially aspiring lower-middles like Sandra in *The Liver Birds* also call their mother 'Mummy'. Trendy lefties and women who are reluctant to grow old, insist their children call them by their Christian names. Jen and Bryan Teale call each other 'Mummy' and 'Daddy', the working classes 'Mum' and 'Dad'.

A lot of confusion is caused by the word 'nanny'. To the upper and middle classes it means someone who looks after children for money, although Samantha Upward would prefer to call her 'my girl', or '*the au pair*'. To the working classes 'Nanny', 'Nana' or 'Nan' is one's grandmother who, as all the mothers are rushing back to work, probably also looks after the children—but is not paid for it. To the upper classes Nana

55

means a large dog in *Peter Pan*.

The upper classes call their aunts 'Aunt Mary', the middle classes 'Auntie Mary'. Lower-middle and working-class children are forced to call any friend of their parents 'Auntie' or 'Uncle'. Two working-class expressions that seem to be creeping upwards are 'Baby needs changing', as though you were fed up with her already, and 'I've potted Sharon', as though she was a shiny red billiard ball. Confusion is also caused by the word 'putting down'. The upper classes 'put down' dogs, Jen Teale tends to 'put them to sleep' or 'send them to the Happy Hunting Ground'. The middle classes 'put down' children for schools, but when the working classes say, 'I've put Sharon down', it means they've put her to bed. When they say, 'I mind children,' it doesn't mean that they dislike them but that they look after them.

The sociologist refers to the child as 'The Third Estate of the nuclear family'. The lower-middles and working classes call him a 'kiddy', the middle classes a 'kid'. The upper-middles and uppers talk about 'the children'. But upper-class people, trying to be democratic, have started to call them 'kids'. This unnerves Samantha Upward.

It is also an aristocratic trait to refer to members of one's family by name, assuming automatically that other people will know who one means. Caroline Stow-Crat would say,

'Harry's shooting. Can I bring Fiona and Georgie?'

She would also say the baby, rather than 'my baby', or 'Baby' or the American-influenced 'my little girl' which is very Jen Teale. Harry, on the other hand, if asking a friend how his son is getting on, might easily say: 'How's your boy?'

One of the first events in the baby's life is a trip to the clinic. On rainy days the place is deserted because the Mrs Definitely-Disgustings, who always dress up to wheel their prams to the clinic, don't like getting their best clothes wet. You can tell the middle-class mothers because they are much more scruffy and have smaller prams (to fit into the Volvo). When I visited a clinic in Putney there were naturally no upper-class mothers because they don't live south of the river and they never go to clinics. Several working-class mothers, in mini-skirts, leather coats and high-heeled shoes, with very done-up babies, were capping each other's crawling and teething stories. Two left-wing middle-class mothers with eager, unpainted faces, ragged hair and dirndl skirts were talking about an anti-aircraft noise meeting that night. Behind them a pretty Samantha Upward appeared to be carrying on a very enunciated conversation with another upper middle-class mum to which no one could help listening. Suddenly one realized that she was addressing a non-stop monologue to her own six-month-old baby, having obviously read somewhere that the more you talk to your baby, the sooner it talks back. The ratlet race had begun.

THE CHRISTENING

The next *big event* in a child's life is the Christening. The Queen was christened in a private chapel at Buckingham Palace at five weeks, baptised with water from the Jordan, and dressed in christening robes of cream Brussels lace, worn by every baby in the royal family since Queen Victoria's children.

The aristocracy tend to be christened in their own thirteenth century churches, wearing slightly yellowing christening robes embroidered with the family crest. *The Times* will report it on the social page. A London christening takes place at the Guards Chapel or in the Crypt Chapel at the House of Commons, with lunch at Boodles afterwards.

Sloane Ranger christenings tend to have Earl Grey tea, not enough champagne and, if they're short of cash, the top layer of their wedding cake re-iced. Christening presents include silver mugs with at least four initials to take in the double barrels, and premium bonds, but not napkin rings or building society shares, which are very lower-middle class.

As the Merrytocracy are fast reaching a state when they can't open their mouths without a glass in their hand, christenings are tending to get later and later, with champagne, chicken drumsticks and leprous quiche at 5:30.

The suburbs and Jen and Bryan Teale tend to go in for multiple christenings with each couple looking beadily at everyone else's baby and thinking how much more 'well spoken' their own godparent is when she names this child. The vicar looks in at all the parties afterwards and has difficulty not shlurring his words at Evenshong.

The left-wing middles, combining parsimony with agnostic puritanism, don't have their kids christened.

Mr Definitely-Disgusting goes out mini-cabbing to pay for the party and a new costume for Mrs Definitely-Disgusting who makes all the food, which includes pork pie, apple pie with pastry leaves, sponge cakes and fruit punch. The godparents probably keep the local pub.

Social climbers choose famous or successful godparents who might advance their children's careers or improve their status. They've dropped all their childhood friends. Sloane Rangers' mothers advise them not to ask that awfully nice girl from next door in Fulham, because you probably won't see her again after you move to the country. Jean Cocteau once acted as a godparent, then promptly forgot about the child. Years later he met the father who reproached him for neglecting his duties. Mortified, Cocteau at once sent his godson a large teddy bear.

'Was he pleased,' he asked next time he met the father.

'Not awfully,' came the reply. 'He's a colonel now.'

The christening, like the wedding, is frequently an occasion when two different classes meet head-on. The baby's mother, for example, may be lower-middle and determined not to put a foot wrong, while the baby's father's family may be upper-middle and equally determined to patronize. Less smart relations are kept in the background or ruthlessly excluded. Examples of this can be found in Colin Bell's fascinating book, *Middle Class Families*, in which he devotes a chapter to describing three Welsh christenings.

The first involved a lower-middle-class couple, who asked a hundred guests to the church. Of these only six were manual workers and their wives. The baby's mother was awfully pleased that her cousin (the sole member of the family who'd been to a public school) had bothered to come. Only one manual worker and his wife, however, was asked back to the party at home after the service. The husband worked on the railways and they lived in a council house.

'But she's my auntie,' said the baby's mother, 'and they're the salt of the earth.' (An expression used by all classes to excuse those of lower station.) As a first grandchild, the baby was given a staggering £1000 by his grandparents and enough clothes to keep Dr Barnado's going for a year.

The second christening involved a slightly less smart family. The father was described as a 'geographically mobile plant superintendent', which actually meant he'd moved around the country in the course of his career, upping his salary each time. On this occasion their daily woman came to the church to keep the older children quiet, but was not invited back to the house for tea afterwards, even to help—a classic example of the *nouveau-riche* not knowing how to treat servants—and presumably because she was close enough to the family in class to be mistaken for a relation. In spite of this she sent the baby a coodly toy. Unsmart relations weren't asked, even though they lived nearby.

'Not because I'm a snob,' said the mother untruthfully, 'but he's a porter or something.'

In the final christening the parents were both bright children of working-class parents, who'd met at university and promptly moved to another part of the country, away from any embarrassing roots. The relations were mercifully too poor to come to the christening. Godparents were friends from work. The grandparents didn't send any presents, only vastly elaborate christening cards.

Another example of the clash between classes occurred at a recent middle-class christening I attended. One of the godfathers, a working-class actor who'd done very well for himself but had never been to a christening before, missed the church service and rolled up in time for tea, armed with a christening cake decorated with primrose yellow icing, the baby's name in mauve and a stork and a baby made out of a sugared almond with its features slipping. Alas, the baby's grandmother had also provided a large white christening cake complete with stork and slipping-featured sugared almond. The cakes were placed side by side— with Storky and Co gazing sourly at one another.

And while we're on the subject of cakes, Caroline Stow-Crat would never call marzipan 'almond paste'.

THE RATLET RACE

The christening over, the ratlet race starts in earnest. The battle is particularly vicious among the middle classes, where if you can't boast an 'int'risting' career, you justify your existence by rearing a little genius. This is another part of the backlash against women going out to work. Newspapers and women's magazines are constantly stressing the importance of the child being mentally stimulated during the first five years of its life. Journalists like Mary Kenny recant on women's lib principles and expound the joys of motherhood. This is very easy for lady journalists who can always write at home *and* see their babies when they want to. Middle-class society is teeming with women having nervous breakdowns because they feel so in-

'Oh Gideon—do you think he's having his first breakdown?'

adequate about only being a wife and mother.

At plonk-and-pâté-tasting-of-old-socks-parties be-loved by the upper-middle classes, you can hear the battle raging. Samantha Upward who, in spite of having a degree, believes in staying at home to raise little Zacharias 'creatively', is talking to a career mum:

SAMANTHA (who knows one is never regarded as a cabbage if one's 'intristed' in other people): How's the job?

CAREER MUM: Oh exhausting. I had to lunch George Best on Monday, look after Graham Greene all week, then we had a press party for Isherwood last night. (Fifteen-love to Career Mum).

SAMANTHA: And how's Damian?

CAREER MUM: All right, I think. How's the baby? (*Not being round much she doesn't even know Zacharias's name.*)

SAMANTHA: Oh he's just finished *Alice in Won-*

derland. Simply couldn't put it down. I do recommend flash cards. And he can already beat Gideon at chess. We're a bit worried he's a Gifted Child, but you can't really tell at two. (Thirty-fifteen to Samantha.)

Harry Stow-Crat doesn't believe in wives working, or husbands for that matter. It would interfere with shooting and fishing.

The upper classes have nurseries upstairs. The upper-middles call them 'playrooms' and tend to have them downstairs so the children won't miss any cultural pearls dropped by their parents. In the kitchen a cork board groans with Zacharias's first drawings. Jen Teale, who is determined that little Wayne shall get on in life, has the nursery in the lounge with model soldiers on the mantelpiece and children's posters on the wall. The garden will be filled with Wendy huts and social climbing frames.

Dive Definitely-Disgusting has no room set aside for him and often sleeps in the same room, or even bed, as his brothers and sisters. The reason they go to bed so late is because Mrs Definitely-Disgusting has to ensure that one child is soundly asleep before she can put the next one to bed, and so on. The cot is often bought with Embassy coupons.

The upper classes send their children to bed at six-thirty so that they'll be out of the way before their father comes back from shooting or the city. The role-reversed upper-middles who believe that contact with the father is essential, tend to keep them up slightly later so they'll have half an hour with Daddy before going to sleep. Gideon Upward, knackered after a hard day, is corrected by little Zacharias every time he tries to skip a page of Paddington Bear and longs for a bit of upper-class peace downstairs with a large gin and tonic.

Sleeping alone, the middle-class child is often frightened of the dark, but his parents can afford to leave a light on all night outside his room.

The middle classes have always given a lot of parental authority to the father. The upper and working classes tend to leave discipline to the mother, nanny or grandmother. But, with shorter working hours and less shift work, the working-class father is tending to be at home more, take more interest in his children and no longer be ashamed to be seen pushing the pram.

'Vic takes baby up the park on the weekend, while I get the dinner on,' is a typical working-class remark.

Equally, as the upper classes get poorer and can't afford servants, the fathers are forced to pay more attention to the children.

'I used to shove the baby into his arms,' said one monthly nurse, 'and walk out of the room. He'd hold it like a rattlesnake; but by the time I left he was pushing the pram and changing nappies.' One upper-class husband, she said, refused to push the pram, but would walk behind his wife when she was pushing it, pushing her.

By the time the middle-class child is a year old, say the statisticians, he will be less likely to have a tantrum than the working-class child, will have had a much better diet and be off the bottle (as though he'd been on an alcoholic binge for the first twelve months). Harry Stow-Crat will have had a grille put in the back of the estate car to stop Georgie bothering Snipe. Georgie will have had his first party, which he won't remember, but which was a great show-off occasion for his nanny. Jen Teale's child will now be referred to as a 'toddler' or a 'tiny tot'. Samantha will be out on the culture beat hawking little Zacharias round museums and art galleries to stop herself becoming a cabbage. The Hayward Gallery won't allow prams inside but provides baby slings to help Mummy appreciate Dada.

CHILDREN'S CLOTHES

Little Georgie Stow-Crat will be out of long dresses now and into romper suits with Peter Pan collars, or short trousers which he will wear until he's half-way through prep school. Occasionally in Hyde Park on cold days one sees the camp sight of little upper-class boys wearing tights under their shorts. He might occasionally be allowed to wear jeans like the middle classes, but never ones that fit, in case their tightness stops him carrying on the line. Upper-class little girls are smock-marked.

The middle classes dress their children like small adults in the hope that they'll grow brighter and more adult earlier. In the same way that the upper classes force boy babies into little dresses, the middle classes force little girls into jeans. Jen Teale's daughter, Chris-

Tracey-Diane Nouveau-Richards in casual clothes

tine, wears her dresses slightly too short, to display hen's bum knickers.

All little girls, in fact, are lower-middle by inclination. If allowed, they would always dress like Christine in peasant blouses with elasticated waists and sleeves, their hair in bunches, sticking out above the ears; or like Tracey-Diane Nouveau-Richards in earrings, with painted toenails, huge nylon bows in the hair, pink plastic butterfly slides and white slingback or even high-heeled shoes. The Teales and the Nouveau-Richards encourage such prissiness by saying, 'Always try to be a little lady', or 'Isn't Tracey-Diane a little flirt?' Mrs Nouveau-Richards, who believes in getting her pound of flesh from the nanny, insists that all Tracey's clothes are 'hand' washed as she calls it. Mrs Definitely-Disgusting dresses her children in brightly coloured polyester and acrylic—shocking pink, mauve, royal blue and turquoise being the most popular. They also wear very shiny T-shirts with 'Ars-nel' on them and mock suede coats with nylon fur collars. The upper classes only used to allow their children to wear anoraks on the ski slopes, but have now given in.

Hair is also a class indicator. Upper-class little boys have their curls brushed flat and cut in the shape of a pudding basin. The middle classes have their hair tapered like Cliff Richard. Upper-class little girls either wear their fringe on the eyebrows like Shetland ponies or drawn off their foreheads (pronounced 'forrids') with a small velvet bow at the side or the crown of the head. They sometimes wear Alice bands, but sewn and with proper velvet, not made out of stretch material. Jen Teale cuts Christine's fringe half-way down the forehead, so there is no danger she won't be able to see out. She cuts Wayne's hair short at the back so that half an inch or two of neck shows. The working classes no longer Brylcreem their kiddies' hair into tight curls—too much like the 'darkies'—but they do brush Baby's hair upwards like a Sioux Indian's.

Until recently it was much easier to tell a child's

65

background from its clothes than its mother's. But since the entire nation's youth is now clad in spin-offs from whatever film is fashionable and since Mary Quant (who staged the great 'sixties revolution, making duchesses interchangeable with shop girls) has gone into children's clothes, all children will soon look alike.

THE RÉGIME

Upper-class mothers believe in fresh air and walks to feed the ducks in the afternoon. They're very park conscious. Ducks in Kensington Gardens ought to be members of Weight Watchers, so stuffed are they with bread (but never sliced, because the upper classes think its common.) Ducks that live near the Round Pond in Hampstead get whole-wheat crusts. As soon as Georgie Stow-Crat can walk he is put on a pony. From Monday to Friday upper-class London children have to make do with the rocking horse at Harrods.

Conventional upper-class children have cake, sandwiches and perhaps as a treat an ice at four o'clock, what the working classes describe as 'afternoon tea'. Middle-class children have high tea at about six consisting of baked beans, beef-burgers or fish fingers and yoghurt. The working classes tend to have the same, but if any of the food is cooked the meal is called 'a dinner': 'Karen has a dinner at lunchtime and a dinner in the evening'. The working classes might also say, 'I gave Baby juice and cereal at three'. The upper classes would specify 'orange juice', and 'cornflakes' or 'Weetabix'. The lower you get down the social scale the more likely people are to use convenience words, like 'teacher' for 'schoolmaster' or 'mistress'. The lower-working classes eat chip butties and sweets all day—they don't have meals.

Upper-class children tend to have other children over to tea at four as a social occasion. Middle-class children come over to play at any time. When the middle classes send their children to state schools the children ask their working-class schoolmates to tea, then feel hurt because they never get asked back. It never occurs to Zacharias Upward that Dive Definitely-Disgusting might feel ashamed of the smallness of his house and the fact that he doesn't have a bedroom to himself.

The working classes tend to cram their children with sweets, cheap placebos like 'Molteasers', 'Croonchy' and 'Cadbury's Fruit and Not'. Samantha Upward, having read about nutrition, tends to restrict Zacharias's sweet-eating, although career mums, conscious of being away too much, bombard their children with guilt presents every time they're late home. Little Zacharias, who is only allowed two sweets after lunch and is fed up with museums, wishes Samantha would get a part-time job, so he could get guilt presents too.

Upper-class children are taught nursery rhymes by their nannies and know them all by the time they're eighteen months, giving them a vocabulary of about 500 words. Traditionally a lot of nursery rhymes chronicle the activities of their forbears anyway. Little Jack Horner pulling out a plum, for instance, refers to the fat pickings culled by the Horner family during the dissolution of the monasteries.

Sharon Definitely-Disgusting only knows television jingles. In a recent quiz at a state school none of the eleven-year-olds could say what Little Miss Muffet sat on.

STAYING WITH GRANNY

Working-class children, as has been said before, often live with or near their grandmother, so the working-class Nan is much the best with children because she's had the most practice. Georgie Stow-Crat's grandparents live in the country, have lots of room and servants to take the children off their hands. Zacharias Upward's grandparents live on their nerves and an ever-dwindling fixed income. They move into smaller and smaller houses but hang on to all the ornaments, which are double-parked on every piece of furniture, so that the place looks like an antique shop. All the china is moved up a shelf when the grandchildren come to stay, but eventually they break the place up because they're fed up with not being allowed to touch anything and with playing the same old brought-out game of bagatelle. A terrible family row develops because one ball-bearing disappears. Both daughters and daughters-in-law feel on trial all the time and the tension is transmitted to the children. If they're let out into the garden, footballs snap the regalia lilies. Mealtimes are a nightmare because the middle classes are obsessively hot on table manners.

'Why do all my grandchildren eat as though they're gardening?' is a typical upper-middle-class granny remark.

Children invariably let the side down by saying, 'Why can't we have baked beans in front of the telly like we do at home?'

Upper-middle-class grannies invariably had nannies to bring up their own children and cannot understand why their grandchildren should be so exhausting, or so much more badly behaved than their own children were. They forget that they only saw them when they were presented, newly washed, for an hour after tea.

Samantha Upward drives her mother-in-law crackers. Every time Zacharias interrupts, she stops whatever adult conversation she is having to answer his question.

The middle classes tend to reason.

The working classes tend to clout.

The working classes have dummies. Middle-class children are more likely to suck their thumbs.

Sexual modesty is also a good index of social class. The majority of the working classes never see their parents naked, which must be quite an achievement as they often sleep in the same room—rather like undressing on the beach.

Social class 1 (which according to the Census, includes scientists, doctors and structural engineers) are much more likely to let their children see them with no clothes on. Pretty horrifying really, and enough to put one off sex for life, having a hairy scientist streaking round the house.

The upper-middle classes are less likely to worry about masturbation and more likely to tell their children the facts of life. They are aided in this by Althea, of Dinosaur Books fame, who has written a very explicit children's book about having a baby. Known locally as the 'rude' book, it is a great favourite to read aloud when Granny comes to stay.

To Jen Teale the word 'rude' means 'slightly smutty', to the upper class it means 'impertinent'. Similarly the uppers use 'cheeky' to mean impertinent whereas to Jen Teale it means a bit risque or near the knuckle.

The working classes have difficulty explaining things so you get their children coming into the public library and saying,

'I want a book about life.'

'Whose life?' asks the librarian. 'Biographies are over there.'

'Facts of life, Miss.'

Georgie Stow-Crat doesn't need to be told about sex because he's seen plenty of farm animals copulating. As a result upper-class men often take their wives from behind.

My husband heard about sex for the first time when he was walking in a prep-school crocodile along the beach.

'I say, chaps,' said a boy called the Hon. James Stewart, 'I know how babies are made.'

Whereupon they all gathered round saying, 'Go on, Stewart, tell us.'

'The man lies on top of the woman,' said Stewart portentously, 'and is excused into her.'

The middle classes will start taking their children to the dentist almost before they've got teeth; the working classes tend only to go when their teeth ache. 'You can tell what class a person is the moment he opens his mouth,' said John Braine, 'by the state of his teeth.' That's why Sharon Definitely-Disgusting claps her hands over her mouth whenever she laughs.

The upper classes give their children 10p from the fairies when a tooth comes out. Inflation and indulgence have pushed the middle classes up to 50p. Among the upper-middle merrytocracy the fairies often get drunk and forget to put the money under the pillow and have to compensate with twice as much the next day. When the fair arrives each year, children have been known to tug teeth out with forceps for more money to spend on the fruit machines.

People are gradually realising that illiteracy in schools today is nothing to do with the teaching, but simply because children have been turned into a race of zombies by watching television. Soon the middle classes will start banning television altogether, and illicit watch-easys will be set up in darkened dives round the country.

Samantha Upward doesn't let Zacharias read comics or watch more than an hours' television a day. Upper-class children go into the kitchen and read the housekeeper's children's comics. Samantha reads out loud to Zacharias in a clear voice altering words she thinks are common and remembering to say 'orf'.

The Queen evidently read very early because in the evenings her mother used to read her books 'about animals and horses and they would recite gay poetry.'

(Marlowe and Oscar Wilde perhaps.) Before he reads, the working class child can write C.F.C. and SHED and SOD and FUK on bus shelters.

By the age of two little George Stow-Crat will be looking out on life with a clear blue gaze, frightened of no one, totally self-confident. He will also have a frightful accent from playing in the stable but no one is in the least bit worried. Working-class children always hold their noses in the country.

The middle-class child will already be shell-shocked with instructions. Don't tread in Doggie's duty; put your hand over your mouth when you cough; don't turn your fork over to eat peas; it's rude to whisper; it's rude to shout; talk in a low clear voice like Anna Ford or Mrs Thatcher. Class is beginning to creep in. Middle-class children twig that they can bully the char's children, but the char's children can't beat them up in return. They also know that there are certain children in the road their mother prefers them playing with to others. Samantha has great difficulty explaining to little Zacharias why he may sprinkle his pepper but not his salt.

I once heard my son regaling his friends:

'Mummy says "pardon" is a much worse word than "fuck".'

Jen Teale's child will be constantly pulled up for some real or imagined coarseness of speech or enunciation. It's so important to be 'well-spoken'.

Middle-class children put cherry stones on the side of their plate with their spoon and chant, 'Tinker, Tailor, Soldier, Sailor, Rich man, Poor man, Beggarman, Thief'. Upper-class children conceal the journey from mouth to plate with curled fist and say 'Army, Navy, Law, Divinity, Independent, Medicine, Trade'. The working classes only eat cherries out of tins of fruit salad with the stones already removed.

Children's parties are a sophisticated form of torture. The upper classes tend to give parties just for

71

nannies and children, mid-week, and ending at six so as not to involve the husbands. No drink is offered to collecting parents.

Nanny Stow-Crat couldn't stop Fiona inviting Tracey Nouveau-Richards as they sit next to each other at nursery school, but Caroline says she's not having those ghastly parents in the house: 'They never know when to leave and once through the door, they might make a habit of dropping in.'

Samantha Upward, being very democratic, encourages Zacharias to invite all his little state school friends who run absolutely wild all over the newly planted perennials that were once going to make an herbaceous border. They refuse to play party games and drive the conjuror into hysterics by explaining in loud voices how every trick is done.

Mr Nouveau-Richards, who feels that only the best is good enough for my Tracey-Diane, employs Searcy's to do the catering, Dick Emery for the cabaret, gives each child a Tiger Tiger doll's house as a going-away present, and shows the premiere of *Star Wars II* after the interval. All the surrounding middle-class mums would like to refuse, but daren't because they'd get such flak from their children.

The upper-middle merrytocracy mix drink, nannies and mothers, thereby making the children's party a much more jolly occasion. Parties in Putney are rather like singles bars with separated fathers turning up to collect children and meeting pretty divorced mothers and getting nose to nose over the Soave and the hassle of bringing up children on one's own.

3 THE NANNY

*'The daughters of tradespeople, however well
educated, must necessarily be underbred,
and as such unfit to be the inmates of our
dwellings or guardians of our children's
minds, and persons.'*

Charlotte Brontë.

Anyone studying the English class system will have
noticed certain similarities between the extreme upper
and lower classes; toughness, xenophobia, indifference
to public opinion, passion for racing and gambling,
fondness for plain speaking and plain untampered food.
Jonathan Gathorne-Hardy, in *The Rise and Fall of the
British Nanny*, says the reason is that the ruling classes
for the last two hundred years have been brought up
almost entirely by working-class nannies, their parents
abdicating all responsibility.

'With monthly nurses, nannies, prep school and public school,' admitted one mother, 'it's almost as though
we put them in care.'

Certainly one of the reasons why the aristocracy has
always notched up so many marriages has been because thay never had any boring middle-class worries
about how it might affect the children. Nanny would
always be there to look after them and provide conti-
nuity.

Working for the great, nannies took on their own
snobbisms, not unlike suburban crones working in
Knightsbridge dress shops for £50 a week who make
you feel bitterly ashamed of your scuffed heels and the
fact that you can't afford £500 for a little black dress.

There was a group of nannies who ruled Hyde Park.

'Are you a titled mummy's nanny?' said one gorgon, when a newly employed nanny sat down beside her.

The new nanny shook her head.

'Well I'm afraid,' said the gorgon, 'that this bench is reserved for titled mummies' nannies.'

Until a few years ago nanny was a fixture in the upper-class house, taking on the surname of the family and often staying with them until she died, when an announcement would appear in *The Times* expressing the family's gratitude and giving her length of service. When her charges grew up, there were always grandchildren. Sometimes she regained her ascendancy when the master became senile and needed looking after, or when Miss Caroline became an alcoholic. One friend of mine spends £6000 a year keeping a large house in Sussex going simply as a base for his old nanny and her dog. Another nanny, when her children grew up, took over the care of the three family dogs, keeping them in baskets upstairs and giving them the same nursery routine of brushing, walks, mealtimes and early beds. While another old nanny keeps an eye on visiting dogs. When a friend's golden retriever had been cavorting in the loch for an hour, she sidled up and said, 'I think Porridge has been in for long enough.'

Today, alas, the old-fashioned nanny whose life was her children, who welcomed the role of surrogate mother, imposed on her by her employers, delighting in the challenge of coping with everything, never taking a holiday, is virtually an extinct breed.

'You'll be lucky if you get a girl to stay six months,' said Nannies of Kensington. 'They just don't want to get involved for too long.' A few years ago Mrs Walters of Knightsbridge Nannies, who provided 'treasures' for half the crowned heads of Europe, said her telephone was permanently jammed with cries of 'Help me, Help me' from harassed society women left in the lurch by their nannies and faced with the appalling prospect of having to forego a game of bridge or a trip to Fortnums. It also suits the agencies to foster this myth of unavailability. The more often a nanny moves around, the more often they get their rake off.

By the end of the 'seventies, however, the position had changed slightly. The rocketing cost of living has made the nanny's job much more attractive. If she lives in, she gets all her bills paid: rent, telephone, rates, electricity, gas and food, and £25–35 tax-free pocket money on top of that, which makes her far better off than a secretary on £5,500 a year. The only way you distinguish the nannies from the mothers picking children up from school is that the nannies are younger and better dressed.

'Well I make it that you'll have to get a rise of £15,000 just to pay for Nanny.'

On the other hand the more women go out to work, the more they are dependent on others to look after their children. If the nanny is working for a divorced or separated woman, or even in a household where the woman is the chief breadwinner, her power is absolute. If she walks out, her employer will have to jeopardize her job staying at home and looking after the children, or fork out for a temporary at £50 a week.

Before the war, the upper and middle classes tended to be undomesticated (my grandmother once went into the kitchen, saw a dishcloth and fled, never to return) and were therefore neurotically dependent on servants. Today any career woman or working mother who has to rely on a recalcitrant daily woman (someone once said they were called 'dailys' because they leave after one day) or a capricious nanny in order to go out to work will understand this neurosis.

One sees this absolute power developing so often. A plump little lower-middle-class girl arrives from the country with rosy cheeks and a Yorkshire accent. She starts off doing absolutely everything for £10 a week, but gradually she makes herself indispensable. She also starts aping the mannerisms of her employers and goes to a West End hairdresser, her accent disappears as do the inches off her hips. Next she meets a boyfriend and, terrified of losing her because she's become such a treasure, her employers let the boyfriend move in. Soon there's a broad-shouldered denim-jacketed back watching television every time the parents come in from an evening out, which is soon followed by additional aggro because he's having fry-ups in the morning, drinking the house Carafino and using the bath.

The employers are by now frightened of using the car in case the nanny is intending to take it home for the weekend, and start fighting as to which one of them is going to ask her to baby-sit, if they occasionally want to go out, standing outside her door, saying, 'No, you do it. No, *you* do it.'

By now the boyfriend starts shop-stewarding around,

76

telling the nanny she oughtn't to be working those hours: 'Girls in our office only do nine to five, and you never get a lunch hour.' More and more concessions are made, anything to avoid the hassle of working in a new girl.

Usually a row blows up about once a month, whereupon the nanny sits in the kitchen muttering to next door's nanny and ringing ads in the *Evening Standard*, or *The Times*. While her employer doesn't feel up to going to work and sits nervously writing an ad for *The Lady*, or ringing up agencies on the upstairs telephone: 'Tell anyone who might be interested to ring my husband at the office, or she can ring here at weekends.' Usually she and the nanny get bored of rowing by the evening, and make it up over a litre bottle of Pedrotti. By the time the husband comes home all wound up to read the riot act, wife and nanny are plastered but fondly tearful over an empty bottle.

A few years ago middle-class husbands used traditionally to knock off the *au pair*. Today, far more often you find husbands getting jealous of the mutually sycophantic, love-hate relationship that exists between the wife and the nanny, particularly since the advent of the permissive society, when nanny often covers up for the wife's sexual peccadilloes and therefore has even more power over her.

Samantha Upward only works part-time and doesn't feel this justifies a nanny so she gets *au pairs* to help Zacharias with his French and says, 'Go and do your *devoir*, darling,' when he gets home from school. Gideon hopes every time for someone like Brigitte Bardot, but Samantha has so much middle-class guilt about employing anyone, and spends so much time scurrying round doing all the work, that the various Claudines and Marie Josés soon become au pear-shaped.

No such scruples overcome Mrs Nouveau-Richards, who, as a first-generation employer, is determined to get several pounds of flesh off the nannies. She expects them to work six days a week for only £12, to wear uniform, to keep the children upstairs and to address her as 'Mrs Nouveau-Richards'. One nanny told us that her newly rich employer allowed her to call her by her Christian name only if they went out together in the evening, never during the day. She also allowed the nanny to use the front stairs, but the other servants had to use the back stairs.

One of nanny's least enviable tasks is helping with the playgroup. The rich send their children to nursery schools, where trained nannies take them over for three hours a day and teach them the rudiments of reading, writing and making castles out of lavatory paper rolls. The less rich have to make do with playgroups, where different mothers take it in turns to supervise the children. Here the lower-middle Jen Teales are *far* more bossy than the upper-middle mums and if a working mother sends her nanny or her *au pair* instead of going herself, the Jen Teales, probably feeling themselves perilously close to the status of the nanny, refuse to talk to her, except for telling her to do all the dirty work. When my own nanny used to do it she was the only adult who wasn't offered a cup of coffee.

Many people who didn't have nannies themselves regard them as a status symbol. One *nouveau riche* family who employed a nanny, insisted she wear a uniform but gave her a nervous breakdown by never allowing her near the baby.

Esther Rantzen devoted a whole column in the *Evening News* to her daughter's 'lovely Nanny, who even likes the mucky bits', but who only has to wear uniform when she goes to official B.B.C. events like Miss United Kingdom. A Birmingham journalist, who had a baby at 42, had a nanny she described as a 'lovely lady, who we call Auntie Margaret'. Being called 'a lovely lady' in the national or provincial press is worth at least £10 a week.

Many permanent nannies today act as managing director for the whole household, but for some reasons they hate admitting to the outside world what their job is. I had one girl who used to tell her boyfriends that she was on the dole and just staying with me. Another nanny was getting her employers and the children off for a weekend when some man rang up.

'Hang on,' her employers heard her saying, 'I'm just saying goodbye to some friends.'

On another occasion, when a commercial was being made in her boss's house, she asked him to carry his newly-ironed shirts upstairs because she didn't want the film crew to realize she was a nanny. If asked what she does she says she's a P.A.

The nanny-employer relationship is interesting because it is one of the few occasions when the classes meet head on, not just during the day, as people do in offices, but at all times, and the nanny has to adjust to a completely different lifestyle.

Nannies divide households into 'upstairs' and 'downstairs' families. The upstairs families keep the children upstairs and allow the nanny complete if lonely autonomy. Downstairs families are usually middle class; the nanny and the mother muddle along, both looking after the children in uneasy complicity.

Differing taste, of course, is frequently a bone of contention in the nanny-employer relationship and there's often a problem when a member of the serviette union goes into a family which says 'napkin'. Children soon suss out areas of discord. Samantha Upward's *au pair* comes in very red in the face, saying, 'Zacharias refuses to say "Pardon".'

Whereupon Samantha goes even redder and stands on one leg, saying, 'Well actually we always say "What". I don't know why.'

Nannies in the past have tried to impose gracious living on our household: mauve bath crystals, Freshaire, white plastic flower vases filled with plastic flowers, plastic punch bowls with eight little matching cups and a glass ladle, short back and sides for both children, an acrylic white cardigan edged with pink tulips which my daughter thought was absolute heaven, as she did a pair of wedge-heeled walking shoes. Nothing could illustrate my innate middle-classness more than the fact that I was too wet to put my foot down and insist they should either be taken back or not used.

Caroline Stow-Crat wouldn't have had any such problem. On the other hand she would never correct her nanny in front of anyone else like a woman with her nanny and child who passed me and my dog in the street.

'Look at the lovely doggie,' said the nanny to the child.

'That is a dog, not a doggie,' said her employer in chilling tones.

Jonathan Gathorne-Hardy claims that there was never any strain between the upper-class 'What', the lower-middle 'Pardon' or the working-class 'Eh'. Nannies simply became bilingual and said 'lounge' to their friends and 'drawing-room' to their employers.

Nannies in the past, however, made up their own little snobbish rules: 'Nanny Ellis said it was common to stare, common to play with children whose friends were in trade, however rich, common to play in the front garden, or to eat jelly with anything but a fork. Vulgar children say "Hip Hip Hooray" and eat Fry's chocolate. We say "Hip Hip Hurrah" and eat Cadbury's.'

Nannies today don't ask the wilder state school children to tea because, instead of please and thank you, they say, 'Cor what's this crap?' when last night's réchauffé Boeuf Bourgignon is served up to them. If they don't eat up nanny doesn't allow them any dream topping or fruit salad, so they don't want to be asked again either.

Mrs Nouveau-Richards, who pays her nanny a pittance, is careful to steer her away from the fast piece at No 10 who gets £35 a week and every weekend off, and who might preach subersive ideas. Even the Philippinos are getting less biddable, Conceptione, who used to do everything for £7, has got herself a job in

a hotel for £8. An actress I know had a Philippino girl
for a second interview to finalize details. Suddenly she
got to her feet and said:

'Mrs Francis, I must be level with you. I cannot after
all come to work for you. I have fallen in love with Mrs
X (her previous employer). She is going to leave her
husband and live with me, but as she is used to a certain
standard of living, I am honour bound to support her
so I am going to train to be doctor.'

4 EDUCATION

O Teacher mine! Where are you roaming?

After three years at a private day school, the upper classes pack their children off to prep school at eight because they're too stupid to do the homework any more, because they can't cope with the complications of the milk run, and because, even though they're not at all afraid of the school staff, they have no desire to mix with them socially at the string of fund-raising events laid on by day schools. Even at eight, little Georgie Stow-Crat misses home less than a middle-class child because his affection is divided between his mother and nanny. He misses Snipe, the labrador, most of all and calls Caroline Stow-Crat 'sir' in the holidays. Any boisterousness or subversive tendencies are ironed out of him at school, and everyone, particularly his grandmother, says how much he has improved. No one, on the other hand, can explain why the housekeeper's cat has been strangled.

Samantha Upward, trying to be enlightened, starts Zacharias off at a state primary which she refers to as 'the village school', but, even with his head start, little Zacharias doesn't do as well as expected and develops a frightful accent which makes his grandmother wince and his cousins at Summerfields take the mickey out of him. After a lot of heart-searching and Gideon having to give up smoking and drink wine instead of whisky, Zacharias is sent to the local day prep school at eight, to find that all the upper-middles by now have been sent off to boarding school, and the place is crawling with pushy lower-middles and Nouveau-Richards. Against such competition Zacharias does less and less well. He's called 'Zacharine' and beaten up in the playground by Jison Nouveau-Richards and his gang and is eventually sent off to a crammer at eleven, because the headmaster has hinted at the horrible possibility that he might not pass Common Entrance, and because Gideon and Samantha can't get him to do three hours' homework a night against a background of *The Sweeney*.

Left-wing intellectuals pack their children off to the local comprehensive, rejoicing in the spare cash and the first glottal stop. Actually their children are bright enough to waltz through any system; if not, they have them coached. The parents shriek like hell when they have to fork out for a university.

The middle classes, of course, always work the system. They have cars to take them to the better state schools, and they deliberately buy houses in the right area. The Oxford local papers, for example, advertise houses with swimming pools, four bedrooms and location in the catchment area of a fashionable state school.

Often a group of middle-class parents picks on a school and enforces its own standards, until it's so oversubscribed that the head can pick and choose. There is a school in Berkshire known as 'the Trojan horse of the state system', where the headmaster only takes children whose parents have been to boarding school or a university, or whose mothers are extremely pretty. The result is scholarships to all the top public schools, and speech days full of headscarves and labradors, not unlike the Fourth of June at Eton. The only difference between this and the local day prep school is that the mothers picking up their children from the state school are better dressed because they have more cash to spend.

'Hooray, we can afford a Volvo,' said one mother when she heard her child had got a place.

Meanwhile Jen Teale is tearing her hair out because she can't get Wayne or Christine in, and has to fork out for a day prep. Having forked out, she is extremely pushy. She always goes along to open day to see what she's paying for, and says she's 'very satisfied' because little Wayne is bound to get qualifications later, and that's all that matters. Wayne has also brought home some very nice boys, which could never have happened at the local primary, where the hazard of him chumming up with the local dustman's son was always a terrifying possibility. In conversation with friends who have children at state schools she often mentions Wayne's French or asks them if they've got a Latin dictionary.

The Nouveau-Richards dispatch Jison to a day prep, and then to one of the top boarding schools, paying exorbitant fees to buy a little upper-middle-class child on the never-never.

The Tory press recently reported that a docker, a warehouseman and a gasmeter reader were sending their children to private schools, while a vast number of middle-class parents couldn't afford it any more. How ironic, the report went on, if the working classes comandeered private education as it moved further and further out of the reach of the middle classes. I think this is unlikely. Traditionally the financial situation of working-class parents make them accept the state system as normal. Mrs Definitely-Disgusting, for example, wouldn't dream of sending a child to a fee-paying school: too many Arabs, and far too many 'soap dodgers' as she calls the black coloured. Cheltenham Ladies even had a black head girl. The working classes also have a traditional resistance to uniform, punishment, homework and 'posh' but useless subjects like music and French.

Both in streamed and unstreamed schools, the middle classes receive different and longer education and are educationally more successful. The chances of the child of an unskilled worker being a poor reader at seven are six times greater than the upper-middle-class child, who arrives at school tuned in to educational demands, and who, when he gets home, has someone to help him with the homework and somewhere quiet to do it.

While half the children in the Census Social Class I (the upper-middles) reach higher education, either at university or polytechnic, only one in a thousand of Class V (unskilled workers) stays on after 16. Leaving school young is deeply embedded in working-class sections of the community, where parents keep their children at home to babysit or do housework, or, if money is short, send them out to work.

The middle-class child is realistic about prospects and sees success in terms of steady progress and cumulative success, while the working-class child sees it in terms of a quiet life, or sudden fame as a pop star or a footballer.

PARENTAL INVOLVEMENT

The National Foundation for Educational Research, who ought to be collectively shot, is convinced that the greater the parental involvement the more able the child will be. Parental involvement is the main hobby of the non-working mother who sees it as an extension of justifying her existence by creative child-rearing. The frightfully lower-middle expression, a 'caring and concerned parent', is bandied around a great deal both by the press and the teaching profession. If a child isn't doing well at school the teacher rings up the parents and tells them that the home back-up isn't 'caring' enough. Another trick is to ask the children to write essays entitled 'My Mummy' or 'My Daddy'. If Zacharias Upward writes: 'My Daddy drinks whisky all day, and my mother looks like a princess, but never comes to kiss me goodnight,' you get a black mark. You also rate as a bad parent if you don't visit the school enough—but if you visit and criticize rather than help with the jumble sale, you are marked down as 'overzealous'.

'The middle classes can be a frightful bore,' said one schoolmaster. 'The ideal pupil would be an industrious middle-class child with working-class parents who kept out of your hair.' The worst parents are evidently middle-class intellectuals, who can't accept that their child is average and the child gets so pressurized it just cops out.

A daunting idea put forward by all schools today is that parents should educate themselves in order to help their children—'father education' my husband calls it. Samantha Upward is taking an Open University course in absolutely everything in an attempt to push Zacharias. Jen Teale has gone back to part-time teaching to catch up on the latest techniques.

Parents are advised to join the P.T.A. and bully for their own maths workshops. As communists monopolize union meetings, so the middle classes, even in a comprehensive school, tend to take over the P.T.A., leading to a serious distortion of influence. Mrs Definitely-Disgusting doesn't speak the same language as the staff and is often frightened of them. With massive condescension, one schoolmaster suggested starting a school playgroup, or a building project, or even a car mechanics club to attract the working classes into the P.T.A.

FUNCTIONS

Not only are the middle classes being taxed out of existence and struggling to pay the fees, they are also made to feel guilty if they're not pouring money into the school kitty and taking afternoons off to be present at school events. If they asked one to sponsor a walk to save-the-parents it would make more sense.

The schools themselves never let up—coffee mornings, knit-ins, jumble sales, P.T.A. dances. These are usually organized by the Friends of the School, a posse of busybodies in tweed skirts who call the headmistress

87

by her Christian name, and haven't enough to do in the afternoons. The good parent has to be there on Saturday afternoon manning a stall. It's not enough to send a cheque for £5 on the Monday after.

The Nouveau-Richards go to everything because you meet such a nice class of parent there. Samantha Upward goes to everything because she feels it helps Zacharias. Her social life is entirely taken up with school events, from biology workshops and concerts to P.T.A. dances, and, as she insists on Gideon coming as well to create an impression of solidarity, they have to spend a bomb on baby-sitters.

The Stow-Crats never go to anything. Mrs Definitely-Disgusting arrives at the door, hears the Hampstead middle-class whine and goes home again. The upper-middles often feel it their duty to patronize events of this kind, have several drinks at home first and refuse to dance.

About once a week a note about forthcoming events with a perforated slip at the bottom is sent round; full of lower-middle-class words like 'nearly new', 'refreshments', 'pleasant' and 'enjoyable', it ends, rather wildly, 'If you can be of service as a helper please tear off your slip and send it to one of the committee.'

At Christmas there's a nativity play, which, at state schools, is often held in the morning. This means lots of working-class fathers on shift work and Gideon Upward looking at his watch and wondering how late he dare be at the office. The Virgin Mary's parents are invariably divorced and acrimonious; they turn up and sit glaring from opposite ends of a school bench, but in the end are forced to sit next to one another through lack of space. No one can hear the kiddies tunelessly chanting ''Ark and 'erald' or 'Once in Royal Divid' because of all the baby brothers and sisters squawking their heads off.

At fee-paying schools there are no babies because the parents pay someone to look after them for the afternoon. The following announcement was once sent out by my son's old day prep school:

'We hope you will all come to our informal Carol Service on December 15. This year we shall be having kindergarten boys for the first time. I'm sure we shall all enjoy them.'

SCHOOL MEALS

When my son first went to a primary school five years ago, faced with the utter impossibility of having the right dinner money every day, I asked if I could pay by cheque for the whole term. The school was extremely shocked. It was good for discipline, they said, for the children to bring the right money each day; and was I too insensitive to realize that it was beyond most working-class budgets to fork out all at once for a whole term? Now I notice that most state schools allow parents to pay by cheque. Private schools call it 'lunch' and put it on the bill. State school dinners are supervised by someone grandiosely called a 'dinner lady'.

The working classes, being picky eaters, often take their own.

'My Mum packs me sandwiches,' says Sharon Definitely-Disgusting, 'and I buy a sweet off the ice-cream van.'

THE MILK RUN

The routine of parents taking children to school by car on a rota basis, often known as the 'milk run', causes more aggravation than any other part of the school day, particularly when mothers are trying to collect children from three different schools all coming out at the same time. Where the children are concerned it's one of the last bastions of snobbery—the bigger and shinier the car you're picked up in the better. On the whole, mothers dress more scruffily the higher-class they are. Caroline Stow-Crat turns up in jeans in a

89

'Why can't we get a motorbike Dad?'

filthy Range Rover and is admonished by George who thinks she ought to wear smarter trousers and clean the car more often. Why can't she be more like Mrs Nouveau-Richards who is always dressed up to the nines and takes the 'show-*fur*' and the Rolls?

Jen Teale, who is terrified her children may miss a second of school that's being paid for, gets quite hysterical when Samantha's French *au pair* oversleeps and picks up the Teale children ten minutes late.

Caroline Stow-Crat is always getting stuck in the country at weekends and ringing up at midnight saying she's snowed up and can Samantha do the milk run. Samantha is furious, but doesn't say so. 'A lady never lets herself go.' Nor can she get any sympathy out of Mrs Nouveau-Richards, who is only too glad to put her show-*fur* at Caroline's disposal at any time. Jen Teale, who cleans the Volkswagen herself, thinks Caroline's Range Rover is much too draughty, and she's fed up with having Snipe's hairs all over little Wayne's newly brushed blazer.

On Wednesday the milk run to the doctored state primary, where the music's so good, is like the bus of the L.S.O. with all the children's instruments sticking out of the window.

Georgie Stow-Crat complicates matters on Samantha's milk run by telling everyone that he's being allowed to stay up till midnight tonight because his mother is giving a party for eighty people, to which none of the milk run mothers have been asked.

A friend's child went to a pre-school open day at one of the most fashionable London High Schools. All the little new girls were told:

'At the end of the afternoon you stand in the hall, and the moment you see your Mummy's car coming up the drive you tell your form mistress and go and meet Mummy.' It was automatically assumed that all the parents had cars. In state schools many of the children walk or go by bus. When Samantha suggested Zacharias might go by bus, so she could take a part-time job, Zacharias refused. He didn't want his cap knocked off by 'comprehensile' boys.

The most relentless upstaging goes on between children on the school runs.

'My mother went to Princess Anne's wedding,' said one child.

After a long pause, the second child replied,

'My parents were asked, but they didn't want to go.'

The attitude towards chauffeurs is interesting, too. One working-class boy, whose father had made good, made the chauffeur drop him a quarter of a mile from his primary school and walked the rest of the way, so the other boys wouldn't mob him up. Two teenagers at a day public school had a different problem. The younger sister hated the chauffeur wearing his cap because the other girls would think it snobbish. The older girl, on the other hand, hated him not wearing his cap:

'It would be so awful, if anyone thought he was Daddy.'

> *Primary Mary, teacher wary,*
> *How does your accent grow?*
> *With cockney vowels, and Mummy's scowls*
> *And glottal stops all in a row.*

An English upper-class accent is often called a 'public school accent'. But, as Jonathan Gathorne-Hardy has pointed out in *The Public School Phenomenon*, accent became a socially distinguishable characteristic long before the founding of the public schools. The dialect of London, Cambridge and Oxford was originally South-East Midland but by the sixteenth century London English (hence the King's English) was regarded as the only language for a literary man or a gentleman, and remained so throughout the seventeenth and eighteenth centuries. The public schools only intensified this.

In the nineteen-sixties, during the hippy revolution against materialism and never-having-had-it-so-good, the upper and middle classes identified profoundly with the new culture and became devotees of long hair and pop music. Working class became beautiful and everyone from Princess Unne downwards spat the plums out of their mouths, embraced the flat 'a' and talked with a working-class accent. Even today you can invariably tell the age of twenty-two to thirty-year-olds by their voices. Prince Charles preceded the revolution and speaks his mother's English; Prince Andrew came after it. Nicholas Monson, who is one of the more enlightened and intelligent of the new wave of right-wing writers, said that during that period he got very embarrassed about being at Eton and having a smart background, but, by listening carefully to the housemaid and watching 'Rossel Harty', he learned to talk with a modulated regional accent.

'After Eton,' he said, 'I put off trekking to Katmandu and discovering Zen. Instead I went to Kingston Poly-technic. As I was mixing with 'real' people, I put on sweaty T-shirts and dirty jeans, let my hair collapse in rat-tails over my shoulders and affected an accent that owed its origins to Cilla Black, California and the East End of London. I was uncomfortable with this voice, so I said little, but nodded vigorously and tried to look tough. We also sneered at a certain lecturer who wore a pinstriped suit and talked posh. It was at such an airing of bigotry that I realized to my acute embarrassment that I was guilty of the same crime as before. I was a snob.'

It must have been about this time in the 'seventies that many other people were undergoing the same re-alization. The prosperity ran out and the working classes, the simple life and dropping out became less attractive, because there were no jobs to drop back into when you'd had enough. Upper- and middle-class schoolchildren became more conventional again and shed most of their working-class accent. As my niece said:

'It simply isn't cool to talk like a yobbo any more.'

The result is a different kind of speech, much more clipped: 'awf'ly' and 'frightf'ly', 'ya' or ''y'p' instead of 'yer' or 'yeah'. Georgie Stow-Crat might say 'funtustic' and 'whole' to rhyme with 'doll', but he wouldn't say 'amizing' like the cockney child. He is often bi-lingual and will lapse into mid-atlantic or disc-jockey when he's with his friends. And when he wants to irritate Caroline in the holidays he cultivates a glottal stop and asks her to pass the 'bu-er'. To the middle classes, although they won't admit it, a fee-paying school means 'no more ghastly accent'. Or, as a headmaster said euphemistically, 'We try to get rid of accents. They're a lazy way of speaking.'

Alas for the Nouveau-Richards, the effect often isn't lasting. When I lived in Yorkshire the rich manufac-turers all sent their sons to Oopingham and Roogby to iron out their accents, but a few years after they left they were speaking broad Yorkshire again.

'It's extraordinary,' said a don at Radley, 'how bucolic some of the old boys sound when they come back after a few years.'

Quite often you get marked class discrepancies in a family because a father has made his pile while his children were growing up and has only been able to send the younger children to boarding school, or equally gone bankrupt in the middle and been forced to send the youngest child to a comprehensive.

The left-wing trendies send their children off to the local state school and go into ecstasies over the first flat 'a'. She has not failed us, she has not failed us. Accent makes the heart grow fonder.

The socially ambitious Jen Teales often regard moving from place to place as an advantage, not only does Bry-an up his salary, but there is more likelihood of Wayne and Charlene being well spoken and not picking up a regional accent.

CLASS CONSCIOUSNESS

> *A gentleman has good table manners and should not make wild gestures when speaking at banquets, so that he sweeps a bowl of semolina into his neighbour's lap.*
> King's House School, Richmond, magazine

There is no worse snob than the prep-school boy, but he is usually a possession snob, status being dependent on the size of his parents' car, how many rooms his house has, whether they have a swimming pool, where he went on holiday, and the intricacies of his digital watch.

The dawnings of true class consciousness vary. A duke's daughter said she was aware of her position for the first time when she was four; she was playing in the garden and a particularly oily butler said, 'Would my lady like some luncheon?' She was very clever, however, and said that at school her intellect was much more of an embarrassment than her title. Rather like my niece the other day asking my nephew what subjects he was planning to take for A levels.

'Maths I and II, and Physics,' came the reply.

My niece gave a gasp of horror:

"Oh Henry, what *will* you talk about at dinner parties?'

My daughter, at seven, is unaware of class, except in so far as she'll suddenly lapse into a Liverpool accent to make her friends laugh. My son, at ten, is beginning to come out with remarks like, 'How many Lords do we know?' And when my husband told him to undo the top button of his shirt he said,

'Well Ken doesn't.'

'Ken,' snapped my husband, 'is not a gentleman.'

'Of course he is,' said my son. 'He's a millionaire.'

When he spent the day with one of his old state-school friends, however, he came back and said in passing that he didn't like their house—the colours were too bright and shiny and you couldn't see through it. After pondering for a long time, I realized he meant there were net curtains on the windows.

'My family used to own most of Bath,' announced one of his school friends, 'but unfortunately they lost it in a game of cards.'

Most snobbery, in fact, is instilled by the parents. For a brief period an earl's son was sent to my son's day school, and it was horrifying the way the mothers urged their sons to ask him to tea and birthday parties. He must have seen Star Wars about fifteen times.

There is beautiful story of a very aristocratic child going away to prep school for the first time, who got hauled up before the headmaster because he insisted on calling his form master 'Mr Brown' instead of 'Sir'.

'I suppose,' said the headmaster with infinite sarcasm, 'you expected Mr Brown to call *you* Sir.'

'Yes,' said the boy simply.

At boarding school, as has already been pointed out, where a child is divorced from its origins and everyone wears uniform, it is often difficult to tell what class someone is.

'The twins are awfully grand,' I remember a friend telling me in awe.

'Why?' I asked in surprise. They were much younger than us.

'Oh, they flip through *The Tatler* and know absolutely *everyone*.'

One becomes suddenly aware that people are different, like the reporter on the *Daily Mail* who said how jealous she felt of the one girl in the class whose parents had a telephone. A girl at Oakham was teased for being the only girl in the class who didn't say lounge.

You find the same upstaging in George Orwell:

'My father's got three miles of river.'

'My Pater's giving me a new gun for the 12th. They're jolly good blackcock where we go. Get out, Smith, what are you listening for? You've never been to Scotland. I bet you don't know what a blackcock looks like.'

Today, in most boarding schools, considering the number of Africans and Indians, he certainly would.

I also talked to a girl who had just left a London fee-paying school in the City.

'No one ever talked about class,' she said, 'but one day a friend whispered, "You and I are upper-middle, but the rest of the class are incredibly lower-middle." Most of them come from Romford and Loughton. Their parents have scraped the money together to send them. One girl's father is a chartered accountant from a grammar school. Another girl's father is the head of a local primary school. He won't let her out in the evening. She has to work. If you ask her where she lives, she always says "the back of beyond". Actually it's somewhere like East Ham. One girl lives in a council house. Her father's a postman, but she wants to be an ac-

96

countant and go to the L.S.E. Because they tend to be alderman class, they're very job-conscious and materialistic. They have no desire to do good for other people, only themselves. They're very impressed by the professions, probably because they regard it as a step up. We went round the class; 17 out of 25 wanted to do law, solicitors rather than barristers, because it's more secure, and probably in local government. I was the only one who wanted to do English.

'The rest all dress very neatly—white shirts that stay tucked in, and clean shoes and skirts. They think I'm incredibly scruffy. They buy a lot of cheap shoes, but never any books.

'Their idea of social success is to be asked to a tennis club or cricket club dance. They talk a lot about losing their virginity but are more interested in whether it will ruin the relationship than the moral aspect. And they endlessly discuss the pill, but there again, because they might put on weight. They're all terribly competitive, but the main battleground, apart from the academic, is the rush to drive. They're obsessed with provisional licenses and three-point turns. One girl's father gave her a car when she passed her A levels.'

These girls, as can be seen, are the same class as Bryan and Jen Teale.

WARFARE—OR THE ETON/JARROW MATCH

'I am conscious, moreover, of a marked distaste for those who have not benefited from a public school education. This distaste is based on no superficial prejudice, it is founded on experience. People who have not endured the restrictive shaping of an English public school are apt in after life to be egocentric, formless and inconsiderate. These are irri-

97

tating faults. They are inclined also to show off. This objectionable form of vanity is in its turn destructive of the more creative forms of intelligence.'

Harold Nicolson.

Whenever people attack the English class system they start slinging mud at the public schools. I say 'English' deliberately because there aren't any famous public schools in Wales and because education in Scotland is far more democratic. Anyone wanting to explore the splendours and miseries of the public school system should read Jonathan Gathorne-Hardy's excellent book on the subject, *The Public School Phenomenon*. One interesting point he makes is that the expression 'working class' was only used pejoratively for the first time in the 1830s, when the industrial revolution was spewing forth Nouveau-Richards in unprecedented droves. 'There is a natural tendency,' he writes, 'for those who have just made money to join the company, and ape the manners of those who have always had it, and despise those they have left behind. In the nineteenth century this was hugely reinforced by the fact that the newly rich appeared at a time when the land-owning upper classes still held political power.'

The easiest way for the Nouveau-Richards to join the upper classes was via a public school. Obviously you could never become a gentleman if you remained jammed up against a lot of common tradesmen. The upper classes, as Gathorne-Hardy goes on, had evolved distinct ways of speaking, dressing, holding their knives and forks, writing letters and so on. And boarding schools, where everyone was in view of everyone else, and away from the coarsening influences of home, were a particularly good way of elaborating and enforcing these aspects of behaviour.

In the nineteenth century the difference between the old landed gentry and the manufacturing classes was that the first had inherited his money, the second had earned it. And paradoxically, although the ambitious merchant or industrialist exalted work, once his son went to a public school and then on to Oxford or Cambridge, and mixed with the upper classes and espoused country house life (probably the most seductive of all life styles), he had then to value idleness as the supreme mark of status. The point of the aristocrat was that he did not need to work for his living. This is crucial to an understanding of English class attitudes. It underpins the idealization of the amateur, it explains why money went on houses and horses and beautiful things, rather than back into the business; it explains the horror of trade, and why the English, unlike the French, Americans or Germans, have always regarded intellectual as a dirty word. The public schools were not required to educate, they taught strength of character, leadership and self-reliance. This, in turn, explains why, until a few years ago, the upper and upper-middle classes took little interest in education. The English gentleman, wrote Douglas Sutherland as recently as the middle 'seventies, regards any child who comes more than half way up the class with extreme suspicion.

Things have changed, however, during the last twenty-five years. Death duties and capital transfer tax made it impossible to leave much money to one's children; taxes were eating into capital and income. The only inheritance one could be sure of giving one's child was a good education. When the Russians come a good engineering or physics degree might save him from the salt mines. In the nick of time, most public schools abandoned their role as character-builders and gentleman-factories and became academically excellent. The Old Boy Network was a thing of the past.

This obsession with education spread down the classes, because, according to the Census, you can't be in Social Class I unless you've got a degree (nuns for some reason being the only exception). To the working classes barristers, doctors and dentists are upper class.

To them an 'educated' voice means an upper-class voice. A good education therefore means climbing the social scale. It gives the bright child the chance to leap from Class V to Class I, and enables the middle-class child to stay put.

Education, as a result, has become a complete rat-race—with nine-year-old day-school children working ten hours a day, with no Arthur Scargill to protect them, with teenagers being offered holidays in Bermuda if they pass A levels and whole families, including the cat, going on tranquillisers before O-Dear levels.

Last year 67% of middle-class children interviewed in one sample said they would rather work for an exam than go to a party, and one working-class family knifed their father collectively because he pushed them so hard to get into university. Even the upper classes are infected and in August the beaches at Bembridge and the grouse moors echo with Caroline Stow-Crat and

''is teacher says 'e's gifted at writing.'

100

her friends upstaging each other over how many A levels Fiona's got.

Consequently the crammers are overflowing, coaches are having a field-day teaching new maths in the holidays, and the paediatricians are coining it in testing middle-class children because they aren't coming top of the class. They've even evolved a new category called 'Gifted Children', who are the new educationally deprived, according to the *Daily Mail*, because they're not being sufficiently stretched. One can't think how poor Beethoven and Shakespeare managed in the old days. The Great Train Robbers are all supposed to have been gifted children.

We now see that the aim to produce 'extra-bright' children is common to all classes. The pressure on the middle classes to stand firm against competition from below not only kept the private and direct-grant schools full, in spite of increased fees, but has also been a factor in people having smaller families.

In *The Anatomy of Britain* Anthony Sampson expressed his doubt as to whether the public schools could maintain their dominant position in the '80s. The middle classes would no longer be able to afford them and the great lower-middle-class movement, the growth of the grammar schools, was acting as a bridge between the lower classes and the corridors of power. Getting into a grammar school was the crucial step for upward mobility, since this made entry into the middle classes and the professions much easier. But in 1975, with the abolition of the grammar schools, the bridge was smashed. The direct-grant schools joined the public schools, as did several of the old maintained grammar schools. In fact, with the scrapping of the grammar schools, the schism has been intensified. With the fee-paying and the comprehensive schools glaring at each other across the abyss, the result is well and truly a class war.

Traditionally the public schools look down on the

grammar schools, and equally the boarders at public schools looked down on the day boys because they pay less for their education. Etonians look down on everyone, and the smartest Catholic school, Ampleforth, looks down on Eton. The big London public schools tended to be superior academically, but it wasn't smart to be academic, and most of the St Pauls and Westminster intake lived in and around London, and no gentleman lived in London. And so it goes on. The great public schools, Eton, Harrow, Winchester, Rugby and Marlborough look down on the minor public schools. And the boarding prep looks down on the day prep, who looks down on state school boys who, in return for such contumely, duff prep school boys up on the way home. Finally the good comprehensives despise the 'sink' schools, where the brighter children despise the dumber ones, and the dumber ones actually refer, according to one schoolmistress, to the bright ones as 'snobs'.

Harry Stow-Crat thinks streaming has something to do with trout.

The 'seventies also ushered in another great movement: the fight-back of the middle classes, they were soon selling their houses, giving up drink and holidays, the fathers taking highly paid jobs with the Arabs, grandparents digging into capital and flogging the silver—all to keep their children at boarding school, or, as my daughter calls it, a 'balding school'. You go bald worrying about paying the fees.

The independent schools themselves are also showing a strong will to survive. Godolphin and Latymer, one of the London direct-grant schools, rather than become a mini-comprehensive, accepted the challenge of independence. Their plight appealed to the middle classes; legacies and covenants poured in; old ladies sent postal orders. 'Old Dolphins' ran Christmas bazaars, girls organized mammoth sponsored skip-ins. Parents coughed up. Industry helped with £1000-a-year bursaries.

Meanwhile, headmasters have taken up fund-raising with a vengeance, producing glossy brochures with photographs of scaffolding with the word *Erection* printed underneath, and whizzing round the country giving appeal parties, which, after all, is far more fun than teaching. Suddenly it became all-important for them to become financial wizards. The Headmaster of Millfield, for example, is the consultant to a firm of brokers in the City. Radley got their half million for a new complex devoted to industry in under a year. My son's old prep school raised £42,000 in a few months.

But how long can they all survive? At first sight the fee-paying schools seem to be booming, and all appear to be heavily over-subscribed. In fact, as John Rae, Headmaster of Westminster, pointed out recently in *The Sunday Telegraph* more and more public schools are losing boarders, the extent of the loss being concealed by the recruitment of girls and foreign pupils. There are well over 7,000 girls in boys' schools now, stripping, as it's delightfully put, the girls' schools of their sixth form, and making it increasingly difficult for them to hang on to their staff. Recently a leading girls' school refused a reference to any girl who sloped off to a boys' school.

Apart from general fund-raising, the schools are devising all sorts of schemes such as enabling parents to pay on the never-never and establishing recruitment agencies in Hong Kong and the Middle East, which conjures up a marvellous picture of masters in lovat green tweed coats and baggy trousers sidling up to rich Arabs muttering, 'Not-at-all-feelthy public schools'.

The public and private school holidays are also getting longer and longer: nine weeks in the summer, compared with six weeks in the state schools and four-and-a-half weeks at Christmas and Easter (compared with the state schools' two-and-a-half weeks) and the children allowed home nearly every weekend, which means food and train fares, particularly if they bring school friends with them. One father said having teen-

'Your father is making *every* sacrifice to pay for your
education!'

agers home for the weekend was like entertaining mediaeval barons. The massive increase in rail fares also
means that parents are tending to send their children
to schools much nearer home, so in a way public schools
are becoming more local.

In the future, according to John Rae, it looks as
though the middle and upper classes will shop around.
Some will try state schools up to thirteen, then use the
independent schools to try and get their children
through A levels; alternatively state schools up to sixteen, then a sixth-form college. Others will send them
to a good prep school and hope that the discipline will
carry them through comprehensive school. The direct-
grant schools have places at eleven and so cream boys
off the prep schools. Public schools, suspecting that
parents can't afford to fork out from eight to eighteen,
may lower the entrance age to eleven, juggling to catch
a new market of parents who sent their children to a
state primary. Whereupon the prep schools, feeling the

draft, may extend the curriculum through to 0 levels, thus knocking the small public schools. A glorious free-for-all is envisaged with parents getting more and more muddled and obsessive.

Except for the inner cities, Mr Rae feels, the comprehensive schools are likely to improve to a point when the middle classes opt out of the private system, and when they do it's likely to be in droves.

'We must abolish the private schools,' writes C.E. Daunt, a schoolmaster who had moved over to the state system, 'for they more than any single institution perpetuate the hoary social curse of our uniquely divisive and persistent English class system.' On the other hand in the next chapter he lists the obvious advantages of boarding schools: 'the education, the widening of horizons, the stimulus of new activities, friendships, a relief from the tensions commonly built up in the nuclear family during adolescence, and above all the development of autonomy.'

One of the saddest passages in a book called *The Hothouse Society*, which consists of interviews with schoolchildren, comes from an East End boy in a state boarding school in East Anglia:

'I leave in four weeks time, and have been very happy here. Just you try living in Bethnal Green, instead of watching it on T.V. or reading those sociological books about it by people who live in Hampstead. I'll never live in a lovely house like this again, the grounds, the birds, the trees, the space here all helped me, and the people, they're kind and interested.'

In fact, if you examine the rigors of public-school life, it's amazing people feel any envy at all. It seems that beautiful, glass-wall, modern buildings are for children of unskilled workers and are free; while mediaeval ruins with ancient, ink-stained desks all jumbled up on top of each other are for sons of managing directors and peers of the realm.

Boarding schools in the old days were far worse than Borstal: Marlborough used to toss people in blankets over the stairs until one boy missed and fell to his death; in another school new boys had to crawl along boiling hot radiators, singing 'Clementine' and have their faces slapped at the end.

But although schools are now less spartan than they used to be, the younger boys still suffer: Take another extract from *The Hothouse Society*:

'My teddy helps me when I cry,' said a seven-year-old prep-school boy. 'It is from home. He's old but I like him. I miss my mother tucking me up. I worry because when I'm eight in the big boys' dormitory they take teddies away.'

In fact Mrs Definitely-Disgusting, who charges round to schools threatening to duff up a form master if he so much as lays a finger on one of her children, would never put up with weeping on Waterloo Station as her darling was towed away to a one-sex borstal with all the risks of beating and buggery behind the squash courts.

But one can't believe that the abolitionists lose a wink of sleep over teddyless small boys, or the flogging and the buggery. What irritates them is that these products of what seems like a cross between the Weimar Republic and a concentration camp somehow make people who haven't been there feel inferior.

The difference, too, is that the public schools select while the comprehensive schools are meant to take everyone. The grammar schools accepted the able minority and discarded the incompetent. Comprehensive schools are supposed to encourage a wide standard of excellence and protect the incompetent—a sort of Non-Utopia. 'You realize X can't read, and you respect him for it,' said one state school master pompously, which is all very well as long as you go on respecting the boy who can. The Labour Government wanted to introduce F levels which will be far less demanding than A levels, in order that more children will leave school with qualifications.

The situation has now been reached that the more 'disadvantaged' a school is (a euphemism for the more problem pupils it has) the more money it gets from the Government. As a result our local state school, which has an impeccable reputation and no hooligans, gets its subsidies slashed every year, and has to rely more and more on contributions from parents. Equally, all comprehensive schools have three bands like a deb dance: 25% in band one for bright children, 50% for average children, and 25% for below average, so you often find a bright child can't go to the school she wants because band one is over-subscribed.

There is also the belief that fee-paying schools push you harder:

'I'm sending Darren to a fee-paying school,' said a Mr Nouveau-Richards from Cheam, 'because they teach you to *com*-pete.'

'Independent schools have a different attitude to work,' said a girl at Godolphin and Latymer. 'My friends at comprehensive school don't care if they work or not. Someone like me who is basically lazy needs the push of a school like Godolphin and Latymer.'

A comprehensive school mistress told me that she would beg, borrow and steal to send her daughter to an independent school over the next ten years until the dust settles. The most pessimistic say it will take 75 years to sort the mess out.

ETON

'Our chaps often get scholarships to Winchester and Bryanston,' said a Surrey prep-school master, 'but not Eton. We don't aim that high.'

On the same note, Simon Raven, an Old Carthusian, tells a horrible story about a Jewish boy who was a brilliant cricketer who'd played regularly in the eleven, but who was dropped when the team went to Eton. Where boarding schools are concerned Eton is the *crème de la crème*.

'Roddy Llewellyn went to Shrewsbury,' wrote Paul Callan in the *Daily Mirror*, 'a school low in the pecking order of the élitist world; for the strata of society he hoped to move in Eton was essential.'

Eton is a very large school, which means that there are a lot of Old Etonians about. They have long had a tradition of political dominance, stemming from the days when power lay in the hands of the land-owning aristocracy who automatically sent their sons to Eton. They still hold considerable sway in the Tory Party. Six members of Mrs Thatcher's first Cabinet were Old Etonians. Coutts' only branch outside London is in Eton High Street.

Eton is also a prime example of self-perpetuating selectivity. Seventy per cent of the boys are the sons of Old Etonians.

All gentlemen go to Eton but all Etonians are not necessarily gentlemen. It is very vulgar to wear an Old Etonian tie except with a morning coat. There is a belief that Eton is secure enough to assimilate all types, that the Nouveau-Richards will be less pilloried there than at other schools, that intellectuals and eccentrics are more tolerated. Recently, however, a boy who said he supported Labour had his study covered in red paint.

To muddle *les autres*, Etonians often refer to the school as Slough Comprehensive. They call masters 'beaks', the matron 'm'dame', terms 'halves', and use quaint expressions like 'Lower Boy Pulling', which is a rowing race, having been in 'pop', which means one of the élite, not a fizzy drinks manufacturer. In the school list Hons are called 'Mr'.

Eton's activities are closely reported by the *Daily Mail* which regularly quotes the *Eton College Chronicle,* as though it were the bible of upper-class behaviour.

The press also regards Harrow as very up-market.

'Harrow boys may all come from the upper classes,' a housemaster's wife is quoted as saying a year ago, 'but they are not all rich. Some of the boys do their own laundry, and we've even got two Punk Rockers' (rather like token blacks).

One is reminded of the Winchester headmaster, chided in the nineteenth century by the authorities for taking rich boys, who somewhat irrelevantly replied: 'The boys are not rich. In fact most of them are extremely poor. It's their parents who are rich.'

SPORTS DAY

The upper classes, regarding the word 'sports' as vulgar, call sports day things like 'the Fourth of June' or 'Gaudy'. At Eton it is rather like a race meeting without the horses, but the deficiency is more than made up for by the braying voices. Everyone knows everyone, so the din is tremendous. Picnics of megalomaniac lavishness are unpacked and dog bowls are laid on the long grass. The place is stiff with dogs, barking with delight at seeing their young masters again.

In the middle-class sector sports day used to be a great hassle, but now that parents are far more interested in academic laurels they are very relaxed occasions. At prep schools a lot of little boys run round a daisied lawn for 'silver' cups. Every time the starting pistol goes off all the labradors look up, expecting a large duck to fall out of the sky, rather like Chekhov with fairy cakes. There are a lot of masters in lovat green tweed jackets and baggy grey flannels swaying from one leg to another. At state school sports day, the masters wear off-the-peg suits or T-shirts and track suits. At state schools the children all wave back at their parents. At prep schools they insist you turn up and then ignore you; it is the beginning of middle-class inhibition.

What is amazing at middle-class sports days is the number of fathers present. Are they all 'concerned and caring parents', or just skiving or on the dole?

The pattern is always the same. Harassed working mothers talking about *au pairs*, and non-working mothers having grisly heartburn that Simpkins minor might not make Oxbridge. There's always a sprinkling of bra-less earth mothers, with John Innes and whole-meal flour under their finger nails, wearing long skirts because they've been caught on a hot day with un-shaven legs. Their tits always wobble in the mother's race—perhaps that's why all the fathers go.

VOCABULARY

Both the upper and upper-middle classes consider it very vulgar to use the word 'teacher'. In ordinary adult conversation the upper classes say 'schoolmaster' or 'schoolmistress'. Jen Teale resists the word 'mistress' because it has sexual overtones, so she says 'school-teacher'. It is all right to describe someone as a good teacher if you mean that he is good at teaching, but very common if you mean that he is a morally irre-proachable schoolmaster. 'Teacher' without an article (e.g. teacher says...) is even worse.

'Youngster' is another very lower-class word, em-ployed by Shirley Williams and Mr Wedgwood Benn when they're trying to be democratic. So are 'lad' and 'lass': 'I've got two fine lads at college'. Harry Stow-Crat would say 'Georgie is up at Oxford'. 'Youth' and 'teenager' (perhaps because they are American) are somehow more acceptable. Other taboo expressions in-clude 'plimsolls' for 'gym shoes', 'P.E.' for 'gym', and 'bathing costume' or 'swimsuit' for 'bathing suit'. 'Scholar' should not be used as a synonym for 'pupil'. It means a child who has won a scholarship.

Here is an example of lower-middle-class journalism. It is a report on Prince Andrew's girlfriend.

'A scholar at exclusive Gordonstoun School, Scot-land, she penned an excited note to her Gran on Palace notepaper. Among the Xmas cards gathered on the mantelpiece above a coal fire was a card from Prince Andrew.

'"We are not particularly wealthy," enthused her Gran. "At the moment she is studying for an examination. She's very keen on sports."'

There are at least nineteen socially suspect words here. Journalists invariably use the words 'exclusive' and 'select' as euphemisms for 'rich' or 'upper class'.

It is very bad form to ask someone where they went to school. The expression 'public school' is also very lower-middle-class in the sentence, 'Wayne is going to public school next term'. Among the upper classes it would be assumed the child was going to Eton anyway.

LES VICES ANGLAISES

> *You can't expect a boy to be vicious till he's been to a good school.*
>
> Saki

If, when you're looking round for a suitable boy's boarding school, you tell someone you've decided on X, they promptly say 'Oh, they're just a bunch of queers there,' so you say, 'Well, Y's my second choice,' to which they reply, 'Oh, they're a bunch of queers there too.' So you say, 'Well, what about Z? All the masters are married, and they've just introduced girls.' 'Oh,' comes the reply, 'that's just a blind. They're still just a bunch of queers.'

Perhaps that's why the Labour Party never bothered to abolish the public schools. If they're only producing queers, they're less likely to marry and produce lots of upper- and middle-class children. Certainly in no other country do boys spend the years from eight to eighteen away from home locked up in single-sex schools.

Not long ago, in the debating society of one of the most famous public schools, a master rashly asked one of the more glamorously decadent of the senior boys how widespread homosexuality was.

111

'Well,' drawled the boy, echoing Mrs Patrick Campbell, 'at least we don't do it in the passages.'

The deliberate segregation and mutual dependence of English public school life, has, Jonathan Gathorne-Hardy suggests, led not only to the Old Boy Network but also to a strong strain of homosexuality (and I would add mysogyny) in upper- and upper-middle-class men. It is interesting, too, that only in England—home of *le vice anglais*—does the word 'stroke' mean both a caress and the lash of the cane. The fact, too, that tarts say that a high proportion of their clients who want to be beaten, or to watch beatings, come from the upper- and upper-middle classes must be something to do with older boys being allowed to cane younger boys, or to watch their compeers inflict the punishment.

In the old days the only glimpses schoolboys got of naked women were in carefully secreted copies of *Health and Efficiency*, or of black ladies in *The National Geographic*. Now, instead of sporting prints on the study walls, they have posters of near-nude Bardots and Jacqueline Bissetts. The latter, with her small-breasted, androgynous figure, is a significant choice, because, as John Mortimer, an Old Harrovian, points out in *My Oxford*: 'When emerging from the chrysalis of schoolboy homosexuality, the girls we preferred were notably boyish. Veronica Lake rather than Betty Grable, and Katherine Hepburn in *Philadelphia Story*, described by Frank Hauser as the natural bridge into the heterosexual world.

'The only women we saw at school,' he goes on, 'were elderly and fierce matrons. We were waited on at table by footmen in blue tailed coats, and settled down for the night by a butler called George. Our homosexuality was therefore dictated by necessity rather than choice. We were like a generation of diners condemned to cold cuts of beef because the steak and kidney was off.'

One of the great panics of upper- and middle-class mothers is that their sons may turn out homosexual. Samantha Upward feels a Becher's Brook has been cleared when Zacharias surreptitiously buys the *Daily Star*, tears out the coloured page with the nude and pins it over the poster of John Travolta above his bed. Mrs Nouveau-Richards, however, who is too working-class to be looking out for homosexuality, is enchanted that Jison has a photograph of his schoolfriend, little Lord X, by his bed in the holidays. The latest generation of public school children, reacting presumably against their parents idiocies during the permissive age, are much calmer and straighter than their predecessors. The drug problem, which haunted the 'sixties, is supposed to have been cured by inflation and fashion, although a Harrovian was recently caught buying cocaine by mail order. Drink has now taken its place. Every public schoolboy worth his salt has a bottle of Southern Comfort hidden under the floorboards, and gout has become the fashionable disease among teenagers. The punishment does not necessarily fit the crime, however. Thirteen-year-old Viscount Linley was recently caught drinking whisky at Bedales with a couple of mates, and made to weed the garden for a couple of hours, but thirty less august children were suspended for holding a midnight party—perhaps it's a question of the Royal Weed. No one gets sacked for homosexuality any more—they wouldn't have any boys left.

GIRLS' SCHOOLS

Be good, sweet Maid, and let who can be clever.

Animosity against the public schools is aimed far more at boys' schools than girls', because it is still the men, rather than the girls, who are bagging the top jobs, because girls' schools are far less snobbish, and because among the upper echelons it matters far less where girls went to school, a lot of people still believing it's nice for a girl to stay at home.

The upper and middle classes traditionally spend far less on their daughters' education than their sons'. A feeling still persists that it doesn't matter so much for girls, as long as they learn French, and nice manners, and get a few O levels and make some jolly nice 'gairl' friends.

A classic example of this was the diplomat quoted in *Harper's* who sent his secretary to find a boarding school for his daughter, adding that if she had been a boy, 'I'd have had to do it myself'.

Girls at boarding schools are seldom taught any domestic science beyond making cod in cheese sauce and rhubarb crumble, nor do they ever learn how to clean a room. This is a hangover from the old days when it was assumed they would always have servants when they grew up.

Comprehensive schools have home economics sections, often grander than those of any finishing school, but the girls get so good at housework that this often leads to conflict at home.

Some girls' schools pretend the class barriers are breaking down, but the old prejudices remain. Gathorne-Hardy quotes one headmistress as saying she would love her girls to go to dances with neighbouring boys' schools, but alas there were none in the area. Actually there were several comprehensives: what she meant was no public schools.

5 UNIVERSITY

I'm afraid the fellows in Putney rather
  wish they had
The social ease and manners of a 'varsity
  undergrad,
For tho' they're awf'lly decent and
  up to a lark as a rule
You want to have the 'varsity touch after
  a public school.
                                              John Betjeman

The expression an 'Oxford accent' was once used syn-
onymously for an upper-class accent. And certainly
among the lower and lower-middle classes, going to a
university gives one social cachet. I remember a Jen
Teale in one office in which I worked, who fell for one
of the more degenerate copywriters, saying she knew
that her mother would approve of him because he was
'a graduate and nicely spoken'. Mr Definitely-
Disgusting thinks his sons have 'gone up in the world,
because they've got letters after their names'. Howard
Weybridge and the more entrenched right wing of the
middle classes, however, might disapprove of undergraduates. To them 'intellectual' means wishy-washy
lefty, and why should young layabouts looking like
trainee Old Testament prophets spend three years at
some fun palace at the taxpayers' expense? The words
'hotbed of communism' are often on their lips. Like the
Leicester businessman who said that most of the people
he knew were Conservative—'But I've got a brother
who's a Socialist, one of the things he picked up at
Oxford.'

Mrs Nouveau-Richards gets frightfully excited about Oxford and everything wrong. She tells all her friends Jison is going to New. Harry Stow-Crat didn't go to university; he'd acquired quite enough character at Eton by the time he was 18, but his great-great-grand-father, being a nobleman, was allowed to graduate after two years, and Georgie Stow-Crat—now that the upper classes are beginning to take education seri-ously—worked hard at Eton and managed to scrape a place in geography at the House (Christ Church, Oxford).

'Christ Church undergraduates,' wrote Sir John Betjeman, 'gave the impression of dropping in at Oxford on the way to a seat in the House of Lords, that they were coming in for a term or two but mostly stay-ing away from college in country houses. They hunted, fished and shot, but I never heard of any of them play-ing football or hockey or even cricket, although cricket was played on the grounds of country houses within motoring distance of Oxford, and men from the House might have been called in to swell a village team.'

The House was still the mecca of the socially am-bitious in the 'fifties when I was camp-following at an Oxford typing school. I had one or two boyfriends at Christ Church and went to several parties there. I'd never encountered people so noisy, wild and totally self-assured. Freed from the restrictions of National Service, they were like a lot of oated-up thoroughbreds suddenly let loose in the paddock. They always seemed to be drinking champagne, whizzing up to London in fast cars to go to nightclubs, or breaking up the rooms of luckless grammar school boys. One of them was sent down for shooting a don through the foot with a 12 bore. All of them ran up the most frightful debts. For-tunately for them, they were surrounded by a galaxy of Nouveau-Richards who were always ready to pick up the bill. None of them appeared to do any work or go to any lectures. I was totally intoxicated by their sophistication and their ancient names: Mowbray, Bathurst, Gage, Stormonth Darling. But for me it was a time of great insecurity. Not only did I feel intellectually inferior because I wasn't an undergraduate, but also socially inferior because I was middle-class. It was the first time I'd met the upper classes *en masse*. If school, with its private and state sectors, is the great divider, university should be the great bringer-together. For many undergraduates it's the first time they meet people of different classes.

My thrill at Oxford was that I met the aristocracy, but for Angus Wilson, it was rubbing shoulders, and goodness knows what else, with the working classes:

'There had of course, been my London sexual encounters, many of them with cockney working-class young men, but the glory of Merton was I found myself meeting for the first time working-class men who came from the Midlands and the North.'

This, and the earlier quotation from John Betjeman, comes from *My Oxford*. Recently published together with *My Cambridge*, this is a book in which well known people each wrote a chapter describing their experiences as undergraduates. What is remarkable—apart from the high standard of writing—is what incredibly class-conscious documents they are. One feels that the authors wrote with an honesty about their origins they would never have displayed if they hadn't been so successful.

Eleanor Bron, for example, found herself mixing with an upper-middle-class intellectual élite, which made her unable to communicate with her own family (working-class Jewish) when she went home:

'I was too clever; like Alice I had grown and couldn't fit in the door anymore.'

Alan Coren arrived at Oxford at the beginning of the 'Flat-"a"-working-class-is-beautiful era' and capitalized on his own self-admittedly humble origins:

'I had a great success with *Isis* on the strength of a donkey jacket from a second-hand shop, an accent that went with it, cracking knuckles, narrowing eyes to slits and spitting out pips with no concern for target. This was how I became an authentic working-class voice, and sold many stories to a succession of gentlemanly editors.

'This was in the post-Angry days, when people referred to themselves as "one", blushed and started referring to themselves as "you", and tall willowy lads with inbred conks and hyphens stood before mirrors abbreviating their drawl, dropping aitches, and justifying a family that went back to the fourteenth century by saying they were all solidly behind Wat Tyler.'

Piers Paul Reid, upper-middle-class and second generation intellectual, arrived a few years later at Cambridge when the egalitarian movement had reached its height and the middle classes actually sought out working-class company. One of his friends recounted with a frisson of delight that there was actually a miner's son with rooms in the same building. Alas, in Piers Paul Reid's college 'There was only *one* boy who lived in a council flat. But he could grasp logic and metaphysics, and at the same time amass a variety of scholarships and grants by the judicious exploitation of his background. He avoided paying bills and was treated leniently because colleges were as eager to cultivate those proletarian seedlings as were American colleagues to cultivate black students.'

Having ferociously despised Etonians at the Pitt Club, Piers Paul Reid then reluctantly discovered that they were rather nice. Finally he went to a May Ball at St Johns, 'where there were girls in long dresses, and men in hired white tie and tails, not Etonians, instead bright guys from the grammar schools, and minor public schools, intoxicated by the mirage of success'—Jen Teales, in fact, trying to maintain some standard of gracious living in the face of rampant egalitarianism.

By 1968 the 'working-class-is-beautiful' movement was coming to a head with student power joining forces with militant workers (a far cry from the undergrad-

uates who rallied in 1926 to break the General Strike).
But from then on things began to change. The austerity
years arrived and, instead of power, undergraduates
started worrying about survival, about fast-diminish-
ing grants and getting a job when one went down. The
possibility of actually joining the working classes in
the dole queue suddenly made them seem less attractive. People no longer wanted to get a job helping people
or burned to do something in the Third World. Instead,
they wanted to amass a fortune in the Middle East.

'Apart from medics and Indians,' said one Oxford
undergraduate, 'all anyone wants to do when they
leave here is to make a fast buck.'

According to *The Sunday Telegraph,* in recent years
the main scramble has been into those twin middle-
class havens of indispensability—law and accountancy.
The proportion has doubled in the last two years. Soon,
no doubt, the market will be flooded and there'll be
hundreds of out-of-work accountants working as waiters. (At least they'll be better at adding up the bill than
out-of-work actresses.)

'A few years ago,' confirmed a don, 'I spent my time
convincing people that Marx hadn't said the last word
on everything. Now I spend the same amount of time
persuading them everything he said wasn't complete
rubbish.'

The universities, in fact, have become bourgeois.
How then have the classes re-aligned?

'One does generally mix with people of one's own
type (i.e. class),' said an upper-middle-class undergraduate from Oriel, 'though this is by no means a
conscious or rigid principle—but it does seem that
many comprehensive and grammar school types are
not very interesting people, or at least seem to have
less in common with one because of their background.'

'At teacher training college,' said a working-class
boy, 'we found our own level and stuck together. Particularly in evidence was a stuck-up group we called
"the semis" (lower-middle, Jen Teale again) who got

engaged in the first year. All they talked about was houses and cars. The only aggro I got was at Christmas dinner when the principal told me to leave the table for not wearing a tie.'

'You don't notice people's backgrounds,' said an old Harrovian now at Reading, 'until someone almost beats you up for asking his name. Yobbos are less tolerant of having the piss taken out of them, and tend to over-react, which public school boys don't understand. When they get a bit of confidence, yobbos who've been up for three or four years take a delight in mimicking one's accent, which can get very offensive.

'I went out with a grammar school girl,' he went on 'and I shared a flat with a boy from a comprehensive school. Apart from his talking about "lounge", "settee" and "toilet", we got on very well, although communal eating was a problem. He wanted to eat early, I wanted to eat late. Dinner in hall was a sore point—between 5.30 and 6.30, but I expect that's for economic reasons. You get so hungry you have to buy something from the bar to eat later.

'One thing I did learn was that, if I got drunk, I broke up public school boys' rooms, and they always broke up mine. It's much easier to break up rooms of those who you know will take it well. Public school boys don't seem to mind so much about their possessions or other people's whereas yobbos do seem to care.'

Today at university the classes seem principally to be re-aligning into the upper- and middle-class guilty, the lower-middle materialistic and working-class cross. And although the middle and upper classes are no longer assiduously courting the working classes, a terrible inverted snobbery has now developed. 'The young,' said Anne Thwaite in the Introduction to *My Oxford*, 'tend to avoid Oxford and Cambridge for egalitarian reasons, opting for Sussex, York or East Anglia, as somehow being more mysteriously like real life.' There was a don at a redbrick university who said he would never dare write a book about the middle classes because he couldn't possibly justify it to his students.

Nicholas Monson overheard two sociology students having a passionate row over which of them was more working class: 'One said his father was a miner in Darlington, while the other countered victoriously that, although his father had worked as an insurance clerk, his grandfather had gone on the Jarrow march. The first refused to concede his superior origins because his opponent's origins had been partially diluted by the capitalist occupation of his *petit bourgeois* father.

'They clearly needed the assistance of a recognized authority,' added Nicholas Monson dryly. 'Perhaps next year we might see the first edition of *Burke's Peasantry*.'

Even upper-middle-class at Oxford are worried about their image at the moment. They were perfectly beastly to Princess Anne, priestess of the flat 'a', when she visited the Union recently. Gay libbers, women's libbers and general lefties jostled her and shouted four-letter words outside; inside there was intense heckling and a ghastly audience participation exercises in which everyone had to turn to the person on their right and 'say in your poshest voice "Hullo dahling".'

Then *The Cherwell* also runs a competition for the pushiest freshman: 'He who hacks most people in the most disgusting way in his first term.' A hack is someone who solicits, pesters, toadies, and generally social climbs, in order to cunningly gain an advantage over others, by boring the pants off people in the Union bar, and then relying on their vote. Rather like Eton running an Upper-Class Twit of the Year contest.

Oxford, in some way, is more a target for egalitarianism than Cambridge. As Eleanor Bron pointed out, 'At Oxford all acquire a veneer of upper-middle-classiness, while at Cambridge, home of scientists and fact rather than opinions, they simmer down to a vague middle and lower-middleness.' Oxford's trouble is that, despite efforts to the contrary, they get more and more élitist. 'In the old days considerable gifts of spirit and intellect were needed to counter severe economic disadvantage,' said J.I.M. Stewart, 'but now most people are hard up, no college is noticeably cluttered up with hopelessly thick or incorrigibly idle youths from privileged homes.'

Ironically, although they may no longer be idle and overprivileged, 50 per cent are still from fee-paying schools because Oxford can't get enough candidates from the state system.

'Chaps from comprehensives simply aren't up to it,' said one don. 'You look for promise not achievement, then you say, "Dash it, would they ever pass prelims if we let them in?" and so in the end you say, "No, go somewhere else where they'll feed you compulsive lectures".'

An interesting statistic is that women graduates as a whole tend to be socially superior to men. Most of them come from Social Class 1 in the Census which means they are daughters of lawyers, doctors, engineers and accountants. This is probably because the upper-middles are the least male chauvinist of all the classes and therefore, unlike the aristocracy, the lower-middles and the working classes aren't so resistant to women being educated.

The exception to the upper-class rule is, of course, the Pakenham family, who were all expected to get a first. Evidently when Lady Antonia broke the terrible news to Lord Longford that she'd only got a second, there was a long pause; then he said with characteristic charity, 'Never mind, darling, I expect you'll get married.'

According to the Old Harrovian at Reading University, 'A lot of girls go to university to find a husband, although they would be livid to be told that. I fancied a girl who'd been to grammar school. Very clever—three As at A level—who I started to go out with, but she would only allow me to kiss her, saying if I wanted more I'd have to promise more. Well I ran away like a coward, and in my absence a creepy sort of chap

122

stepped in and having promised all, i.e. an engagement which he'll never keep, is enjoying her favours.'

The undergraduate at Oriel said that, in almost every case, people take sexual partners from the same class. 'If they're socially mis-matched there's usually not enough common ground to keep a conversation going.'

'Nice girls,' wrote Antonia Fraser about Oxford in the fifties, 'never accepted invitations from unknown undergraduates in the libraries, and lived in mortal fear of being seen out with men in college scarves and blazers with badges on,' and adds, with commendable hindsight now that she's living with the far from patrician Harold Pinter, 'no doubt missing the company of almost every interesting man in Oxford.'

'But Wayne, dear—are you *sure* that's the sort of tails they meant?'

Dive Definitely-Disgusting, however, is so proud of getting to a university that he wants to advertise the fact by wearing college scarves and blazers with badges, at the same time dissociating himself from the plebs in the street, showing that he's 'ge-own', not 'te-own'.

In the conventional late 'seventies sales of college scarves went up sevenfold in Oxford and sales of blazers with badges fourfold. This may be because the campus look is fashionable, because in a time of uncertainty people search for identity, or because they're all being bought by Zacharias Upward trying desperately to look like a yobbo.

An upper-middle Old Rugbeian up at Cambridge said it was certainly not done to wear college scarves, but the upper-middle Old Wellingtonian at Oriel said he thought they were O.K. now, although old school scarves were smarter, and in fact college scarves tended to be worn by those who didn't have a respectable old school scarf. Badges with blazers were never worn by the upper and upper-middle classes.

The Old Harrovian at Reading said the only thing he and his friends considered 'not on' was another piece of advertising: a T-shirt with 'Reading University' printed across the front of it, which some undergraduates insisted on wearing on the campus—again distinguishing ge-own from te-own.

Georgie Stow-Crat imports crumpet from London, spends about three hours a week reading geography (a traditionally thick yock-yock's subject) and runs the college beagles. One fellow of All Souls put a low gate on his stairs, not to keep his children in, but to keep hounds out. Jison Nouveau-Richards, who calls himself Jason now, has given his college scarf and blazer with a badge to a jumble sale, after one acid comment from Georgie, and now wears cavalry twill trousers, a tweed jacket and fine green check shirt, and looks more straight than Georgie, all of whose gambling debts he's paid off.

Mrs Nouveau-Richards is ecstatic about the whole experience. She knows Magdelene should be pronounced 'Maudlin' and Caius 'Keys', but she makes Jason wince by talking about the 'varsity' and 'freshers' and 'undergrads' which is almost as common as 'students'. Zacharias Upward wishes Georgie and Jason would ask him to their 'dos', as he calls parties. With seven men to one girl, he never gets even a fumble. Where Stow-Crats rush in, Upwards fear to tread.

When Samantha and Gideon take their daughter Thalia back to Sussex, Samantha in her ethnic and Gideon in his jeans, it looks as though Birnam Wood has arrived at Dunsinane, the car is so thick with potted plants for her room. Samantha was certain she would be the youngest and trendiest mother, and was disappointed to find the entire campus swarming with identical middle-aged Bolivian peasant ladies.

Dive Definitely-Disgusting feels horribly disorientated and homesick his first year. He's never been away from home before, and this is his introduction to 'adollt' life, and his college doesn't even look 'ollde'. Since her latest baby, Joanne, was taken on by a modelling agency, Mrs Definitely-Disgusting has had a telephone installed, so Dive rings her every night, holding the telephone miles away because Mrs D-D talks so loudly. Dive is reading maths or science. Used to being a big fish in a small comprehensive pool, he find no one takes much notice of him here; they all seem to be in 'clicks'. No wonder he eats in hall every night and sticks to his rooms. He doesn't meet any girls and in desperation imports his steady girlfriend from home, but is so broke on his grant that he has to smuggle marmalade rolls for her from Hall. Mrs Definitely-Disgusting doesn't quite appreciate the glory of having a son at Oxford until she sees him on *University Challenge* and hears that Bambi Gaskett telling him, 'Well interrupted, St Cats'.

Games, it seems, are the one great social mixing ground. Social divisions are genuinely forgotten and genuine friends are made between people of different classes. The smart set would never bother to know any-one who didn't go to a public school if it weren't for rowing or cricket.

Rowing used to be élitist, but although Old Etonians have gained 650 Blues since the boat race began, (schools such as Radley and Shrewsbury failing to get within 500 of that score), times are changing. Over the last 10 years, Eton still leads with 22 Blues, but Hampton Grammar is now third. In 1978 there were three undergraduates in the Oxford boat who would formerly have been dismissed as colonials, four grammar school boys, and three public school boys.

The old sneer, 'You never see a blue on a bicycle,' no longer applies. Most of the crew were, according to the *Daily Mail* 'reading unsmart subjects like engineering, science or economics, which demand not waffle but unequivocal answers in exams, and who you know or how you rowed are no help at all.'

'The class thing is going fast,' said one of the crew. 'Last year there was a touch of class feeling, a sort of "them" and "us" in the boat, but not this year. Perhaps it's something to do with the whole sport opening up. All along the river are clubs who want good rowers and don't care where they went to school.'

In the national eight there are now more dockers and lightermen than people who went to a university.

6 WORK

Oh let us love our occupations,
Bless the squire and his relations,
Live upon our daily rations,
And always know our proper stations.

According to the sociologists the two most important factors affecting upward mobility are your job and your marriage. But this may be partly due to the fact that the Census, upon which most government and sociological statistics are based, judges a person's class entirely by the occupation of the head of the house in which they live. In all societies there is a division of labour and consequently a hierarchy of prestige, but such arbitrary distinctions as the Census makes lead to a gross over-simplification of the class system. Photographers, for example, are rated Class III which puts Patrick Lichfield, Anthony Armstrong-Jones and Christopher Thynne in the same social bracket as David Bailey and Terry Donovan. Brewers like the Guinnesses and the Cobbolds are even lower, in Class IV. Athletes all rates Class III which puts Princess Anne on a level with Kevin Keegan. While the Marquess of Anglesey, as a writer, is rated lower than all the dentists, chemists and opticians in Class 1. The deb, working as a waitress (Class IV) and having *nostalgie de la boue* fantasies about lorry drivers, is actually bettering herself because they're rated Class III. Peers of the realm don't get a rating at all, and if they don't work are lumped together with the disabled, undergraduates, ex-convicts and the chronically sick. Did

127

SOCIAL CLASS I — Professional – 4%

Accountants, chemists, university dons, lawyers, vets, opticians, ornithologists, scientists, vicars, engineers, architects, dentists.

SOCIAL CLASS II — Intermediate occupations – 18%

Airline pilots, chiropodists, farmers, members of parliament, schoolmasters, police inspectors, artists, nurses, publicans, journalists, sculptors, diplomats, chicken sexers, actors, company directors.

SOCIAL CLASS III(N) – Skilled occupations – Non Manual – 21%

Sales reps, secretaries, shop girls, bank clerks, photographers, restaurateurs, policemen, cashiers, models, undertakers.

SOCIAL CLASS III (M) – Skilled occupations – Manual – 28%

Bus drivers, cooks, miners, guards in trains, upholsterers, butchers, all athletes including horseback riders and footballers, plumbers, shoemakers, printers, brewers.

SOCIAL CLASS IV – Partly skilled – 21%

Farm labourers, barmen, bus conductors, fishermen, postmen, telephonists, milkmen, gardeners, hawkers, ambulance men, barmaids, brewers, waiters and waitresses.

SOCIAL CLASS V – Unskilled – 8%

Office cleaners, porters, builders' labourers, messenger boys, lorry drivers' mates, stevedores, window cleaners, chimney sweeps, ticket collectors, charwomen.

Lady Chatterley, as the wife of a non-working baronet, enhance her social status when she embarked on an affair with a Class III gamekeeper?

Cabinet Ministers, M.P.s and diplomats are only graded Class II, which is logical. Once upon a time diplomats used to be Old Etonians with firsts, now they're parvenus like Peter Jay, and all the British embassies, according to a recent observer, ring with flat 'a's and regional accents. You also get a judge like Lord Denning, who would be rated Class I by the Census and upper class by the majority of the population because he's a peer, using such unpatrician expressions in an interview as having 'no help' in the house, 'a roast' for lunch on Sunday, and referring to his wife as 'Lady Denning'.

When you marry you automatically take on the class of your husband, which means that the day a duke's daughter (even if she's qualified as a Class I barrister) marries a chimney sweep she is promptly assessed with him as Class V.

What one does is certainly indicative of one's class. One thinks of solicitors as being middle-class and lorry drivers as working class—but I know of a peer of ancient lineage whose daughter has been a long-distance lorry driver for the last five years. Again and again one is struck by the relativity of the whole situation. To the working class, barristers and solicitors seem not middle but upper class while to the aristocracy they are definitely middle class. A solicitor told me that lower-class women invariably put on a hat when they come to see him, and Michael Young, in *Family and Class in a London Suburb,* quotes a man from Woodford Green:

'We have a very dear friend who's a practising barrister, and it amazed us that people might want to know us because we knew him and called him by his Christian name.'

Similarly we had a lower-middle-class nanny who

129

stopped going out with a solicitor because he made her feel socially inferior.

The other day I met a woman at a party who said her daughter had just got engaged to a dustman. Uncertain of her political affiliations, I was wondering whether to compose my features into a 'How Splendid!' or 'How Awful!' expression when she went on complacently,

'But it's quite all right. His father's a general.'

But of course a general who'd started his career in the cavalry would probably be of a very different class to one who had begun in the Royal Corps of Transport.

One poll conducted among the working classes showed that a footballer was regarded as the most prestigious career, followed by a chauffeur. My daily woman was grumbling one day that her daughter didn't speak to her any more since she'd married into the professional classes. What did her son-in-law do, I asked.

'Oh,' she said, 'he's an undertaker.'

One notices, too, that occupations that have a slightly ludicrous image acquire new, more euphemistic and therefore more Jen Teale titles: 'dental surgeon' instead of 'dentist'; 'rodent operative' for 'rat catcher'; 'public health inspector' for 'sanitary inspector'; and, worst of all, 'refuse collector' (presumably because they refuse to collect) for 'dustman'.

The position of the doctor is also ambiguous. The working classes think of him as upper-class. He has even usurped the lord as the most popular hero in romantic fiction. But a publisher I know was driving down the village street with a very grand old woman when he saw a man on the pavement waving to her.

'Some friend's trying to attract your attention,' he said.

'That's not a friend,' snorted the old lady. 'That's my doctor.'

I recently heard a very upper-class girl say she must go home to Lancashire because 'I've got to help Mummy with a horrors party for the doctor, the dentist, the solicitor and the agent.'

Medicine, except in the private sector, is fast dropping caste, along with teaching, nursing and the army, because they're all dependent on state pay, too ethical to go on strike, and getting broker and broker and more and more demoralized as the system breaks down.

Doctors, too, used to get invited to a lot of smartish parties, but now your G.P. won't come and see you any more, and you can't welcome him in a glamorous nightie in the privacy of your home, people tend not to know them socially. Certain doctors are also to blame for this loss of status. A friend who hadn't been to her doctor for over a year was greeted with the words, 'Not you again'.

The upper-class attitude to farmers is curious, too. Many aristocrats have land run by farm managers with whom they enjoy talking shop, and who they far prefer to businessmen or people in the professions who don't know their place—'more genuine' is the phrase used. Harry Stow-Crat also has to suck up to neighbouring farmers in case he should want to hunt over their land. Upper-class young men often go and work on farms as apprentices, before going home to manage their own estates, and say 'How sooper the farm blokes are', although they don't drink in the same pubs as them. This preference of the upper classes for the working class because they are far enough away socially is exquisitely summed up by Jane Austen's Emma (who, I suppose, could be described as landed gentry):

'A young farmer, whether on horseback or on foot, is the very last sort of person to raise my curiosity. The Yeomanry are precisely the order of people with whom I feel I can have nothing to do. A degree or two lower and a creditable appearance might interest me, I might hope to be useful to their families in some way. But a farmer can need none of my help and is therefore in one sense above my notice, as in every other sense he is below it.'

Emma, believing her young friend Harriet to be the illegitimate daughter of a *gentleman*, firmly discourages her from marrying this particular young farmer as being far beneath her. When, however, Emma discovers Harriet is only the daughter of a rich *tradesman*, she changes her mind and finds the farmer a perfectly suitable match.

Which brings us to the upper-class horror of trade. A gentleman didn't have to earn his living, as has been pointed out in chapter 4. 'The acceptance of high living and leisure,' wrote Evelyn Waugh in *Noblesse Oblige*, 'as part of the natural order, is a prerequisite of the aristocratic qualities and achievements. [The aristocrat] who goes into business and sticks to it and makes good, is soon indistinguishable from his neighbour in Sunningdale. You should have said, not that aristocrats can't make money in commerce, but that when they do they become middle-class.'

In fact, if one looks back at most of the great families one will find that they started off in trade. Many of them got rich lending money to both sides in the Wars of the Roses, and then bought land. But once one's pile was made, the life of leisure was espoused and one's origins rejected, which goes a long way to explain the parlous state of British industry today.

This horror of commerce is further expressed by John Betjeman:

> *Businessmen with awkward hips*
> *And dirty jokes upon their lips,*
> *And plump white fingers made to curl*
> *Round some anaemic city girl.*

Conversely the moment the businessman gets his foot on the ladder he'll start gathering round him upper-class trappings: going out hunting, buying boats, leasing a reach of a good salmon river and joining several smart clubs.

Firms like Plessey even employ upper-class ex-army

types to organize shooting parties and get very grand people along to impress the customers, often with disastrous results. One adviser remembers a peer arriving drunk from shooting with President Giscard, and telling such filthy stories at dinner that the great industrialist invited to meet him left the table in high dudgeon and cancelled the order.

Trade seems less despised if one is flogging works of art, and somehow shipping or oil seem to be more respectable.

'Wouldn't it be heaven if Hamish got a job in Shell at £600 a year,' wrote Nancy Mitford in the 'thirties, and the Onassis and Niarchos families seem to have been totally accepted by the English and French aristocracy, if not by the Greeks, which is often the case. One's social deficiencies always seem more glaring to one's fellow-countrymen than they do abroad. Onassis and Niarchos have been brilliantly described as 'parachutists', people who drop out of nowhere into a new class. The French have a splendid word, *rastaquouère*, to describe foreign nobility of dubious origin.

Social advancement is also dependent on access. Businessmen tend not to meet the upper classes. But members of the 'professions'—architects, doctors, dentists, estate agents, solicitors—encounter all classes, as do West End tailors, interior decorators, dressmakers and some journalists, while chauffeurs, nannies and masters at boarding schools have long-term access. All these people not only see the upper classes at close range and have ample opportunity to observe them and ape their manners, but also, if they have charm and a certain deference, often get taken up. When Michael Fish was invited to some frightfully smart house, the housekeeper was overheard saying to the butler:

'Things have come to a pretty pass when they ask the shirt-maker to stay.'

In Germany and America the businessman is of a far higher caste, and at the same time more democratic. In America, even though the men on the shop floor call the managing director by his Christian name, no one looks down on him socially. Advertising is also much smarter in America because Ad men get paid such vast sums of money.

'Advertising is still not considered a fit occupation for a gentleman,' said David Ogilvy recently. 'If I were top of another profession, such as law, I would be in the House of Lords today. If I were an actor or even a jockey I would have been knighted. As it is I get the C.B.E. When the Queen heard what I did her expression was a mixture of amazement and amusement.'

On the other hand, the laid-back, lotus-eating entrepreneurial atmosphere of advertising is very well suited to the upper classes.

'What do you do?'
'Nothing.'
'In which agency?'

THE ARISTOCRACY

Lord Finchley tried to mend the Electric Light
Himself. It struck him dead: And serve him right!
It is the business of the wealthy man
To give employment to the artisan.

Hilaire Belloc

Nobility of birth commonly abateth industry, said Bacon, but during the twentieth century the gospel of work has spread to the upper classes. What career, then, is open to Georgie Stow-Crat? He's unlikely to go into any of the professions (Lord Colwyn as a trumpeter and a dentist being a rare exception) because he lacks the application to train for six years and he'd find the people too stuffy and boring. One aristocrat who actually managed to pass his bar finals left the legal profession after a year:

'I couldn't stand the other barristers. They were so pompous and middle-class, and only interested in talking shop.'

134

Georgie might temporarily become a stockbroker, like the Marquess of Tavistock, or dabble in accountancy, like Lord Greenock. This would help him run his estate later and teach him the rudiments of tax evasion. Others take up 'head-hunting' or go into property where they do very well because they know all the right people and get hot tips about whose land is coming on the market. Georgie might also run a restaurant or add kudos to a smart nightclub, acting as bait to rich upper-class friends, and even richer nouveaus.

Some aristocrats try photography because it gives them the chance to get at pretty girls; others flatten their 'a's and go into the pop music business or produce films. They are very good as front men in P.R. because they know the right people, but they are better at charming the press and clients than dealing with all the follow-up work.

A lot of them go into Sotheby's or Christie's or smart art galleries, because, being surrounded by beautiful things at home, they're supposed to know something about furniture and pictures. They don't, of course. One Christie's valuer told me that only once, in all the houses he'd visited, was he made to dine in the kitchen with the servants, although in another house there was an old nanny in residence who wouldn't let him watch television after 8:30.

Then there are the Whore Lords, who get their names on to as many firms' writing paper as possible. Kind hearts may mean more than coronets, but a lord on the board means business and impresses customers, particularly Americans.

Georgie is most likely to end up farming his own land. If he were a younger son, he'd probably go into the army. Cirencester Agricultural College prepares heirs for the task of managing their estates, and currently (1979) boasts three sons of earls, three sons of viscounts, two barons' sons, a peer and, much to the joy of the popular press, a bewildered-looking Captain Mark Phillips. Sandhurst takes second and subsequent

'I don't mind you working at Christies, Georgie, but why on earth do they want to come and look over the place?'

sons for training in the martial arts. All that shooting is such good practice for the grouse moors later.

There is also a strong correlation between the aristocracy and the arts. Genius, being unbridled, is very upper-class. 'Look in thy heart, and write' said Sir Philip Sidney, but don't get paid for it. No one worries about that today. Lord Kilbracken and Lord Oaksey are journalists. The Marquess of Anglesey is writing a four-volume history of the British Cavalry. Dukes and earls burst joyously into print publishing their memoirs, or extolling the merits of their ancient houses. Lord Weymouth paints murals and writes thrillers.

In the same way, there's nothing unsmart about science as long as it's not applied. It is perfectly all right for his lordship to potter around in the west wing letting off stink bombs and making hot air balloons. But it should be pointed out that, in the arts and among academics, social snobbery is invariably suspended in favour of intellectual snobbery.

'When I find myself among scientists,' said Auden, 'I feel like a shabby curate who has strayed by mistake into a drawing-room full of dukes.'

Or as John Betjeman, gently taking the mickey out of donnish attitudes, put it:

> Objectively, our Common Room
> Is like a small Athenian state
> Except for Lewis; he's all right
> But do you think he's *quite* first-rate?

That tentative, fusty '*quite* first rate' seems to sum up the whole world of academic snobbery. The egghead is mightier than the strawberry leaf.

'Scientists,' said one sociologist pompously, 'tend to have a classless image, which can be embraced by working-class students without involving a denial of biological self,' which means they have very short hair and are all so common they have to go abroad to achieve

137

any status, or hide themselves in laboratories engaged in what they call '*ree*-search'.

Most academics get on together talking shop, but all hell breaks out when their wives meet and are expected to get on.

'It was dreadful,' said one sociologist's wife after a dinner party. 'All the walls of the lounge were papered in different colours.'

You may be a giant among bio-chemists but a pygmy at the local P.T.A.

COMPUTE, COMPETE AND COMMUTE

'To the middle classes,' wrote Dahrendorf, 'the career is the supreme reality.' Fear of failing is almost as strong as the urge to succeed. The fittest survive and escape to another rung up the ladder, the unsuccessful are ostracized. The historical origins of the middle classes lie in trade. They can be traced back to the bourgeoisie in the chartered towns where they grouped together to demand their rights and govern the towns, terrifying the aristocracy in much the same way that the Trade Unions scare the middle classes today. (Samantha Upward's mother thinks T.U.C. stands for 'Terribly Unkind Communists').

The middle classes didn't become really powerful until the Industrial Revolution, when the development of industry brought the need for new types of work: insurance, banking, accounting, engineering and science. Many of the people who entered these professions were successful craftsmen or farmers who had left the land. The penalty of failure was to sink back into the ranks of the working classes, so a gulf grew between them. As the big towns grew, so did the middle classes. They moved out of the towns and built suburbs and dormitory towns, and this seclusion enabled them to copy the way of life of the upper classes. Their children, as has been pointed out in chapter 4, were sent to the new boarding schools and developed refinements of dress and speech and, like all newly risen classes, walked through life gingerly as though they were treading on eggs. Their distinctive characteristic was that their work was not manual. Like the working classes, however, they had numerous rankings within themselves, which included manufacturers above the grade of foreman, most farmers, the majority of civil servants, professional people, businessmen and shop-keepers who owned their own shops, as well as independent craftsmen. It seems ludicrous to lump the small shopkeeper with the great banker, but all were united by their dedication, persistence and desire to get on.

Ever since the Middle Ages the 'professions' have considered themselves superior to bankers and businessmen and regarded themselves as a class on their own. Medicine, law and the church were suitable occupations for a gentleman; they did not dull the brain like manual work, nor corrupt the soul like commerce. They did not advertise. Some sort of qualification was needed, so they formed professional associations and became members of closely knit, protective groups.

The smartness of the various professions is subject to changes. Architects are considered smart today because there is something creative about their work. There was not, until recently, any stigma attached to a young man going into the Church, because the upper classes have to believe in God. Indeed a country parish was traditionally the destiny of younger sons with small private incomes. Medicine, as we have pointed out, is on the way down, except in the private sector. Dentists, on the other hand, are on the way up. They tend to make much more money than doctors, because they've escaped the clutches of the National Health, and because the desire for perfectly capped teeth has spread from America. Vets are also on the way up, aided by a little touch of Heriot in the night.

Schoolmasters could be described as middle-class,

but again there is a vast difference between the headmaster of one of the great public schools, or fashionable prep schools, and the junior master in an urban sink school. On the whole the private sector look down on, but feel guilty about not being part of, the public sector. On the other hand they make exceptions. I was talking about the headmaster of an élitist primary school the other day.

'Oh yes,' said the head of my son's prep school. 'He's obviously a coming man. *I've met him at a dinner party*.'

Engineering has always been an unsmart profession, partly because no one knows what it involves. Harry Stow-Crat thinks it is something to do with driving a train. When people asked me what my father did I always used to say he was in the army or that he was a scientist because I thought that sounded more romantic and boffinish than being an engineer. But once again things are changing.

Among the great variety of middle-class occupations there are three main strands which are particularly in evidence: the 'burgesses', the 'spiralists' and the lower middle class. The terms 'burgess' and 'spiralist' were coined by W. Watson in his article 'Social Mobility and Social Class in Industrial Communities' (1964). The burgess tends to stay put in the neighbourhood where he was brought up or started work, and establish prestige in the community. He is often the country solicitor, accountant or local businessman; he takes an interest in the community and often gets into local government to further his business interests.

In *Middle Class Families* Colin Bell quotes a burgess describing his life. He is a typical Howard Weybridge. The Weybridge expressions are italicized.

'My *people* have always been *comfortably off*. After going into the *forces,* I went into *Dad's* business. We have several *representatives,* who have come up from the shop floor . . . I am a very keen member of *Rotary* [on a par with Teacher and Doctor]. I belong to many clubs and associations because I think it's a good thing other Swansea *folk* see me at the right *functions*, and realize we are not just tradesmen. I also belong to several *social clubs* as a duty, so that I meet the important Swansea people.'

This is typical middle-class behaviour, the careerist socializing, the pomposity of expression, the desire to be a power in the community, a big fish in a small pool, and the joining of clubs, which would all be unthinkable to the working or upper classes.

The second category, the spiralist, moves from job to job and place to place, upping his salary and his status as he goes. Colin Bell quotes a chemist from a working-class background who is far more upper-class and direct in his language than the burgess.

'I went to a grammar school and then to a university, very red brick and provincial. I worked like hell and got a first, then did a Ph.D in chemistry to avoid going out in the world. Meantime I got married and had several children; after that I moved from firm to firm, upping my salary every time. Then I was promoted to Holland' (where class and accent didn't matter).

He then left the research side, because, if he didn't, he wouldn't get on, and went into the middle-class admin' side, which was far more cut-throat, but which counted for more. Now, as the head of a large industrial plant, he had to decide whether to move to head office in London to up his salary or change jobs. His only friends were people he worked with, his wife's only friends their wives. The only way to get on, he felt, was to move. He hoped it didn't interfere too much with the children's education.

'If I get a couple of notches further up,' he concluded, 'I'll send them to boarding school. Not that I really approve of it, but it will make moving about easier.'

Here you have a man, sometimes working-class, sometimes lower-middle in origin, who is prepared to sacrifice friends, children and principles to his career. In fact he's eager to leave his family and the friends of his childhood because they might be a social em-

141

barrassment. Later the spiralists often jettison their wives and trade them in for a Mark II model that goes with a new life-style.

Interesting, too, that this particular spiralist showed working-class shyness by cocooning himself against the world and taking a Ph.D. He made a typically working-class early marriage to combat the loneliness, but then made a deliberate decision to move over to the middle-class admin' side because it would further his career.

In a survey of managers' wives, it was shown that they all wanted their daughters to marry a 'burgess' in the professions. All believed this would provide more security and status than industry. They did not realize how many young barristers have to tramp the streets for months after qualifying before they get any work. Nor could they appreciate the status props that go with the spiralist's job: the houses, the company cars, trips for wives, gardeners and chauffeurs, the source of which can all be concealed from the neighbours.

'It's great, Angela! I've been promoted to Patagonia!'

The salient characteristic of the spiralist, whether he is from the working classes or the lower-middles is his adaptability and his total ruthlessness. He is the cog in the wheel, the corporation man who can charm his colleagues while trampling them under foot with his slip-on Guccis. His mecca is the conference.

'I've come a long way,' said one spiralist. 'My parents were working-class in the North-East; my expectations were at best tradesman. When I'm at conferences I feel how far I've come.'

On the other hand his social mecca would be Sunningdale or East Horsley, so he often ends up turning into a Howard Weybridge.

I went to a conference recently where the spiralists were rampant. The 'venue', as they would call it, was the Café Royal, and it was all firm handshakes and announcing of names:

'Vic Taylor. Pleased to meet you Ji-ell' (always two syllables), accompanied by a card pressed into one's hand.

Another favourite gesture on seeing an acquaintance was the thumbs-up sign, or jerking the head to one side and winking simultaneously. (The middle classes, particularly schoolmasters, tend to raise one arm at about 20 degrees.) The smell of *Brut* fought frantically with that of deodorant. Most of the spiralists had goalpost moustaches and brushed-forward thatched-cottage hair, with that flattened lack of sheen which comes from being washed every day under the shower, rather than in the bath. They all wore natty light-weight suits in very light colours.

On their lapels, like the faded square on Harry Stow-Crat's drawing-room wall where the Romney's been flogged, are unfaded circles which have been protected by conference badges. One could hear the rattle of Valium as they took off their lightweight long-vented jackets to reveal belted trousers. Their accent is mid-Atlantic, justified by the fact that they've spent a lot of time in the States (Non-U for America), which usually means a cheap weekend on a Thomson flight.

Their vocabulary is peppered with expressions like 'product attributes', 'growth potential', 'viability' and 'good thinking'. Perhaps it is some unconscious search for roots, but whenever they meet, they start tracing advertising genealogy.

'That's Les Brace, he used to be Saatchi and Saatchi, Garland Compton, before they became...', with the same intensity with which Caroline Stow-Crat and her group of jolly nice girl-friends are always saying:

'Sukie Stafford-Cross, she was...'

Conscious of their seemingly effortless mobility, spiralists always have razors, toothbrushes, Gold Spot, pyjamas and a drip-dry shirt in their briefcases.

Our third strand is the lower-middles, who don't rise and who Orwell described as 'that shivering army of clerks and shopwalkers. You scare them by talking about class war, so they forget their incomes, remember their accents, and fly to the defence of the class that's exploiting them.' They are also the sergeant-majors, the police sergeants, the toastmasters, Prufrockian, neatly dressed, cautious, thrifty. 'In the old days,' as Len Murray pointed out, 'they had an affinity with the boss, who saw them as people who could be confided in and trusted. They haven't the bargaining power, now there's more education about.' The nineteenth century entrepreneur has gone, and in his place have come huge management empires, where the smooth pegs thrive in round holes.

If the ex-working-class spiralists's mecca is the conference, the lower-middle's mecca is the 'function', where, in hired dinner jackets (which they call dinner 'suits'), they play at gracious living and the 'Ollde Days'. Howard Weybridge goes to lots of such occasions and rather takes them for granted. But Bryan Teale's ambition is to be president of the Stationery Trade Representatives' Association for one year, and stand with a chain round his neck, beside his wife, who has a smaller chain and a maidenhair corsage, graciously welcoming new arrivals, and being stood up for and politely applauded when they come in to dinner. Throughout the five-course dinner which starts at 6.30 they will 'take wane' with each other and various dignitaries and past presidents and their ladies down the table. As this is a Ladies' Night, each lady will get a gift of a manicure set or an evening 'pochette' in uncut moquette by her plate. Later there will be Ollde Tyme dancing, interspersed with popular favourites. Bryan will 'partner' Jen in the valeta. They both enjoy 'ballroom dancing'. The conference gang, on the other hand, bop until their thatched hair nearly falls off. The difference between the lower-middle 'function' set and the spiralists is that the former crave the 'dignity' of a bygone age, while the latter, with their natty suits, their bonhomie and their slimline briefcases, are geared towards America and the future.

But the real battleground in the late 1970s was between the 'function' brigade of the clerks and insurance salesmen, and the skilled manual worker one rung below. For a long time the skilled worker has been earning far more money than most clerical workers, and because the former tend to live in rented council flats, rather than paying commercial rents or buying houses on mortgage, and have all the kiddies at state schools, they have far more money to play around with.

One notices, too, that, in the light of extra cash, people tend to think of themselves as being in a far higher class than they really are. In Woodford, which is a predominately lower-middle-class area, 48 per cent of the skilled workers interviewed said they were middle-class, but in Greenwich, a more down-market area, only 23 per cent said they were middle-class, whereas in Dagenham, which is a working-class and principally socialist stronghold, only 13 per cent claimed middle-class status. The working classes tend to think that class depends not so much on education and income as production and consumption. Large numbers of miners interviewed in a similar survey called themselves upper-middle-class, whereas the Census would have called them upper-working-class.

BARRIERS

Although the barriers are slowly breaking down, there are still jobs from which you will be excluded unless you come from a particular class. Many firms in the city—stockbrokers, insurance and shipping brokers, commodity dealers—still appreciate what they call 'polish and mixability (which is a euphemism for upper- and upper-middle-class background) beyond academic qualification.

The discrimination, however, is now going both ways. A company director recently said that if he interviewed two graduates, one working-class and one from a public school, he took the working-class boy, because he'd had to fight harder to get there. Nicholas Monson, an Old Etonian, was sacked from a provincial newspaper because of what was loosely called his 'background'. A fortnight later he was told by a London advertising agency that his credentials were fine, but he couldn't have the job because the staff objected to Old Etonians.

You can't get a job as a disc jockey if you're upper-class nor as a television reporter, particularly if you're an upper-class woman. Time and again one hears the terrible flat 'a's and dreary, characterless Midlands accent of the reporter, which conjure up a picture of some folk-weave goon. Then suddenly the camera pans on to a ravishing creature in a trench coat, tawny mane blowing. Jison Richards, having dropped the 'Nouveau' and gone back to being Jison, by dint of touting his mother round all the interviews has got a job interviewing on ITN. Georgie Stow-Crat, on the other hand, despite brushing his hair forward and taking elocution lessons from the gardener, forgot to say 'As-cót' and 'Sollisbury' at the interview and was turned down.

A public school accent, said the *Daily Mail*, is a positive disadvantage in acting. So you get Ian Ogilvie, an Old Etonian, playing the Saint as a transatlantic spiralist. RADA advises one even more confusingly to keep your regional accent but speak the Queen's English. Vivat Regions presumably.

Many people, particularly rock stars, find they can only hit the big time if they go abroad. Vidal Sassoon went to America, which he described as 'a society where there are no class barriers, where the cop's son can become president of a great corporation, and where profit isn't a dirty word'. Mr Sassoon was wrong. There are plenty of class barriers in America, but he, as a foreigner, wouldn't be aware of them, nor feel self-conscious if he transgressed them.

No one now is more in demand with the American television cameras than Mr Sassoon, who attributes his success to his stepfather, who taught him how to cut hair and made him take elocution lessons to smooth out his cockney accent.

But despite the film *Shampoo*, which portrayed the hairdresser as a superstud, and Mr Sassoon making the gossip columns as 'millionaire crimper and health food freak inviting 400 close friends to the Hilton', hairdressers are not likely to be accepted by the upper classes because of their pansified and plebeian image. Her hairdresser may be the recipient of Caroline Stow-Crat's indiscreet confidences, but he'll never be asked to dinner, although, as a token working-class, he might get asked to her wedding.

THE WORKING CLASSES

'While I was at University, I took a vacation job. To a nicely brought-up girl from an academic family the horror of sitting at a conveyer belt eight hours a day packing chocolates was indescribable. I also remember the feeling of being a non-person to the manager and the secretaries of a small firm. I hope the

147

> *custom of students doing manual work con-
> tinues. For many of us it is the first time we
> have been in close contact as equals with the
> working classes.'*
>
> Letter in The Sunday Times

The use of the words 'working classes' is interesting.
The girl who wrote this letter must have met people
from working-class backgrounds at university, but
then, perhaps by definition, they had already become
middle-class. Recently, when a Sunday paper published
a middle-class man's account of how he swept the
streets for six months as an experiment, what came
across was the monotony, the hard grind, and the way
people in the street behaved as though he didn't exist
—was a 'non-person' in fact. Evidently the only compensation for working in a factory is that it teaches
you to lip-read.

If the career is the supreme reality to the middle
classes, the worst thing about the working classes, said
Ernest Bevin, was their poverty of ambition. They are
far more interested in good pay than job satisfaction.
In a recent survey 96 per cent of clerks interviewed
thought that pay was less important than prospects,
but only 20 per cent of the manual workers wanted to
be promoted to foreman. Promotion would involve too
much commitment to the management and much less
overtime pay. If Mr Definitely-Disgusting is made a
foreman, he finds himself in an ambiguous position.
The management think of him as a junior executive,
but he wants his fellow workers to think of him as one
of the boys. He also finds he has to cajole and threaten
to make the slacker on the assembly line pull his finger
out. The only thing Mr D-D's really good at is assembling cars—and he doesn't do that any more. If he
works too hard, even on the factory floor, he'll show up
his colleagues and they'll resent it. To rise is to feel
less secure; paranoia is the disease of the upwardly
mobile.

If Mr D-D wants to get on, therefore, it's far easier to become a shop steward and rise through the unions. Then he can have a chauffeur-driven car, expense-account lunches, first-class tickets, trips to Brighton, Blackpool and abroad, and the ear of the Prime Minister, all without losing the respect of the shop floor.

For the middle classes it is much easier to move upwards. By hard work and a bit of luck, a man in Unilever can become managing director of sausages at 28, then move on through soap, and toothpaste up to the central board.

The tradition of the working classes is a fatalistic acceptance of hierarchy and status. Mr D-D's hopes for the future are based on the price he and his mates can get for the work they do. This is emphasized by the belief that they will do better by collective bargaining under appointed union leaders, who often manipulate their demands, rigging ballots and forcing them to come out on strike. Striking is also a good way for union leaders, shop stewards, pickets, even Mr Definitely-Disgusting to get on Telly, and have Auntie Edna ringing up from Darlington after *News at Ten*, screaming excitedly, 'We've just seen you'. Even Mrs Definitely-Disgusting was asked for her autograph the time she attacked a picket with her shopping bag during the lorry drivers' strike.

It's significant that two of the great working-classes heroes are Harvey Smith and Oliver Reed, two bruisers who are totally unafraid of, and repeatedly raise two-fingers at, the Establishment.

As work on the whole is hell, the working-class man likes to keep home and work quite separate. Mr Definitely-Disgusting comes home, having been bossed about all day, and wants his tea on the table. Nor does he see work as a place where he makes new friends or joins social clubs. He couldn't go to one of these clubs in his overalls, all sweaty from work, and once he's out of the place, he doesn't want to have to go home, clean up, change and come back. Firm's social clubs and societies for this reason are almost exclusively middle-class.

When work is so exacting, monotonous and unrewarding, it is hardly surprising that workers seeing people having candle-lit dinners, frisking on sun-drenched beaches and driving blondes in fast cars every night on television, often fail to clock in.

At British Leyland if Mr Definitely-Disgusting works for three months without taking a weekday off, his and Mrs D-D's names are included in a draw for a fortnight in Majorca. For those who can go for two months without playing hooky there's a chance of five days in Belgian beer halls, after which you'll probably need a month to recover. If you don't go to work because you're ill, the working class refer to it as being 'on the sick', which sounds awfully slippery.

Within the working classes themselves, there are also numerous rankings. We know of the Respectable and the Rough, and those in work despising those who are unemployed. There are also great divides between skilled, semi-skilled and unskilled. There is great kudos in being skilled as my hairdresser pointed out: 'My Dad works at Vauxhall on the cars—skilled of course. Then there's my father-in-law on nights at Fords, earns £200 a week, but he only does two hours a night, spends the rest of the time learning Spanish. He's skilled too.'

There is also status in having the power to paralyse. The biggest rewards go to the workers who, if they stop work, do the most harm to the country collectively. Thus miners, power workers, dockers, engineers and lorry drivers are the new élite who can bring the country to its knees, while the poor postmen, firemen and ambulance men, who have less clout, slink home without a decent rise. (The spiralist would call it a 'raise'.)

Mining and quarrying is regarded as much grander than building, because it's not casual work. Engineers regard themselves as the cream of the working class. Printers are evidently the most imaginative and intelligent. Miners in Britain know that their counterparts in Poland are payed twice as much as dons and doctors, and are biding their time.

CHOOSING A CAREER

The great problem when the working-class school leaver looks for a career is the discrepancy between fantasy and actuality. According to a Careers Officer: 'Jasmin comes in with one C.S.E. in needlework and says she wants to be a brain surgeon. "How about nursing?" you say. No, if she can't be a brain surgeon, she wants to be an architect. Some school leavers fancy science, but they think it's going to be all "Eureka! I've discovered a new gas and I'll be awarded the Nobel prize my first week." They also love anything with a 'y': psychiatry, psychology—not having a clue what it involves. Of course all the E.S.N. automatically go into a factory.'

E.S.N. stands for educationally sub-normal, which Dive Definitely-Disgusting is not. With one C.S.E., he wants to be a helicopter pilot; he doesn't know how to fly, but they'll learn him. A few years ago he might have gone into 'The Print' as he calls newspapers, but they're not taking on any more apprentices; or he might have trained as a motor mechanic, because it would have been his only chance of handling a car, but now his father's got a second-hand Vauxhall, the job has rather lost its appeal.

Mrs Definitely-Disgusting, who accompanied Dive to the interview with the careers officer, thinks he ought to learn a trade, then he'd be skilled, definitely. Dive rather likes the idea of being a tool-setter, which he thinks is somefink to do with chisels and hammers, like, and he enjoyed woodwork at school. He might go in for television repair, then he can mend the knocked-off telly when it goes wrong, and he's quite drawn to electronics, because he thinks it will involve somefink like that spaceship in *Star Wars*, and it'll help him mend the knocked-off Hi Fi when that goes wrong, like.

As you need a good C.S.E. for bricklaying these days, Dive might have a crack at that. He's read somewhere that hod-carriers earn £200 a week, and anyway it sounds rather grand if you refer to it as the construction industry. Anything to do with shops is known very grandiosely as retail distribution. Dive's mite, Stan, has become a butcher's assistant and refers to himself as a trainee manager.

Mrs Definitely-Disgusting, having scattered Coke tins and crisp packets over Wandsworth Common all weekend, wants to know if they've got anything on The Environment, y'know pollution and all that. Dive thinks this involves rushing around in a Land-Rover with a theodolite. Dive also fancies geology and marine biology, which he sees as whizzing around in jets, personally discovering crude oil. Like many town children, having seen green fields and sheep and cows and pigs and hens on telly, he believes he would enjoy forestry and farming. But the moment he gets to the country, he can't bear the quiet, and there's what he calls 'no life, like'; so he wants to come back to the town again. Because he sees beaches and Martini ads on telly, he would also like to be a courier, anything where a golden-hearted employer will pay him to move about, and as he still identifies with Divid Bailey as a great working-class hero, and because 6/8ths of his holiday snaps came out, he quite wants to be a photographer.

Looking for a job at 16, he'll probably be luckier than little Wayne Teale who'd been persuaded by Jen and Bryan to stay on until he's 18, presuming there must be some lollipop at the end. A headmistress at a comprehensive school admitted that she uses class as a carrot, telling her girls that if they stay on longer and take G.C.E. they will get a job in a better firm, and more nicer girlfriends, and meet a better class of man. In fact, as the Careers Officer pointed out, it's easier to get a job at sixteen because the employer feels he doesn't have to pay you nearly as much as an eighteen-year-old.

Alas too, today's more straight and sober teenagers are reaping the wild oats sown by the last hippy generation, who were so restless that they dropped out of any job after three months. In the end employers got fed up and now tend to employ Old Age Pensioners, rather than office juniors—they're more reliable, they're grateful for the work, and they don't feel jobs like making the tea and doing the post are demeaning.

Even so Sharon Definitely Disgusting will probably end up in an office or a shop, which she always refers to as a 'booteek', unless it's Woolworth, where she will call herself a trainee buyer. Mrs D-D would rather she worked in an office. If 'they learn her to type' she'll become a 'sekkertry', go straight into Class III Non-manual, and cross the great manual divide. She'd quite like Sharon to become a hairdresser—'skilled' again—and then she could do Gran's hair on the weekend. But Sharon doesn't like the idea: On your feet all day, and you have to work Sa-ur-days. She'd enjoy doing something with kiddies. (For 80 places last year Wandsworth Borough Council has 900 applicants.) She'd do anything not to have to work in a factory, or for some reason in a laundry, nor would she touch nursing—far too many soap-dodgers. But nursing is still very popular with West Indian young who regard it as a step up from Mum who used to clean wards when she first arrived from Jamaica.

Ten years ago, Sharon's ambition would have been to become an air hostess, but as it would take her away from her steady boyfriend for such long stretches, she'd prefer to be a ground hostess. Mrs Definitely-Disgusting likes her at home, anyway. She'd like Dive to get on but she doesn't have any real ambitions for Sharon. One working-class school-leaver in a very depressed area of the North managed very creditably against a lot of competition to get herself a job as a hotel receptionist. Her parents refused to let her take the job because they thought it would make her 'too posh' and they didn't want her carrying on like they do in *Crossroads*.

WOMEN

The greatest occupational change in the last twenty-five years has been women going out to work, the telling statistic being that three-fifths of all working women now take non-manual jobs, while three-fifths of all working men do manual work. This is reflected in the vast shift to and swelling of Class III. With increased technology, the top Class I and II jobs have gone to men, and with women filling the increasing array of lower white-collar jobs. Consequently schools, for the first time, are taking seriously the fact that most women will work before and after they're married.

One of the great job phenomena of the 'seventies was the way the upper classes took up cooking. All the debs take *cordon bleu* courses automatically now, instead of learning to type and undo the flowers. All their mothers cook like mad because they've got upper-class husbands with picky appetites, and have to organize grand house parties and dinner parties without servants. So it's like falling off a house for them to cook for other people. The result is Caroline Stow-Crat organizing directors' lunches and working wives' buffet parties, starting take-away food shops and running Mrs Nouveau-Richards' dinner parties.

Fiona Stow-Crat goes and cooks in chalets in Switzerland for free skiing, or in villas in Spain or Majorca in the summer, and is known as a jolly good sort. She was fumbled on the last night by one of the husbands in the kitchen, but turned her head away because her mouth was full of left-over Coq au Vin.

Like the upper-class man who can't cope with the six-year training for a lawyer, the upper-class girl is incapable of long-term sustained effort. If she works in an office she's always on the telephone, or sloping off on Friday morning and not coming back till Tuesday, or far far worse, not recognizing any difference socially between Sharon Definitely-Disgusting in the typing pool, whom she describes as 'absolute heaven', and Thalia Upward who's doing significant research in the art department. As the Principal of a smart London secretarial college can be heard saying on the telephone: 'Saturday morning? Oh, that wouldn't suit my girls. They go to the country on Friday.'

My husband once had a secretary who used to ring up her mother when she was going home for the weekend and arrange to have the train stopped, because the railway ran across their land.

The upper classes sometimes impose their tastes on others as interior decorators. 'I let Caro Stow-Crat have Carte Blank', says Mrs Nouveau-Richards. The Marchioness of Tavistock advises Aston Martin on their colour schemes. Sometimes they run dress shops from which the hoi polloi think they can buy upper-class taste, but in which they get ripped off just as much as Oxford Street. Nude modelling used to be O.K. for the wilder element at the beginning of the 'seventies. By the middle 'seventies women's lib had arrived and any kind of modelling was dismissed as pandering to sexism. But now Antonia Fraser's daughter and the Earl of Dudley's niece are modelling, people have got bored with women's lib and it's quite smart to be a sex object again.

Mayfair Mercs are the glamorous social climbers invented by *Harper's* and are the female equivalents of spiralists. They go into advertising, pop music, commercial radio or television, or they shop for Arabs. They also become stylists in advertising, which means they impose their frightful lower-middle-class taste on all the sets in television commercials and press ads.

It seems insane, too, that all lower-middle and lower-class girls who come from Loughton and Romford and the East End, work in the city, with upper- and upper-middle-class men who wouldn't dream of marrying them. While all the upper- and upper-middle-class girls who live in Knightsbridge, Fulham and Chelsea can't face going any farther than Mayfair on the tube and therefore work with all the middle- and lower-middle-class spiralists in advertising, whom *they* wouldn't dream of marrying either.

Upper-class and working-class husbands don't like their wives going out to work. They want them waiting when they get home, always with a clean house, regular meals and children under control.

Only in the middle classes is a job regarded as a sign of status. Samantha Upward hates saying she's just a housewife, although taking an interesting job is less of an economic necessity than it is for Mrs Definitely-Disgusting.

Mrs Nouveau-Richards has absolutely no desire to work. She saw her own mother working her fingers to the bone and considers herself very lucky to be a 'lady' (she emphasizes the word) of leisure.

Upper-class wives again tend to play at jobs. They counter depression when the children leave home by doing charity work, sitting on committees, visiting the old, or spending one day a week in a smart boutique or a bookshop.

'I wouldn't possibly have time to do a job,' said one upper-class woman. 'If you have a private income you have far too many letters to write.'

IN THE OFFICE

The middle classes tend to take work home from the office and not take nearly so many days off. The working classes, feeling socially out of their depth in offices, do best in backroom jobs—one remembers the spiralist who felt he had to switch over to admin' in order to get on. The lower-middles do best in sales and P.R. because they're so pushy. Gideon Upward is too laid back to sell, but he has polish and self-confidence which makes him good as an account executive, liaising with the client.

According to a fascinating book by J.M. and R.E. Pahl called *Managers and Their Wives* the working-class woman like Mrs Definitely-Disgusting would loathe the firm's dance. But Jen Teale would adore it. The atmosphere is lower-middle anyway, and she likes to practise socializing in a formal atmosphere. Often she's been a typist before she was married and feels very much at home.

Samantha Upward would hate any of Gideon's office parties. She would feel under-rated and neglected. She doesn't like being defined by *who* she is, rather than *what* she is. She can't bear being treated just as Gideon's wife.

Mrs Nouveau-Richards has a ball and kisses all the directors on the mouth.

Eileen Weybridge, because she is house-and kitchen-proud, enjoys entertaining Howard's colleagues at home. She has read magazines and seen commercials emphasizing the wifely role when the boss comes to dinner, and knows about cooking food that is delicious but not so obviously expensive that Howard would not be thought to need a 'raise'.

Samantha Upward doesn't mind entertaining, but she finds it more of a bore than an ordeal. She regards Gideon's boss as such a tedious little man.

Jen Teale, who would love Bryan to get on, gives him more practical help than Samantha gives Gideon. Because they don't often entertain she discusses work with Bryan in the evening and, being an ex-typist, helps him out typing reports when his secretary is off with the curse.

The most terrible story is told of the very shy wife of a spiralist, who was bogged down at home by several little children, but who was invited to her husband's annual dinner dance. As he was doing well, she made a tremendous effort, buying a new dress, going to the hairdresser, arranging for her mother to baby-sit, and scouring the headlines for conversational fodder. The great day dawned and, on arriving at the dance, she discovered she was sitting next to her husband's boss. Despite her trepidation, they got on terribly well and it was only during the main course, when suddenly everything went quiet, that she realized she had cut up all his meat for him.

When Jen Teale worked in an office, she was a flurry of daintiness—fingerettes so she didn't have to lick her finger to turn a page over, plastic soap dishes, a shoe bag for her outdoor shoes, a mauve office cardigan to stop her good clothes getting dirty, a floral plastic sponge bag, and a blue plastic container for her Tampax, in case anyone should see anything. In the Ladies she rustles lavatory paper very noisily from the moment she shuts the door and sometimes coughs, too, so no one will hear anything. Afterwards she washes both hands with soap and water, unlike Samantha who only bothers if there's someone there.

7 SEX AND MARRIAGE

'My period has come upon me' cried the Lady of Shallot

As was pointed out at the beginning of the last chapter,
the chief factors affecting social mobility are career and
marriage. If Sharon Definitely-Disgusting blossoms
into a beauty and lands Georgie Stow-Crat, her future
will be completely different from that of her brother
Dive who marries a factory girl. If you marry beneath
you, and have plenty of money, it is possible to yank
your partner up to your own level. By the time King
Cophetua had given the beggar maid a few elocution
lessons and smothered her in diamonds and sables, she
was probably indistinguishable, save for a few 'tas' and
'pardons', from the other ladies of the court. But take
a plunge both in class *and* financial status, and it's a
different matter. If Queen Cophetua had fallen for a
beggar, however handsome, and been cut off with 10p
and forced to live on his lack of income, they would
both have vanished into obscurity.

Although kings have married beggar maids, and
peers' daughters eloped with garage mechanics, the
fact that gossip columnists get so excited when this
happens stresses both the news value and the rarity
of such an event. Most of us commit endogamy, which
is not a sophisticated form of bestiality, but merely
marrying someone of the same class. In fact, Sir Anthony Wagner, the Clarenceux King at Arms, has gone
so far as to say that a social class for him means 'an
endogamous class, one that is whose members normally
marry within it'. The main reason why the classes have
tended to pick partners in the same stratum is to exclude the classes below. The upper classes, for example,

married each other to keep their land to themselves. The bourgeoisie did the same because they didn't want to share their capital with the working classes.

Much has been written about the social mobility triggered off by the sexual revolution of the 'sixties, with working-class lovers surging up from the East End, public school boys melting down their accents, and upper-class girls, in a glow of egalitarianism, taking on a string of down-market lovers—lorry drivers one year, negroes the next and beards the year after. But as *Harper's* has pointed out, 'Her final choice remains strangely unaffected. Somewhere there is a chartered accountant with her name on him.' Or, in Fiona Stowe-Crat's case, it's back to Squire One.

COURTING

The working classes get off the mark very early. Dive Definitely-Disgusting, having gone to school locally, meets the same members of the opposite sex all the year round, like. He goes about in mixed gangs at first; then one day on the way home from school he offers to pay the bus fare of one of the girls and has the mickey taken out of him by all his mates. From then on he and the girl go round entwined like a three-legged race. As neither has a telephone at home they spend hours on the doorstep necking, or gazing into each other's eyes like cats. If they ever do talk on the telephone, the conversation is punctuated by long, long pauses. Embarrassed by tenderness or compliments, they indulge in permanent badinage and back chat. This behaviour in extreme form was ritualized by the punk rockers:

'When you fancy a girl, you spit in each other's glasses. Then the boy punk says, "Do you?" The girl answers, "Yes," and you go to the toilets.'

Jen Teale is very strict with Christine and hangs around at teenage parties, finally falling asleep at two o'clock in the morning under a pile of crisp packets like a babe in the wood. Naturally Christine reacts against

160

Jen and she and her friends escape to London, live in hostels, go in pairs to wine bars and pick up men with eye-meets. They are very keen on what they call 'Chinese Nosh' or a 'meal e-out', and use expressions like 'a curry' or 'a wine'. Having been told since childhood to behave like little ladies, they are the most overtly flirtatious of all the classes, fluttering their eyelashes, pulling faces and rolling their eyes like Esther Rantzen, which they call being 'unimated'. When she goes into a party or a restaurant Christine always looks round to see what effect she is having on men. The upper classes never bother—and they never fidget either.

Zacharias Upward starts courting much the latest. The upper-middles haven't the self-assurance of the upper classes and, locked into a single sex school, Zacharias makes do with Thalia's friends who've been asked to stay in the holidays. Howard Weybridge and his friends are much better off. Too inhibited to pick

'We're goin' steady!'

each other up, and considering it common anyway, they have evolved an elaborate system of legitimate pick-up places: tennis clubs, rugger, golf and hockey clubs, where sporting events take place to heat the blood, followed by drinking to release the inhibitions before anyone can get going. Jim Callaghan, who was working-class, had to join the tennis club in order to court Audrey, who, by his definition, was middle-class because her parents had a car, a char and went on holiday.

Later the upper-middle classes also escape to London where they share flats with other girls and boys of 'roughly the same sort of background' (their euphemism for 'the same class'). They tend to meet the opposite sex through work, nurses going out with doctors, secretaries with bosses.

The upper classes have far more confidence. They all know each other anyway, and their parents, who they call 'wrinklies' or 'jarryatrics', have full enough social lives not to bother themselves too much about their children's morals. They worry far more about drugs and car smashes after drinking than loss of virginity.

Georgie Stow-Crat meets girls at dances in the holidays, at the Fourth of June, in Scotland in August or at the Feathers Ball, once described by *The Observer* in very unsmart terms, as the 'do of the year for those of first-class stock'.

Unlike Thalia Upward, if Fiona Stow-Crat sees a boy she likes:

'I dance over and hope he notices me. If that doesn't work I find someone who knows him and get that person to introduce me. If he still isn't interested I give up.'

When they're older, the upper classes meet skiing, shooting and at various up-market occasions like Ascot and Henley. At parties they go in for lots of horse play and shrieking. Linda in *Love in a Cold Climate* was far more attractive to the opposite sex than the more beautiful Polly because she was a 'romper'—almost a sort

162

of chap. The upper classes are inclined to lean out of windows and pour champagne on tramps and parked cars, or to charge around at dead of night changing road signs. The sexes also meet each other at drinks parties in the girls' flats in Knightsbridge and Belgravia. Even if the party isn't being given in her flat, the hostess sends out 'At Home' cards, and the recipient automatically runs her thumb over the words 'At Home' to see if they're engraved.

THE SEASON

Up to the late 'fifties most upper-class girls 'came out'. One's mother, who'd been presented herself, presented one to the Queen, and the Nouveau-Richards bribed some impoverished upper-class woman to do the same for Tracey-Diane. In 1958, however, the Queen abolished the whole presentation ceremony, which meant that anyone could become a deb. The season was swamped by social climbers and lost any kind of cachet.

Despite this setback, a few hundred girls still come out every year. The process is to write to Peter Townend, the social editor of *The Tatler* for a list of 'gairls' doing the season. Then follows a string of luncheons where the mothers get together, see that party dates don't clash and make sure that their daughters get asked to as many things as possible. Clued-up mothers have stickers printed with their own and their daughter's addresses on. The minute the first luncheon reaches the coffee stage out come the diaries and everyone charges round seeing how many stickers they can get into other people's diaries.

Many of the upper classes sell farms or woods to pay for dances. It is also necessary to suck up to Peter Townend in order to get your daughter's picture in *The Tatler*. He can also produce young men out of a hat whose background, education, regiment or sheer cashflow make them eligible. Most of the young men live in the country or a precious stone's throw from Harrods.

One of the great dangers is that one's daughter may fall in love with one of them at the beginning of the season and wreck her chances with other men. 'Don't you dare go steady,' I heard one mum say recently. 'Just like the lower classes.'

One has the feeling that the mothers enjoy the season almost more than the daughters. Many of them, still youngish and pretty, have the chance to meet up with old gairlfriends and flirt with old flames.

At the end of the season I asked a deb's mum, did she feel all the expense had been worth it?

'Oh yes,' she replied. 'The gairls have all had such fun, and at the worst, they'll have built up a network of jolly nice gairlfriends.'

'And even if they do go astray', boomed her friend, 'one knows they'll go astray with the right sort of chap,' (which is back to endogamy again).

ROUGH DIAMONDS ARE A GIRL'S BEST FRIEND

'When the mind is full of tit and bum,' a friend of mine once said, 'it tends to be a-critical,' meaning that, in the first flush of love, you don't mind what class a person is. The fact that he's not 'the right sort of chap' makes him even more attractive. When they are young, the insecure of both sexes tend to drop class. Older upper-class men love going to bed with working-class girls. It reminds them of nanny. For the same reason, they adore big strapping Australian girls. One Australian journalist went to interview an earl about wealth tax and only moved out six months later.

Equally, going out with a yobbo gives the middle- and upper-class girl a feeling of superiority. She also finds working-class men more respectful but at the same time more dominating than their public school counterparts. (Geoffrey Gorer claims that the skilled worker has the highest sexual energy—so she's on to a good thing.)

It should be pointed out here that the working and upper classes tend to be far more chauvenistic than the upper-middle and middle-middle classes. This is perhaps because they are more reactionary, but also because they tend to have everything done for them by their mothers or nannies; whereas the middle-class mother, struggling for the first generation without servants, is much more likely to have made her son run around fetching and carrying for her. The middle-class man will therefore be far more prepared to reverse roles. This is important because it is crucial to an understanding of the different attitudes to sex, dating and women in general.

The first great love of my life was a miner's son who'd become a millionaire. I was working on a newspaper in Brentford. He passed by in a vast, open, dark green car, and screeched to a halt. I bolted into my office, but when I sidled out two hours later he was still waiting. He was the most handsome man I'd ever seen, and it was all very disgraceful and wildly exciting. He took me straight back to his house, whereupon he told me to go and make him a cup of tea. I was far more shocked than if he'd tried to seduce me. None of my stuffy middle-class boyfriends had ever bossed me round like that.

We went out for nearly three years . . . Whenever he went abroad on business, and, I suspect, pleasure, he never wrote. This broke my heart. I only discovered years later that he was ashamed of being ill-educated. He was shocked if I said 'blast', and would never come to any of my parties, although I was dying to show him off, because he was shy and probably bored by my friends. He went to see his mother every day.

He was bossy, yet socially tentative, prudish yet unfaithful, and mother-fixated—all working-class qualities; yet we had three marvellous years. He was incredibly generous, showering me with presents which cost a fortune and which were returned (my middle-class background again) whenever we had one of our periodic bust-ups. And he was far more masculine, more reassuring and more fun than any of the uptight barristers, stockbrokers and account executives I'd run about with before. If he had asked me to marry him, I should certainly have said yes, but he had the good sense to realize we were far too different for it ever to work. For when the class war and the sex war are joined, hostilities always break out in the end.

Alan Coren said that, when he was at Oxford, upper-class undergraduates screwed nurses and married upper-class girls, while working-class undergraduates married nurses and screwed upper-class girls, yelling 'One for Jarrow' at the moment of orgasm.

Richard Hoggart, that champion of the lower orders, says that one of the most valuable characteristics of the working classes is the ability to take the mickey and say 'Come off it', which the middle classes usually translate as having a 'bloody great chip on one's shoulder'. This trait frequently comes out in working-class intellectuals when they have affairs with middle-class girls. One remembers Jimmy Porter constantly bitching at his gentle, long-suffering wife.

Another example of working-class chippiness coupled with macho occurred recently with a beautiful girlfriend of mine who was running two men at once, one of them an underwriter and the first man ever to wear full eye make-up to Lloyd's, the other a working-class pop music promoter. One day the Lloyd's underwriter took her for a row in Hyde Park. They were just pulling into shore when the music promoter leapt out of the bushes where he'd been lurking and pushed the underwriter into the lake, where he stood spluttering and threatening to call the police.

'If he'd been working-class,' said the music promoter later, 'he'd have slugged me back. I didn't throw him in the water because I was jealous about you but because he was upper class.'

If Zacharias Upward goes out with Christine Teale, Gideon and Samantha will talk scathingly about 'Not

quite P.L.U. [People Like Us] darling' or 'rather
Pardonia', and pray that their children will grow out of
it. Middle-class parents also become particularly
tolerant in the face of eligibility. If you go out with
someone much grander than yourself, you tend to take
on some of their mannerisms. Friends noticed that when
Roddy Llewellyn was going out with Princess Margaret
he assumed the patrician poker face, used the pronoun
'one' instead of 'I', and started walking around with his
hands behind his back like Prince Philip.

THE DATE

When Dive Definitely-Disgusting takes a girl out on a
date he's likely to be much cleaner than Zacharias
Upward who often goes out straight from the office.
Dive has a bath and a good scrub before getting dressed
for the evening. He'll reek of Brut and over-scented
deodorant and wear an open-necked shirt to reveal a
hairy, muscular chest clanking with medallions. He'll
be very generous with drinks, but he'll tend not to give
the girl dinner (having already had high tea, so as not
to drink on an empty stomach) because he's frightened
of 'resteronts' as he calls them. He can't understand the
menu if it's in French, he doesn't know how to order
wine or how to eat asparagus, and is terrified of making
a fool of himself asking for steak tartare to be well done
or complaining that the Vichysoisse is stone cold. This
is why many restaurants qualify food on the menu, like
'chilled' watercress soup, and probably explains the
popularity of melon because it's the same in French and
English.

Being taken out to dinner is such a treat for Sharon
Definitely-Disgusting that she always goes right through
the menu, and always has pudding. She won't comment
on the food or say 'Thank you' afterwards. One working-
class girl I know went out with a lower-middle sales
rep who had an expense-account acquaintance with
'resteronts'. 'He was so charming and well spoken,' she

'Waiter! There's an eyelash in my friend's soup.'

said afterwards, 'and such a gentlemen. He kept telling me what knife and fork to use and correcting my con-ninenal accent.'

Georgie Stow-Crat would never correct pronunciation or comment on table manners. If his companion wants an 'advocado' pear, let her have one.

The manager of our local restaurant is a great observer of dating couples. 'You can always tell a girl who's escalated,' he says. 'She talks direct to the waiter, instead of letting the man order for her. Artichokes are a great leveller; I saw one girl trying to eat the whole thing.'

'People who belong,' he went on 'always hold their coats in mid-air when they take them off. The *nouveau riche* never say "good evening", are curt with waiters, snap their fingers and then over-tip. They also put vinegar on their chips.'

Both Christine Teale and Sharon Definitely-Disgusting prefer sweet drinks to dry: sweet Cinzano,

Martini, Baby Cham and orange (a sort of Doe's fizz), Tia Maria, Crème de Menthe. If they drink gin, it's with orange.

Sharon also likes a man to be neatly dressed on a date. 'If he had a holey sweater or holey jeans I wouldn't entertain him,' she says. 'And he must be clean. I couldn't stand all those rockers a few years back with dirty hair. I like a boy with a bit of life in him, but not rough.' She would also say, 'I've got a snapshot of him indoors' (which is working-class for 'at home').

Christine Teale refers to a boyfriend over twenty-one as a 'boy' ('I'm going out with a wonderful boy'). Most people say 'boyfriend' or 'man'. The upper classes, when they're trying to be democratic and trendy, say 'guy' in inverted commas. One should never talk about an 'escort'. According to *U and Non-U Revisited* one should say 'male companion', which seems a bit pedantic. Most people merely say the person's Christian name, and leave you to guess who they're talking about. It is also vulgar to say, 'May I bring my girl?' as opposed to 'a girl' when you mean a girlfriend.

Unlike the working classes who don't bother about the morrow, Wayne Teale tends to be tight with money. To splash it around is both prodigal and cheap. He won't buy a girl dinner, so he'll put on a paisley scarf, which he calls a 'cravat', tucked into a sweater, and take her to a bar where he knows the landlord by his Christian name. This he calls 'social drinking'. If he's over thirty, he might wear a white orlon polo-neck jersey which he'll call a 'röllneck' (to rhyme with doll) sweater, because a touch of white is so flattering after a certain age and the neck hides the wrinkles in his throat. He refers to a girl as an 'attractive young lady'. He would prefer her to wear a skirt than jeans, even though his trouser creases are sharp enough to ladder her tights. He's also read somewhere that it's common to say perfume, but scent sounds too foxy, so he settles for 'fragrance'. Gideon would probably say, 'That's a nice pong'.

Caution is the watchword of the lower-middles. Wayne daren't be romantic in case some unsuitable 'young lady' traps him into matrimony. He would call it getting 'invōle-ved' with a long 'o'. He doesn't resort to insults and backchat like the working classes, but his conversation is arch, and rather hearty with an air of continual interrogation, rather like Bob Dale or the non-yokels in *The Archers*. He will use expressions like 'Chop Chop, Young Lady', or, even worse, address his girlfriend as 'Woman'. She will say in reply, 'Stir your stumps, Wayne Teale.' It is frightfully lower-middle to address people by both their Christian name and surname. Any money Bryan makes will be spent on what he calls 'home improvements' or on his car, which has a Christian name and is always referred to as 'she'.

Zacharias Upward likes entertaining girlfriends in his flat where he can show off his gourmet cooking. This is cheaper than going to restaurants, saves on petrol, and is much nearer the bedroom. All his friends say Zak is very 'hos*pit*able' (the upper classes emphasize the first syllable).

Howard Weybridge's idea of an exciting date is to ask his girlfriend to freeze on the touchline while he grapples muddily with a lot of other fifteen-stoners on the rugger field. Later she will be expected to talk to rugger wives about deep freezes while he frolics naked in a plunge bath with the rest of the team, and then make one warm gin and tonic last all evening while he downs pints and pints of beer. In summer she might get taken to cricket, which is sometimes warmer but goes on longer.

Georgie Stow-Crat will be very generous to his girlfriends—like Oscar Wilde who, when asked why he gave champagne to a barrow boy, replied, 'What gentleman would starve his guests?' Georgie can't cook and would starve in a well-equipped kitchen. So, as he is too thick to make conversation for very long, he takes girls to dine in a night club or a disco. Romance, according to Tina Browne in *Over 21*, blooms in the twilight gloom of smart places like Wedgies and Annabels. As the upper classes tend to leave London at the weekend, Fridays and Saturdays are very bad nights at Wedgies.

WHO MARRIES WHOM

> *'Education! I was always led to suppose that no educated person ever spoke of notepaper, and yet I hear poor Fanny asking Sadie for notepaper. What is this education? Fanny talks about mirrors and mantelpieces, handbags and perfume, she takes sugar in her coffee, has a tassel on her umbrella, and I have no doubt if she is ever fortunate enough to catch a husband, she will call his father and mother Father and Mother. Will the wonderful education she is getting make up to the unhappy brute for all these endless pinpricks? Fancy hearing one's wife talk about notepaper—the irritation!'*
>
> Uncle Matthew in
> *The Pursuit of Love*
> by Nancy Mitford.

As the upper classes all know each other, they get in a panic if their children get engaged to someone they haven't heard of.

Georgie Stow-Crat plays around with girls of other classes before and after his marriage, but he'll try and settle for one of his own kind. For what are a few nights of passion for a lifetime at the wrong end of the table? Lord Lichfield took out a string of models and actresses, but he ended up with Lady Leonora Grosvenor. More recently the Marquess of Douro married the Princess of Prussia, the Duke of Roxburghe married Lady Leonora's sister, Lady Jane, while their brother, the 6th Duke of Westminster, chose Miss Natalie Phillips, granddaughter of Sir Harold and Lady Zia Wernher. As the aristocracy are forced 'to straphang through life like the rest of us', they are closing their ranks and marrying the sort of gairl who will bring some cash or property with her, or as one aristocrat put it, 'can make a decent lunch for a shooting party'. 'The reason why my marriage came unstuck,' said a duke's daughter, 'was because I was upper-class and he was only landed gentry.' The moment Georgie Stow-Crat gets engaged he takes the girl to meet nanny, which is far more of an ordeal than meeting Harry and Caroline.

What the upper classes really dread is their child falling for someone middle-class.

'A thoroughly conventional man in good society,' said Edward Lyttelton, a former headmaster of Eton, 'would rather that his son should resort with prostitutes than that he should marry a respectable girl of distinctly lower station than his own. Indeed it is not going too far to say that he probably would rather his son should seduce such a girl, provided there were no scandal, than marry her.'

In order not to be continually irritated by class differences the aristocracy often marry rich Americans or foreigners, who they can instruct in upper-class English behaviour without being too insulting:

'In England, Ortrud, we have a funny national custom of not saying "horse racing".'

If Georgie Stow-Crat did marry down, he would tend to pick a very beautiful girl, which is why the aristocracy is so good-looking. In general, good-looking people marry up—Tony Armstrong-Jones and Captain Mark Phillips being notable examples—and the insecure and ugly tend to marry down. Just as they dropped class while dating, they tend to pick a partner who'll look up to them and make them feel superior.

When people get married for the first time late in life—in their forties or fifties—parents are inclined to waive class prejudices out of sheer relief that their 'child' is finally off their hands.

172

It is debatable whether the middle classes have any real desire to land an aristocrat any more. As has been said already, the peer is no longer the favourite hero of romantic fiction (unless he's in costume of course) and has been replaced by the middle-class doctor or surgeon.

Heather Jenner says her marriage bureau clients 'don't give a hoot' what class people are any more. 'Why should they want to marry a lord and cope with a falling-down overgrown house? On the whole blue-collar men are far better at giving a woman a good time. One upper-class woman was so fed up with the sexual and financial ineptitude of the aristocracy she put "Working Class Only" on her form.'

On the other hand, another girl who ran a marriage bureau, discovering she had a baronet among her clients, promptly whipped him off the books and married him herself. Another friend of mine, born on a council estate, can pinpoint the moment she fell in love with her future husband, who is a peer: 'He signed a cheque to pay for our dinner with his surname only.' Finally one has only to read the small ads in *The Tatler*—'Very attractive blue-blooded academic in his early thirties equally at ease on the hunting field or engaged in economic and political discussion' (sounds hell)—to realize that class does have a pull. The Blue Bloody is still holding his own against the Blue Collar.

The upper-middle-class man, preferring to get his career together before settling down, tends to marry late, between twenty-eight and thirty-two; his bride will be in her mid-twenties. Often they live together first, particularly if one set of parents disapproves. Then gradually, out of sheer force of habit, or desire for grandchildren, the parents come round.

Samantha Upward, who's always taught Zacharias to be unsnobbish, finds the thought of being a mother-in-law awfully trying. First there was Zulanka from the Fiji Islands, who was really wonderfully dark, but who spoilt it all by referring to all those nice Africans

173

as 'no-good blacks'. And now there's Mikki (who's really called Enid) who appears to have no surname. Mikki does something nebulous in the music business, is totally uncultured, but full of pretensions. In referring to herself and Samantha collectively as 'middle-class folk like ourselves' she is obviously totally unaware that Samantha's family is much better than hers is. Even more maddening Gideon obviously thinks that Mikki is quite, quite perfect, particularly as she doesn't wear a stitch in bed. Gideon insists on taking her a cup of tea first thing to admire her early morning teats.

The lower-middle parents, being materialistic, aren't sure whether to oppose early marriage as unsound financially or welcome it as better than pre-marital promiscuity. One lower-middle spiralist said the reason he finally decided to marry his wife was because she'd been brought up in a careful household, and therefore would be a good manager of his money. Believing in deferred satisfaction, Wayne tends to be engaged for several years, rather than live with a girl, so he can put down a deposit on a house. He will 'study for exams' in the evening, his 'fiancay' Shirl will work in a bar, and bank the lot, so they have enough money to move into a perfectly 'decorated home'. Shirl can't stand disorder—she must have everything nice. The upper-middle girl who wanted to get married in a hurry would be perfectly happy to move into a rented box in Fulham and run up an overdraft doing the place up, or expect Daddy to fork out for carpets and things later.

The Nouveau-Richards will be absolutely furious if Tracey-Diane doesn't marry up. In the same way that the middle-class Princess Grace was livid, having hooked a prince herself, that her daughter settled for a middle-class industrialist.

Parents are very seldom cross about upward mobility. Even when engagements are broken off, they can make social capital out of it, like the mother who went round telling her friends:

'It's such a bore having to pick the coronets off all the linen.'

Dive Definitely-Disgusting marries the earliest. This is probably due to frustration. He's likely to have no flat or car to make love in. If he goes home Mrs D-D and the children are watching the telly—and it's too cold outside, except in summer. They also started dating earlier anyway, and if they do screw they don't bother to 'take precautions', get pregnant and can't afford abortions.

'I didn't *have* to get married, I married for love,' a working-class minicab driver told me the other day, as if it were the exception to the rule.

Engaged at seventeen Sharon Definitely-Disgusting gets 'eternized' at eighteen, which means she receives an eternity ring from her betrothed. At Christmas and birthdays she will send him a four-foot-square card padded with red satin, saying 'To my Darling Fiance' (without the accent).

The word 'fiancé', perhaps because so many people live together now, has become distinctly vulgar, particularly when it is pronounced 'fee-on-*cay*' with the weight on the last syllable. Debs get round sometimes by saying 'my fiasco' or 'my intended' in inverted commas.

THE WEDDING

The wedding is another occasion when the classes meet head on. People who marry up choose tiny churches, or have registry office weddings so they don't have to invite less grand relations. It doesn't matter having common friends; everyone thinks one's frightfully democratic. But common relations are quite a different matter. Wedding presents aren't displayed either, because they might cause derisive mirth at the reception. Embarrassing relations also show up less at a stand-

175

up reception with food you can eat with your fingers (which Jen Teale calls a 'finger buffet'), so people's table manners don't show up—and with any luck working-class relations will push off early because they hate not being able to sit down.

There will invariably be a panic about protocol. One girl said her mother poured over *The Tatler* for months, studying every detail of the weddings, muttering 'we're going to get this right if it kills me'. 'We even put a sleeping pill in Grandad's cocoa the night before, because he refused to wear morning dress.'

When John Betjeman married a very upper-class girl, he drove his future mother-in-law insane at the pre-wedding party by wearing a made-up bow tie on elastic and flicking it all the way through dinner.

But, however critical he or she may be of the behaviour of others, the true aristocrat is a law unto himself. The men had just finished dinner at a stag party in a private room at a London club when the bridegroom's father, an aged Earl, suddenly beckoned to a waiter and said, 'Pot'.

'We're not allowed to supply it, Sir,' said the waiter, nervously.

'Don't be bloody silly,' roared the Earl. 'I mean piss-pot.' Whereupon a huge chamber pot was brought down from one of the bedrooms and the Earl proceeded to use it in full view of the other guests.

The upper classes get married in the country in their own churches. As they are accustomed to giving and going to balls and big parties, the wedding is not such an event as it would be in a middle-class family. Quite often the bride wears her mother's wedding dress, and a 200-year-old veil of Brussels lace held in place by the family tiara. (One upper-class bride was so relaxed she spent her wedding morning washing her horse's tail.) She doesn't usually have a long engagement or any of the hassle of finding a house, because her parents or her in-laws have already given them a 'place' with lots of 'pieces' in it.

The wedding invitations are engraved in black; the service cards have the bride and bridegroom's (pronounced 'gr'm' not 'grume') Christian names printed at the bottom. Flowers in the church are usually something unostentatious like lilies of the valley, with the bride's bouquet (pronounced '*book*-kay' not 'buke-*ay*') of white roses or spring flowers.

The men wear their own morning coats. There are usually hordes of little bridesmaids called Sophie and Henrietta, a page with patent leather hair wearing a replica of a Blues and Royals uniform, and a labrador who wriggles ingratiatingly into the wedding photographs. No one minds about the music—'Here Comes the Bride' up, Mendelssohn down. The bride agrees to honour and obey. It used to be unsmart to get married at the weekend, particularly in London, as everyone had gone away. But now that most of the upper classes and their show business friends have jobs it is considered perfectly all right. Saturday police have to be deployed from the local football match to deal with the traffic. Several of the guests arrive by helicopter.

After the service the line-up to shake hands with the couple takes hours and hours. We queued interminably at a royal wedding a few years ago—it was rather like mountaineering. You crawled along for ten minutes, then turned into the next room to find another queue, and then another up a staircase and then another. People kept giving up, and doing U-turns to go out to dinner. One felt they ought to provide something to sustain one during the waiting: champagne at the foothills, or brandy at the South Col, or at least lay on buskers.

At another very grand wedding, having been nervously practising my curtsey all the way, I found, when we finally reached the bride and bridegroom, that everyone was shaking hands with them.

'I thought we were supposed to bob,' I muttered to a friend once I was safely inside.

'I was damned if I was going to bob to that jumped-up trollop,' she said, 'and after that everyone followed suit.'

The reception at an upper-class wedding is a very cheerful occasion, once again because everyone knows each other, and it doesn't matter that there's no introducing. None of the women look the least self-concious in hats. The cake is decorated with white flowers, and often cut with the bridegroom's sword, the nearest it ever gets to active service. Really grand weddings include busloads of tenants from both families. Usually they sit around with red faces, shiny blue suits and tumbrilcreemed hair. But at Earl Grosvenor's wedding recently morning coats were hired for all the tenants, so that they wouldn't feel out of place, and they were all flown down by aeroplane.

Georgie Stow-Crat hates his honeymoon because he misses Snipe. Upper-class girls often take Teddy on honeymoon.

When Georgie marries Tracey Nouveau-Richards no expense is spared. Tracey's tiara is so heavy her head droops like a snowdrop. The 'floral decorations' composed of 'Football Mum' chrysanthemums, nurtured in Mr Nouveau-Richards' conservatory, are described by Mrs N-R's friends as 'tasteful'. Mrs N-R hires a hundred out-of-work actors to pose as relations, and two hundred more as tenants. They rather overdo the Somerset accents and rust-coloured country suits. The wedding takes place in Guildford Cathedral, with a reception at the bridal home in Sunningdale. The marquee extends beyond the garden and covers much of the golf course. Guests keep falling down the holes. Three tons of Joy are squirted into the swimming pool on which float the words 'George' and 'Tracey-Diane', written in salmon-pink carnations.

Mrs Nouveau-Richards has had orchids and maidenhair corsages in little test tubes of preservative liquid made up for herself and Caroline Stow-Crat, who surreptitiously tries to rip off the maidenhair during the service and only succeeds in burning a hole in her new coat and skirt with the preservative. Signing the register takes longer than usual as Mrs N-R's hat gets stuck in the doorway.

Harry Stow-Crat has a wonderful time. There's plenty of champagne—Tracey-Diane's endowment of worldly goods means he needn't worry about death duties anymore. All Mrs Nouveau-Richards' hired relations turn out to be his show business cronies, which persuades him the N-R's do know some quite amusing people after all.

The Upwards are simply furious they haven't been invited.

'You can't ask everyone,' says Samantha bravely, although Mrs Nouveau-Richards seems to have done just that.

The upper-middle wedding is far more depressing. Samantha, wanting to be different and stress how 'cultured' and musical she is, chooses hymns the congregation don't know. Lists are placed at Peter Jones or the General Trading Company, so everyone knows what they're getting. Waiters keep the napkin over the champagne to hide the lack of vintage. No one wears maidenhair behind their carnations except a few *déclassé* cousins in lounge suits.

As the upper-middle classes don't all know each other, and prefer three hours' drinking to a sit-down meal, their weddings are rather heavy going. The women's heels sink into the lawn so they can't circulate. Merriment is not aided by a long speech from the bride's parents' most upper-class friend. No one can clap properly at the end because they're holding empty glasses. Thalia's husband hates his honeymoon and thinks they're so called because they're so sticky.

Howard and Eileen Weybridge's wedding is held in the function room of the Olde White Hart (circa 1937) with French windows opening on to the patio. The women look very self-conscious in floppy hats, and show too much hair at the front. The bride makes her own wedding dress, or buys it off the peg. According

179

to one manufacturer, royalty influences far more wedding dresses than show business, and the less virginal a girl is the more covered-up she wants to look. Howard Weybridge and his ushers are photographed outside the church in hired morning coats with maidenhair rampant behind every foiled carnation, and their top hats on the sides of their heads. The reception starts off with sweet and dry sherry followed by Asti Spumante ('bubbly' is too expensive). Everyone sits down to lunch of a nice smoked trout, chicken and bombe surprise, after frightful rows over the seating arrangements. The speakers, likely to be local councillors or secretaries of the tennis club, who adore the sound of their own voices, go on for ever, and every dismally unfunny telegram is read out.

The bride's mother finds the 'holl' occasion very 'meuving'. 'It's such a nice opportunity to meet and converse with relatives,' and Eileen's had 'some wonderful wedding gifts'. The father says, 'Look after yerself,' as Eileen goes away in the Austin Princess and a navy costume with beige accessories. The honeymoon is spent in the bridal suite of a hotel in Devonshire.

The lower-middles are the tiredest when they get married, because they've just 'decorated and renovated their new property' themselves. (Georgie Stow-Crat would say 'done up the house') all ready to move in.

Bryan Teale has his stag party two nights before the wedding because Auntie Jean has to be met off the train from Scotland on Friday, and the car has to be put through the car-wash before they go away. No one wears a morning coat; the men are in three-piece waisted suits; the best man goes off to buy shoes with built-up heels on the morning of the wedding so his trousers hang better. The 'bridal gown' is based on the latest royal soap opera with Mrs Fitzherbert sleeves. The photographer snaps away throughout the service at all the most solemn moments. People are shown to their seats by 'groomsmen' rather than 'ushers', and the results are put in a white album with spider tissue paper. The service cards are printed in silver gothic script and decorated with silver bells and the bride and groom's initials. The bridegroom has to remove his initialled signet ring to his right hand to make way for his wedding ring, and the happy couple, smothered in confetti and rice, leave the church in a white Rolls-Royce.

The reception is held at the Dainty Maiden Tea Rooms, and thirsty cyclists who've ridden over from Godalming are told to go to the Hand in the Bush Tea Rooms down the road, as the place has been taken over for a 'function'. Sherry is followed by *vin rosé* or sparkling hock. Everyone eats ham, chicken and salad. The wedding cake is topped by a papier mâché replica of the bride and groom both wearing lipstick, and decorated with silver shoes, horseshoes and plastic flowers.

The bride, wearing a tangerine 'skirt suit', and the bridegroom, in an even lighter coloured and more waisted suit, go off to Majorca for the honeymoon where the new Mrs Teale loses her virginity on the third night.

The working-class wedding is the jolliest. Mrs Definitely-Disgusting has even forgiven Stan for putting Sharon in the club—at least he's white. The hall is hired at the Goat and Boots; the bar is open all day; everyone sits down or dances—the working classes never stand because of their corns. Dad soon gets down to the piano, and starts playing 'golden oldies' like 'Deep in the Heart of Texas'. Auntie Eileen leads the singing. Even Mrs Definitely-Disgusting is persuaded to do a knees up. Sharon wears an empire-line dress to hide the bulge and feels sick all the time. The honeymoon is spent in Jersey. Having never been away from home before, Stan and Sharon are very homesick.

OH COME OH COME NON-MANUEL

It is difficult to generalize about sex and class. Hunter Davies, a working-class writer so successful that he has certainly become middle-class in life style, expressed his bewilderment in a recent *Sunday Times* article at his thirteen-year-old daughter going out with boys and demanding parties with drink: 'Brought up on a council estate in the 'sixties, I married the school swot. It took me three weeks even to hold her hand. My dad knew what it was like for me when I was courting, but things have changed so much in the last ten years that I haven't a clue what it's like to be Caitlin. She's a different age, a *different class*, a different society.'

With the advent of the permissive society, one hopes that the young of all classes are getting better at sex and more aware of 'the great discovery of the age', as Hugh MacDiarmid calls it, 'that women like it too.'

But there are still vast pockets of male chauvinism among the upper and lower classes, particularly in the north. It is possible that young Georgie Stow-Crat and Dive Definitely-Disgusting are fairly competent operators, having picked up a few tips from the cinema and Anna Raeburn, but their fathers are probably still floundering around in the dark ages.

Harry Stow-Crat's attitude to sex, for example, is the same as that of our late lamented English setter, who was spoilt, goofy, terrifyingly tenacious and with a totally unbridled sex drive. If he got on the trail of a bitch, he would charge across three main roads, race twenty miles until he caught up with her, and then mount her from the wrong end. His libido was only equalled by his sexual ineptitude—rather like one peer who discovered after three years during which no heir appeared that he'd been buggering his wife all the time.

Another married aristocrat I know was so wild to pull a girl he'd had lunch with that he smuggled her into the Great Western Hotel by a side door, broke into an unoccupied bedroom and was just settling down to work when the management rumbled him. Only a lot of fast talking and a fistful of fivers stopped him being arrested and the most frightful scandal ensuing.

If Harry fancies a girl, particularly a lower-class one,

he will pester her until he gets her, and then it's wham, bam, thank you ma'm. He's far too used to poor Caroline shutting her eyes and thinking of England to believe a woman should derive any pleasure from the act.

The telly-stocrat and the pop singer have the same exalted approach. 'It's so easy,' sighed one rock star. 'You have all these groupies; there's no time to romance (lower-middle for to court) on the road, so you just say, "Get your gear off".' A sort of *droit de Singer*.

My favourite mini-cab driver has a theory that tall people are good in bed because only they can reach the sex books that librarians insist on putting on the top shelves. But this doesn't explain why aristocrats, who are generally tall, tend to be hopeless. Maybe they never go into public libraries, or don't read anything except the *Sporting Life* and Dick Francis. Harry's sole aim is vaginal penetration; he can't even count up to foreplay. When a girl kisses him, she can feel his narrow stoat's head under his straight mousy hair, totally devoid of any Beethoven bumps. As he thinks aftershave and deodorant are vulgar, and he doesn't have any middle-class hangups about being nice to be near, he might even smell rather sweaty.

Aristocrats often break their toes on stone hot-water bottles climbing into other people's beds at house parties. One wonders what the procedure is. Does the hostess sleep with the man in the right-hand bedroom for the first half of the night, and the man in the left-hand bedroom for the second half? Presumably anything goes as long as you're back in your own room by dawn so as not to upset the servants. Most of the upper classes share beds with their dogs for warmth. When a lover leaps into bed and thinks he has encountered something interesting and furry, he may easily get bitten.

As they have all the freedom and restlessness of inherited wealth, there is a wild decadent fringe of the aristocracy, whose sexual appetites are so jaded that they're into every perversion under the eldest son.

Having enjoyed beatings at Eton, both Harry and Georgie Stow-Crat adore being whipped. You can recognize an old school bottom—striped with red, white and blue weals—anywhere.

Most life peers, who have been far too busy making it to the top to get any practice, are absolutely hopeless in bed.

ONCE YOU HAVE FOUND HER NEVER LET HER COME

The upper-middles used to be even worse than the aristocracy. Too inhibited even to have Harry's *joie de vivre*, their upper-middle lips were far too stiff for them to be any good at oral sex. Gideon's parents must have had terrible sex lives because of overhead lights in the bedroom. Once they'd switched the lights off by the door, the room was plunged in darkness, so it is a miracle that they even found each other and managed to produce Gideon.

Moving down a generation, Gideon is very enthusiastic, but a bit mainline—*Playboys* in the lavatory and a finger under his next-door neighbour's roll-on at New Year's Eve parties. He knows all about middle-class sophistication and de-furred satisfaction and longs for Samantha to shave her bush off. She did once but it was awfully itchy, and as the whole family have baths together, it might have put Zacharias off his O-levels. But she's frightfully understanding about Gideon's *Playboys* and allows him to do anything he likes to her in bed, shutting her eyes and thinking of Great Britain and the Common Market. She does her yoga every morning to keep herself young and attractive.

The best lover of all is the upper-middle-class intellectual. Having been made to run round by his mother when he was young, he's into role reversal and a woman having as much pleasure as a man. His already vivid imagination has been encouraged by voracious reading. He's just as randy as the aristocrat, but he tempers it with finesse and humility. Lucky the girl that lays the golden egghead.

A male stud who has done extensive field work agrees that middle-class intellectual women are also best in bed. The *Guardian* reader, he says, is the easiest lay of them all, because she feels she ought to be liberated and knows all about rejection and blows to the male ego. She always refers to coming as 'a climax', says 'penis' and 'vagina' and talks about her friends having 'lovely breasts'.

The lower-middles tend to be too cautious. It's all 'nudge nudge', prurience and not much pleasure. Jen Teale is also terribly difficult to get at because she wears such an armour-plating of full-length petticoats, which she calls 'slips', corselettes, five pairs of 'punties', tights with trousers, which she calls 'punts', and 'punty girdles'. Dainty and fastidious, she would never make love while she has the curse (which she calls a 'period') and she is 'revollted' by anything slightly off-centre. Afterwards she says, 'that was very pleasant, Bryan.'

Mandy Rice-Davies, interviewed in a sex book, is a good example of lower-middle refinement: 'Looking sexy is a very low-class turn-on ... I've had brief affairs with Lord Astor and Douglas Fairbanks Jr. [here she displays parvenu boasting and lack of discretion] but none of those involved anything remotely kinky.'

WORKING-CLASS SEX

The working classes have a reputation for potency and being good in bed—a myth probably started by middle-class novelists and by graphologists who claim that anyone with loopy writing must be highly sexed. Randy they certainly seem to be. According to an Odhams Survey, the working-class couple makes love more than any other class, but the woman enjoys it less.

'We don't fight,' said one builder's wife, 'only over money and sex, especially sex. He always wants it. He'd do it now if he came in and you weren't here.'

'Oh my Gawd!'

Geoffrey Gorer maintains that the skilled worker (Class III) would appear to have more sexual energy than the other classes. But he says that there does not seem to be any factual basis for believing that the working classes in general are more sexually potent. He quotes an upholsterer who only had sex three or four times a month, and a welder who only had it once a month (perhaps he got stuck).

Mrs D-D calls sex 'having relations' or 'in-ercourse'. If there were any sexual problems, she would be far too embarrassed to discuss them. Mr D-D is not into foreplay; he uses that finger to read the racing results.

A divorce lawyer told me that the working classes hardly ever see each other naked, probably because they often sleep in one room with the children, and if Mr D-D takes his clothes off Mrs D-D might see 'Rosy', 'Mum', 'Nancy' and 'Doreen' tattooed all over his body and get jealous. As he also imagines all women have *retrousée* tits, sopping wet hair and full make-up like page 3 of *The Sun*, Mrs D-D undressed might be a bit of a disappointment.

MARRYING UP

No one understood the nuances of class better than Chekhov. At the beginning of *Three Sisters* Natasha, Andrey's fiancée, is seen as a lower-middle-class social outcast. Everyone laughs at her and the three sisters tell her her clothes are all wrong. Then she marries their brother and gradually she gains ascendancy. She starts bossing the sisters about, henpecking her husband and being beastly to the old servants ('I don't like having useless people about'). Soon she is cutting down trees on the estate and moving the sisters into smaller bedrooms, until by the end they are meekly taking criticism from her about their clothes.

People who marry up are more insistent than most on having their new status recognized. I'm sure that Cophetua's beggar maid, despite her lovesome mien, made a perfect nuisance of herself queening it over everyone, and we have all seen how the middle-class Princess Grace became far more regal than royalty once she landed Prince Rainier.

One woman who married a duke suddenly insisted on having a room to herself at the hairdressers, 'because I'm not just anyone anymore.' Often they can't quite master the new vocabulary.

'We're spending the weekend at Bath's seat,' said a secretary who'd just landed a peer.

Women who marry up also become frightfully strict about their children's manners, because they're terrified that any lapse in behaviour will be attributed to a mother who doesn't know what's what. In the same way, stupid women who marry clever men are pushy about their children's education. Middle-class women who marry into the upper classes say 'se-uper' a lot, and become very good cooks to cope with picky aristocratic appetites.

When men marry up, they usually move away from their home town, buy horses and farms and take up patrician pastimes like hunting and shooting. They also become totally bilingual, putting on very grand voices when they're out hunting, and lapsing into their mother tongue when they're talking to garage mechanics.

If you marry someone who constantly tells you you're pretty, you begin to think you are. In the same way if you marry someone who thinks you're frightfully grand, you begin to believe him. As a result lots of middle-class women married to working-class men get very smug and think they're far more upper-class than they really are. Men who marry up often put their wives on pedestals and then run around with other women. Parvenus, in fact, are invariably unfaithful. It's a back-handed blow for the class war. John Osborne's Jimmy Porter is a classic example, as was the late President Kennedy. Upper-class women, brought up to expect infidelity, can handle this; that's why they build up that network of jolly nice gairlfriends to fall back on; and anyway they're so busy sitting on committees, organizing charity balls and wondering what to wear at Ascot that they don't miss sex much.

The middle classes, like Eileen Weybridge and Samantha Upward, can't cope at all.

'Oh Keith,' said one middle-class wife, 'I can't bear to think of your penis in Mrs Peacock.'

Which brings us to....

ADULTERY

The way to helly is paved with bed intentions

Harry Stow-Crat has never been faithful to Caroline, like the earl who made a good start to his marriage by asking all his old girlfriends to sleep with him as a wedding present. Traditionally, as was pointed out in Chapter 1, marriages were arranged to improve one's cash situation and to increase one's land; one got one's fun elsewhere. Not all aristocrats are rich, of course, but it is much easier to play around if you don't have a job, own several places, have a helicopter (chopper) to whisk your mistresses round the country, and plenty of cash to take her to smart restaurants and hotels. Upper-class males also tend to lead separate lives from their wives in any case.

'Where's Daphne,' I remember asking one peer. 'Oh, she's stalking in Scotland,' came the reply (the prey wasn't specified).

If ennobled, aristocrats also have a perfect alibi in the House of Lords. One's wife never knows if one's in the House or not. In fact a friend recently discovered a peer screwing a girl on the woolsack, but no one sneaked on them; there is honour among strawberry leaves. Location can also curb the libido. A girlfriend of mine said her lover, who was an Hon, wouldn't even hold her hand if they were walking across the Knightsbridge side of the Park, but would neck ferociously on the non-smart Bayswater side (because he was unlikely to see any of his wife's smart friends up there). And in the undergrowth of Wimbledon Common he would fornicate freely ('because there's not the slightest possibility of ever bumping into anyone I know in the suburbs').

An aristocrat who came up to London to take me out to lunch booked a table at a restaurant in Holland Park, which he also regarded as suburbia and quite safe. Alas, we couldn't get a taxi afterwards, and to his extreme consternation had to walk all the way to Knightsbridge before we could find one.

Upper-class wives can occasionally be just as unbridled sexually. One even has two telephone numbers, one for business and an ex-directory hot line for lovers. She was livid when one editor (who was an ex-lover) rang her about feature on the lovers' telephone. When one peer's daughter discovered her M.P. lover had ditched her and returned to his wife, she stuck a huge placard on his car, which was parked in the street outside his house, saying:

'Do you really want to vote for an adulterer?'

The upper-middle classes used to concentrate on their careers to keep sin at bay. But all that changed with the advent of the country cottage. With Samantha in the country and Gideon at his little flat in the Barbican, the fun is unconfined, although Gideon's frolics are slightly inhibited when Thalia decides to leave Wycombe Abbey early, take a secretarial course in London and live with Daddy.

The seven-year itch often finds some basis for truth among the middle classes. Samantha marries at twenty-four, has Zacharias at twenty-six and Thalia at twenty-eight. Three years later, when she's been married exactly seven years, Zacharias starts full-time school and Thalia goes to play group. For the first time in years she has the house free; she also has a feeling of nagging inadequacy—that the children are no longer a full-time job, justifying her being just a housewife. Hey Presto, in moves the lover.

The upper-middles, not having living-in servants, often have a sexual renaissance when the children go to boarding school and they have the house to themselves for the first time in years. On the debit side, one friend said it was very difficult to keep lovers at arm's length when one no longer had the excuse after a liquid lunch that one must rush away and pick up the children from school at four o'clock.

All adultery grinds to a halt during the school hols, which is the main reason—not tiredness—why mothers get so bad-tempered. The lower-middles tend to be far too cautious to commit adultery; it might upset the extra bright children. Instead they go to wife-swapping parties and pool all the children with what they call a 'sitter'. Sometimes Bryan Teale, when he's not working out the commission he's made that morning, makes love in the back of his car on the edge of the common in the lunch-hour, which is why he equips his car with cushions, and coat-hangers so that his cheap suit won't crease.

Working-class adultery, however, is much harder to achieve. No telephone to arrange appointments, possibly no car to draw up in lay-bys. Because of shift work and overtime, the lover never knows if the husband will be there or not . . . when the coast is clear the wife puts a packet of OMO in the front window, which stands for 'Old Man Out'.

The upper- and upper-middle classes talk about 'having an affair' with someone. The media and the trendy middle-class call it 'having a relationship'. The working classes say 'going with'; 'I think he's going with another woman.'

IN-LAWS AND PARENTS

Many working-class couples, unable to afford a place of their own, are forced to live with one set of parents after they are married, often with the wife's mother bringing up the children. This is why the mother-in-law problem is more acute among the lower echelons, and is the basis for so many music hall jokes. In the past, when the mortality rate was very high and husbands were likely to desert or be put out of work, the wife had to fend for herself, so she clung to her own family, particularly her mother. As has been pointed out, many working-class men visit their mothers every day and, if their wives are working, go home for lunch. Although the old matriarchies are breaking down now that most couples can afford cars, and move to jobs away from home, working-class mothers tend to be far more possessive. At Christmas and birthdays they have truces and send each other large, spangled 'Dearest Mother-in-Law' or 'Daughter-in-Law' cards.

Among the middle classes the social gradations are so complex that you often get both sets of parents thinking their offspring have married beneath them.

'Oh, Tom has got a nice, little wife,' a mother will say. 'We're getting used to her saying "garridge" and "Port-rait".' ('Little', as in 'little shopgirls', is a euphemism for 'common').

If, however, the 'nice, little wife' looks after her husband well and produces a son fairly quickly, she will soon be forgiven her low caste. Heirs are a daughter-in-law's crowning glory. In many ways, too, a slightly common daughter-in-law is preferable as long as she's respectful, because it makes the mother-in-law feel superior. One girlfriend said she didn't speak to her husband for three days after a weekend with her in-laws. In the middle of dinner her mother-in-law asked her to pass the cruet, and her son, half-jokingly said,

'Oh, Angie thinks the word "cruet" is common.'

In the same way, if Thalia Upward were to marry Dive Definitely-Disgusting, she would start making Mrs D-D feel that her anti-black and generally zenophobic attitudes were uncouth. Mrs D-D, in retaliation, would disapprove of the way Thalia made Dive do the housework, get his own supper when she went to maths workshops, and even went out to work when she needn't.

The middle classes, disliking friction, try to keep a superficial peace with their in-laws, even if they disapprove. The upper classes don't bother. A middle-class friend of mine was pointedly told by her very grand old mother-in-law, 'Divorce is considered perfectly respectable now.'

On the middle-class front, one often gets antagonism between two sets of in-laws if the wife is working. Samantha's parents say, 'You must be getting *so* tired. Gideon really ought to be able to support you, darling.' Colonel and Mrs Upward, nettled by such disapproval, retaliate with 'Poor Gideon being hampered in his career by having to help with the housework and cook dinner when he gets home in the evening'.

Parents whose children marry and move away often complain that young people today are selfish and ungrateful. 'He's become like that Greta Thingamy;' grumbles Mrs D-D. 'He wants to be alone.'

One girl who married a man in the R.A.F. said it was a nightmare everytime her working-class parents came to stay.

'Dad sneers every time Don brings out a bottle of wine at meals, and says, "We *are* pushing the boat out, aren't we?" Then he expects Don to take him for a drink at the Officers' Mess. If only they'd behave like the jolly kind of people they normally are.'

'My daughter goes to sherry parties now,' said another working-class mother sadly, 'and has a little car of her own. She asks me to go and stay but I don't go. I might show her up.' Stay in your own world, you're OK. Move up and you're out of step.

As Tracey Nouveau-Richards says,

'If Dad wasn't my dad, I'd laugh at him myself.'

One lower-middle girl I know describes a horribly embarrassing occasion when she got engaged to a peer's son and his father came for a drink to meet her parents.

Her mother's first words were,

'We're all of a flutter. We don't know whether to call you "Your Grace" or "Dad".'

DIVORCE

As you go down the social scale, the more rigid and unforgiving you find the attitude towards infidelity ... The upper-middle-class couple, according to Geoffrey Gorer, believe in talking over the situation if they discover one of them is having an affair. The lower-middles would try and reconcile their differences, and get over what they hope will be a passing fancy. The skilled worker might advocate separation but not divorce. But Classes IV and V would be all for punitive action: clobber the missus and clobber the bloke, and after that the only answer is divorce.

Of all social classes, in fact, Class V clocks up the most divorces. This is probably because they marry so young, often having to get married, and because they find it impossible to discuss their problems when things go wrong. The husband can't cope with the pressure of so many children, and as he often takes casual labouring jobs in other parts of the country, the temptation to shack up with another woman is very strong. He can sometimes get legal aid, and doesn't have to pay for a divorce, and, finally, because the parental bond is so strong, it is quite easy for both husband and wife to go home and live with their own parents, whereas the middle-class wife, having achieved a measure of independence, would find this far more difficult.

What else wrecks a marriage? The middle classes mind most about selfishness, conflicting personalities and sexual incompatibility, while the working-class wife objects to drinking, gambling and untidyness, and the husband going out on his own with his mates.

Despite all the country cottages, Class I (engineers and oculists) has the fewest divorces, probably because they can't afford two mortgages and two sets of school fees if they marry again, because no one's going to give them legal aid, and because they think divorce would be bad for their careers.

According to Ivan Reid's *Social Class in Britain*, the lower-middles get divorced more frequently than the skilled workers. Maybe this is because the lower-middles, working together in offices, have more opportunity to meet the opposite sex on a long-term basis, while the skilled worker is stuck on the factory floor assembling tools. Maybe, too, the skilled worker has enough potency to keep both girlfriend and wife happy, and has no particular desire for a divorce.

The aristocracy, statistically negligible though they may be, tot up more divorces even than Class V. Since the turn of the century, thirty-three per cent of all marquesses and earls have been married twice, twenty-four per cent of viscounts and twenty per cent of barons. That's why *Debrett's* is such a fat book, listing all the marriages.

'The reason for this,' explained a peer 'is that few blue-blooded aristocrats have inhibitions about what their neighbours think.' Presumably if you live at the end of a long drive the neighbours don't get a chance to see anything.

Only three per cent of life peers get divorced—too busy getting to the top to have anything on the side, and too hopeless in bed for anyone to want them.

One of the saddest victims of the class war is the wife of the ambitious spiralist. While *he's* been living it up in foreign hotels, eating expense-account lunches and playing golf with the boss, she's been stuck at home with the children. He has a whole new life-style, and he wants a new wife to complement it, someone more glamorous and more socially adept. Husbands justify abandoning the first wife by saying:

'Anita didn't travel with me' or 'I married a local girl [euphemism for 'common'] first time round'.

People who've been married several times tend only to mention the grandest ex they've been married to. Woodrow Wyatt has had several wives, but in *Who's Who* only lists the one who was an earl's daughter.

8 HOMOSEXUALITY

*'The middle age of buggers is not to be
contemplated without horror.'*
　　　　　　　　Virginia Woolf.

Heterosexuals, as we have seen tend to marry and go out
with people of their own class. But, as Harry Stow-Crat
might drop class if he had something on the side,
because there would be less likelihood of his own set
finding out, homosexual relationships (because until
recently they were against the law) tend to be between
people of different classes simply for safety reasons.
Harry Stow-Crat pursuing rough trade in Brixton is not
likely to bump into any of Caroline's friends, any more
than Dive Definitely-Disgusting bouncing around in
the four-poster of some stately homo is likely to meet
any of his mates.

Because there are fewer homosexuals (about one in
ten) around than heterosexuals, it's more difficult for
them to find someone of their own class. Nor could you
find a class of people more insecure socially than most
homosexuals and, as we've already pointed out, the
insecure tend to drop class. The upper-class man having
an affair with Dive Definitely-Disgusting is given a nice
feeling of social superiority.

Perhaps most important of all there is the psycho-
logical motive: if you're going to descend into the pit of
Sodom, you might as well degrade yourself further by
dropping class. Hence the often tragic addiction of
upper- and upper-middle-class queens to the criminal
classes, laying themselves open to goodness knows
what blackmail, beatings-up, and being left trussed up

naked like a chicken for the char to discover in the morning.

Sometimes there are happier outcomes. A famous painter surprised a burglar rifling his house and invited the burglar to stay, which he did—for the next twenty years. Another friend has a running affair going with a wonderfully handsome married burglar. He was particularly enchanted the last time the burglar came out of the nick, 'because he lied to his wife about the release date and spent the first night out with me.'

There's no doubt there is something very attractive about a butch, muscular, working-class boy. 'I'm simply not turned on by people who don't have accents,' said one aristocrat. A middle-class man said his father 'warned me never to look below for a friend—how wrong he was.'

'If I want to attract a toff,' said an East-Ender, 'I always thicken my accent and talk about "fevvers". They think it's marvellous.'

On the other hand the queen, whatever his class, always tries to be more upper-class, ironing out his accent like mad, and putting on what my East-End mates call a 'posh telephone voice'. Because the middle classes tend to articulate their words very carefully, the homosexual voice is often very difficult to distinguish from Jen Teale refained. This is why the working classes roar with laughter at people like Larry Grayson, Frankie Howerd, Dick Emery and the two Ronnies when they do drag acts, because they think they are putting on lower-middle airs.

The upper classes are drawn to the working classes not only because they like the butch image, but also because, like women, they are drawn to people who give them a hard time. E.M. Forster, after years of falling in love with unreliables, said he was convinced that the working classes were incapable of passionate love—'All they have is lust and goodwill'. Ironically Forster at last found happiness with a married police-

198

man, who after he died said, with typical lower-middle-class caution, that he'd never realized Forster was a homosexual.

Yet earlier Forster had advised the writer J.M. Ackerley, who suffered from a string of unreliable boxers, burglars, guardsmen and deserters, to bear in mind that the lower-class lover can be quite deeply attached to you, but may suddenly find the journey up the social scale too much.

Certainly if Dive Definitely-Disgusting gets taken up by the upper-class fag mafia he can lead an amazingly grand and glamorous life. A friend says his plumber spends his weekends moving from one stately home to another, the sort of life Mrs Nouveau-Richards would give her capped teeth for. Evidently a famous Oxford queen once took him to stay with Harold Nicolson, which he didn't like because Harold had made him go and put on a tie for breakfast.

'Well Doctor—it's like this—I feel queer.'

One of the problems of staying in very grand houses is that the moment you arrive the servants remove your clothes, wash and press them, and you never have anything to wear. My husband woke up once and, finding no trousers, rang what he thought was a bell for a valet and set off the fire alarm. One homosexual friend who'd packed rather haphazardly and only put in one pair of shoes found they had vanished without trace at breakfast, so he went down with bare feet to find a Royal Duke eating kedgeree.

'I should have thought he'd have seen enough bare feet on deck when he was in the navy,' he said afterwards.

According to Geoffrey Gorer, the higher the social class, or rather the more educated people are, the more likely they are to be tolerant of homosexuality. As he was basing his finding on the census classifications, by the highest classes he would mean Gideon and Samantha Upward rather than Harry Stow-Crat. Certainly Jen Teale and the lower-middles who don't enjoy sex and disapprove passionately of promiscuity would be the most intolerant, not being able to comprehend how anyone could do anything so 'revollting' for pleasure. The top rungs of the working classes are also very intolerant. One thinks of the poor electrician who wrote to *Coal News* saying he was a homosexual and pleading for tolerance, who was promptly sent to Coventry by his workmates. There is even less tolerance in the Midlands and North-East.

In Newcastle working-class homosexuals are so terrified of being rumbled that they always take girlfriends with them to the gay pubs.

'I was chased by fifteen youths in Newcastle,' said a Cockney boy. 'They wanted to beat me up because I was carrying a handbag.'

Some policemen investigating a drug case went up to Wales incognito and tried to ingratiate themselves with the locals. But the locals automatically assumed they were homosexuals and resisted every approach, until the police imported some sexy police women. London, of course, is much more tolerant. When I went to a CHE (Campaign for Homosexual Equality) meeting in Streatham, I was told that one lorry-driver came up from Wales regularly to meetings, because 'you can't come out in Cardiff'. And a boy who worked in a London betting shop said that when he told his mates at work that he was queer they were very understanding about it. 'What they simply couldn't understand—and I think this is a working-class attitude—was how I could sleep with a man and not get paid for it.'

Whereas in the old days the great fear was that one's daughter would become a prostitute now it's the young lads, referred to as 'rent boys', who run away from home, go up to what is known as the 'Meat Rack' in Piccadilly and hawk their bodies for £15 a throw.

One interesting point is that the working classes seem to get less flak than other classes when they tell their parents they're homosexual.

'My parents found out when I was about 18,' said an East-Ender. 'This boy kept writing to me. We don't get many letters in our house, and I told Mum I was going to spend Easter with him. She said, "Is there anything you want to tell me?" I said, "No." Well, I had a lousy Easter worrying about her, and the moment I got home I said, "I have got something to tell you, I'm homosexual." Her reaction was, "Oh, thank God. I thought it was drugs." I went to a shrink and he wasn't any help, so now everyone's accepted it. A lot of my gay mates are frightened of shrinks. The moment you tell them you're gay, they leap on you. There's a change in my Dad too. Before, he was always very undemonstrative, but now we get on very well, and he often puts a hand on my arm and says, "Are you all right, son?" My mum and dad don't mind what friends say, because they haven't got many friends; they're too much into the family.'

One gets the impression that because the mother-son link is so strong in the working classes, a lot of them are subconsciously not displeased if their sons turn out queer: there won't be any daughter-in-law problems and there won't be the macho rivalry between father and son, when the son gets married to some lovely girl and starts jackbooting around the house. Since the working classes have large families, there'll be other children to provide the grandchildren, and anyway there isn't this middle- and upper-class obsession with carrying on the line. Nor, like Jen Teale, do they care much what the neighbours think. In fact they enjoy their sons bringing home all these nice young men.

Further up the social scale parents put appalling pressure on middle-class only sons who turn out to be gay, and don't produce grandchildren to boast about at bridge parties.

'All hell broke loose,' said one middle-class girl, 'when my parents discovered I was a lesbian. They read some of my girlfriend's letters, and immediately started turning it all on themselves: "What have we done to deserve this? Where did we go wrong?" They packed me straight off to a psychiatrist, but as they're both doctors, they made me use a false name. My girlfriend and I are still together after 6 years, but my parents won't accept her, or stop harping on it.'

Rather like the lower-middle-class lesbian who fell in love with a married woman. When the married woman's daughter got married:

'I was allowed to act as chauffeur, fetching the cake and the bouquet, ferrying the bride's mother to the Registry office, where I had to stay outside so no one would associate me with Pauline, then ferrying her to the reception. I wasn't allowed to that either. They were ashamed I looked too masculine and might shock the bridegroom's parents.'

The upper-class attitude to homosexuality is the same as it used to be towards heterosexuality. Marry well and produce an heir at all costs; then do what you like.

Samantha Upward, being terribly 'aware', would be particularly nice to homosexual men, trapping them at parties, because she wants to show them that she feels no animosity towards men she knows can never find her sexually attractive.

Howard Weybridge 'comes out' on the golf course at 45, and suddenly appears at dinner parties in white suits with brushed forward hair. His son, similarily inclined, works in a prep school.

Bryan Teale would have an absolutely miserable time at the office party, avoiding all the secretaries and longing to dance with one of the packers. He also has problems when his boss gives him two tickets for a function. He can't take a man and if he takes a girl she's bound to get ideas and expect him to kiss her goodnight. If the office gets too much he might become a male nurse or a purser, or work in the men's department in a big store.

Some of the happiest marriages, in fact, are when homosexuals marry upper-class ladies, a kind of 'with my buddy I thee worship'. The sex side works, because the upper-class woman doesn't expect much, and the man just shuts his eyes and thinks of Benjamin Britten. Being a raging snob, the homosexual adores all the grand side of it, organizing smart parties and inviting all his prettiest menfriends. The wife, used to the male chauvinism of the aristocracy, is entranced to have a husband who can help her decorate her house, run her social life, advise her on clothes, cook delicious meals, and provide hordes of personable young men to chat away amusingly and quite safely for hours to all the gairlfriends. The two classic examples of such liasons in modern literature are Lady Montdore and Cedric in *The Pursuit of Love* and Norman Chandler and Mrs Foxe in *A Dance to the Music of Time*.

Homosexuals, because they are insecure and sometimes effeminate feel that socially they have to try harder. They worry terribly about accents, vocabulary, and laying the table properly. They always write letters after dinner parties, and send you change of address cards saying 'Crispin and Terence are moving to . . .' Because they have such good taste, their houses are often more upper class than they are.

I think because it's euphemistic, Harry Stow-Crat would not use the word 'gay', nor would he say 'homo' or 'lezzie'. Harry Stow-Crat's mother would say 'roaring pansy'; Harry would probably say 'homosexual' with a long 'o'. Samantha, to show off her knowledge of Greek, would shorten the 'o'. Gideon would say 'queer'. Jen Teale would say 'one of them'. Mr Definitely-Disgusting, luxuriating in alliteration, would talk about 'effing fairies, like'. An old-fashioned expression used to be 'T.B.H.' (which Samantha muddles up with G.B.H.) meaning 'To Be Had'. Also, in the old days, one used to say, 'Is he *So*?'

9 HOUSES

I recall, I recall, the property where I was a happy event.

It is not possible to determine what class a person is solely from the house he lives in. Some of the upper classes have execrable taste and don't give a fig about their surroundings, while some working-class people—probably homosexual—may have an instinctive sense of what is beautiful. How people do up their house is also considerably affected by fashion. A few years ago flying ducks were only acceptable if they were outside and moving. Now they've become *kitsch* and the young and trendy, raising two fingers to convention, are putting them on their walls. Or take someone who's just moved into a new house. The haste with which they explain away the ox-blood fleur-de-lys wallpaper in the drawing-room as the taste of a previous owner might be more an indication of social insecurity than the wallpaper itself.

Electric logs have long been considered a Jen Teale indicator. My husband once worked for a man, whose son (an Old Etonian whom I will call Ambrose) asked us to dinner. The other guests were a very smart couple, whom Ambrose was determined to impress. We arrived first to find him switching off some electric logs in the drawing-room. He was worried the smart couple might think them common.

'My mother, being Spanish, has terrible lapses of taste,' he said apologetically.

So the three of us sat frozen to death until the smart couple arrived an hour later. Instantly some devil overtook my husband. He crossed the room and switched on the logs.

'Have you seen Ambrose's mother's splendid fire?' he asked the smart couple.

There was a ghastly pause. Ambrose's face whitened like that of someone close to death. The merry flickering of the electric logs was nothing to the blaze of rage in his eyes. The evening was a disaster and my husband was fired within three months.

And yet I know two peers of the most ancient lineage who have electric log fires. One even has bright blue water in his lavatory—the upper classes do what they want.

Nevertheless, the house that you live in, like the education you receive and the accent you speak with, is one of the determining factors that indicate the class you belong to. A girl I know was terribly keen on a tall, thin, very aristocratic-looking young man until she discovered that he lived with his mother in a bungalow in East Sheen.

In Putney, where I live, the people in the big Victorian houses on the Common look down slightly, albeit unconsciously, on the people in the large semi-detached houses in the next road who in turn look down on people in similar houses in a street with slightly heavier traffic, who in turn look down on the people in the neo-Georgian houses on the edge on the common, who in turn despise the people in the terrace houses behind them who won't have anything to do with the Council estate beside the river.

In *Voices from the Middle Classes* by Jane Deverson and Katherine Lindsay, a journalist is quoted as saying:

'A house is a complex thing; it represents a social position. We found living where we were (a smartish London suburb) without meaning till we had acquired several friends who see themselves as the same sort of people as we were because they live in the same sort of house. Painting and decorating is a middle-class thing,' he went on. 'You say you've been decorating and you get an immediate response.'

Harry Stow-Crat wouldn't dream of painting his own house or putting up shelves and would regard any such activity as distinctly working-class. Equally, Mr Definitely-Disgusting wouldn't bother to do up his house either because he considers it the council's responsibility. The moment he buys his own house, however, he crosses one of the great class divides from Council Tenant to Owner Occupier and starts to become bourgeois. He'll immediately drop the word 'mortgage' in the public bar, and begin building a new porch or slapping paint on the front of the house to distinguish it from the houses on either side and to show he's not Council anymore.

The expression 'they live in a bought house' would be a term of admiration among the working classes, but of contempt from the upper classes who have usually lived in their own house for generations, inheriting it as they inherit their furniture and silver. (One of the upper-class definitions of the middle classes is the sort of people who buy their own silver—particularly when they call it 'cutlery'.)

Another crucial point to remember is that the Stow-Crats of today were the Nouveau-Richards of a few hundred years ago. 'How often have I wondered,' wrote Lord David Cecil, 'at the difference between the stately beauty of a great house, so exalting and tranquillizing, and the fierce restless unscrupulous character of the men who were so often responsible for its original building. Perhaps a gentler, more contented spirit would not have felt the urge and vitality to create such buildings.'

At the beginning of the eighteenth century the very rich Yorkshire baronet, Sir John Smithson, married Elizabeth, sole heiress of the rich and ancient family of Percy. So great was the extent of their joint estate that Sir John was able to persuade George III to grant him the dukedom of Northumberland. Anxious to establish his new status, the first Duke set about transforming Alnwick, the neglected castle of the Percys. Capability Brown (who'd been such a success at Warwick Castle) was called in to rebuild the towers and add seven turrets and a complete new garrison of stone warriors was stationed on the battlements. At the same time Robert Adam arrived to re-gothicize the interior. Everything was done to make the castle as luxurious and self-consciously picturesque as possible. And no doubt the old aristocracy, who regarded any peer created after the Middle Ages as an upstart, thought the whole thing both phoney and vulgar.

So it was that generations of new noblemen harnessed the best talents of their time, as today David Mlinaric and David Hicks move around forming the tastes of the uncertain and the newly rich.

In the same way the pop star who makes it big immediately buys a large house in the Thames Valley with high walls and installs burglar alarms and vigilante systems as daunting as any medieval drawbridge to keep out the fans. He will decorate it to the nines to impress other rising pop stars, and in his spare time take up market gardening, breeding race horses and farming. The Rolls is replaced by a Range Rover. The Showaddy Waddy even hunt with the Quorn.

What is regarded as the height of vulgarity today—the huge oval bed humming with dials or the onyx and marble double bath with 22-carat gold-plated mixer taps—will probably be considered exquisitely beautiful when it is unearthed from the rubble in the year 2500. Certainly the furniture and building trades would grind to a halt if it weren't for people erecting monuments to new splendour or ripping out the taste of previous owners because they consider it too grandiose or too vulgar.

Although they may have originally been built, to quote Ivy Compton-Burnett, 'as huge monuments to showing off', few buildings quicken the pulses more than the great English country house, with its 'towers and battlements ... bosom'd high in tufted trees', its sneering stone lions at the gate, and long avenue of chestnuts leading up to the russet walls rising gently from soft billowing green lawns which eventually melt into the park.

Harry Stow-Crat does not refer to his house as a stately home but as an ''istoric hice'. Perhaps he pronounces 'house' as 'hice', because he usually has more than one, like mouse and mice. The word 'home' except for putting 'At Home' on an invitation or saying 'I'm going home' is very common. It has been taken up by the media, so now you have the awful 'stately home', 'family home', or, even worse, 'they live in a lovely home'. Other horrors include 'homebuying' instead of 'buying a house' or 'home improvements' instead of 'painting ones house'.

Vita Sackville-West once said that the best historic houses grew in a leisurely way over generations, sprouting a wing here a tower there, like the oaks and elms that surrounded them. They grew inside, she says, in the same way as outside. 'There is no question of the period room, so beloved by professional decorators. Everything is muddled up: Jacobean paintings, Chippendale tables, chinoiserie wallpaper, Carolean love seats, Genoese velvets, Georgian brocades, Burgundian tapestries, Queen Anne embroideries, William and Mary tallboys and Victorian sideboards, all in a mixture to make the purist shudder.' But it is this feeling that each succeeding owners acquired beautiful furniture and pictures as the fashion of his generation dictated that makes up the glorious historical hotchpotch of the great house.

Lord Weymouth, who has contributed his own splendidly colourful murals to the walls of Longleat, says that everyone in his family 'has been raised from birth to be an acolyte in the temple'. This sums up the attitude of the aristocrat: good husbandry rather than good husbands or 'old masters and young mistresses', as Peter de Vries put it. 'I don't mind black sheep in the family,' said Lord Carrington. 'What I can't stand

'One has one's own piped music.'

is people who don't put back something into the house.'
Which explains the fearful chuntering over Lord Brooke
flogging his Canalettos and the famous Warwick vase,
and why so many aristocrats make very considerable
sacrifices to keep their houses going when it would be
so much easier to sell up and go abroad.

Most upper-class houses, therefore, have a certain
shabbiness about them. (There ought to be a shop called
'Shabby-tat' where Mrs Nouveau-Richards could buy
aged-up furniture and materials.) The festoons and ro-
settes on the ceiling show the traces of the years, the
pink and white striped silk cushions are falling to
pieces; the faded red damask sofa is covered in dog
hairs. On the walls, like the circle on the spiralist's
lapel, are squares of much lighter paper, where a Lawrence or a Romney has been flogged to pay taxes. When
you go to bed you draw the pale blue, watered-silk
curtains with care. The aristocracy believe in buying
the best—silks especially woven in the colour they
want—and then making it last. They'll probably only
redecorate their rooms every fifty years. Upper-class
colours therefore tend to be faded into softness by an-
tiquity—like a Beatrix Potter picture. The faded rose-
reds and golds of the Tailor of Gloucester's coat are
particularly popular, and ice blue is very in at the
moment. Green is never popular because there's so
much of it outside in the park. In upper-class London
houses (perhaps because they miss the green of the
country) you get a chilly Eaton Square eau-de-nihilism.

The floors are polished, and three-quarters covered
with very good, very old, patterned carpet. Caroline
Stow-Crat wouldn't dream of buying a modern patterned carpet, but Casa Pupo rugs are somehow considered all right. Until recently she's resisted plain
fitted carpets as being an example of the middle classes
boasting that they've got enough carpet to cover the
entire floor. But convenience is a great leveller and,
if you haven't got a servant to polish the floor, you may

211

sink to a fitted carpet. In the same way duvets are being surreptitiously smuggled into four-posters, particularly for the children, and the silver centrepiece in the dining-room, which is made up of forty individual bits and used to take two men three days to clean, has now been lacquered over.

Caroline also resists any man-made fibres, and certainly anything plastic, which Harry and his mother still call 'plarstic'. The upper classes wear leather on their feet and on the elbows of their coats, but not on their sofas or their backs. Their rooms tend to be very leggy, like the bottom half of the paddock, because all the furniture has long, spindly legs. Huge libraries of memoirs and sermons are kept behind grilles. The bedrooms have slots on the door for the guest's names, and interlocking doors, so people can bedhop easily without the servants finding out. The ceilings are particularly beautiful, so Caroline can admire them when she's in the inevitable missionary position, as a change from shutting her eyes and thinking of England. On the whole the upper classes prefer things to be beautiful or functional. They wouldn't hide the television in a repro cabinet, although they hide plant pots in bowls called cache-pots.

The rooms are lit by crystal chandeliers or candelabra, or by lamps with no tassels. Tassels on anything—umbrellas, lights or chairs—are very vulgar.

The bath and basin are always white; the lavatory is white with a chain that pulls and a wooden seat which is often agonizingly cracked, and gives exquisite pain by nipping the Old School bottom. All upper class loos smell of asparagus pee in June. The kitchens are traditionally hellish because that was where the servants lived.

As the outdoor life has always been more important to the English gentleman than indoors, the field more alluring than the hearth, their houses tend to be terribly cold. (One member of the landed gentry always asked you to bring old telephone directories when you went to stay to feed the insatiable boiler.) On the walls hang huge paintings of battles, hunting scenes and ancestors. There are also portraits of the dogs, the horses and the children. As the last go off to boarding school so early, it's useful to be reminded of what they look like.

The upper-class man always has a dressing room. Even though Harry sleeps in the same room as Caroline, he would refer to it as 'Caroline's bedroom' if he were talking to an equal, 'my wife's bedroom' if he were talking to a higher echelon servant like the woman who shows people over the house, and 'Lady Caroline's bedroom' to a maid.

One very grand old lady said, 'When Willy and I went to stay with some people in Norfolk, they didn't give Willy a dressing room but they provided a screen in the bedroom so we managed very well.' This was when they'd been married forty years—back to the Definitely-Disgustings again!

Because they have had their houses for hundreds of years, the aristocracy take the beautiful things in them for granted, and tend not to comment on them in other people's houses.

'Fellow noticed my chairs,' said a surprised Earl of Derby after a visit from the Duke of Devonshire.

Equally it is not done to show someone over your new house unless they ask specifically or they pay at the gate.

There was an embarrassing moment when an actress we know, who was justifiably proud of her very expensively decorated house, asked an upper-class friend if he'd like to see over it.

'Whatever for?' came the curt reply.

In very grand houses they have an estate carpenter permanently on the premises doing repairs. One friend got locked in the lavatory when she was staying in Yorkshire, and her host fed her Bloody Marys through the keyhole with a straw while they waited for the house carpenter to come and free her.

> *The poor man in his castle*
> *Sells tickets at the gate*
> *While all the rich plebians*
> Have *fun on his estate.*
>
> Leonard Cooper

'Between the duties expected of one during one's lifetime, and the duties exacted from one after one's death,
land has ceased to be either a profit or a pleasure. It
gives one position, and prevents one from keeping it
up, that's all that can be said about land,' said Lady
Bracknell in *The Importance of being Earnest*, admirably summing up the plight of the aristocracy.

In the old days Harry Stow-Crat's ancestor would
have looked out of his top window and owned all he
surveyed. Now someone else probably owns much of it.
Most of the upper classes are feeling the pinch, and the
days when they could man a chauffeurs' second eleven
against a footmen's third eleven are over. Some peers,
like Lord Montagu and the Duke of Bedford, who obviously have a strong streak of showmanship in their
make-up, seem to rather enjoy it. Others hate it, like
an earlier Lord Bath who was found cowering in a
cupboard by one of the visitors, or Vita Sackville-West
who hid in the roses. Some peers try to keep up standards and shock visitors to the house by putting up
signs saying *lavatories* rather than *toilets*, but most of
them descend to the level of public taste by flogging
the most appalling souvenirs—key rings, caps, T-
shirts, replicas of the house in a snow storm, bottled
Welsh or Scottish garden fragrance—in order to keep
going.

When we went to spend the weekend at Longleat,
as we drove up the drive my children's eyes grew rounder and rounder as they took in first the green mist of
flat-bottomed spring trees, the herds of cows and sheep,
then the lions, leopards, rhinoceros, monkeys and a

giraffe. Finally, as the great golden house came into sight my son turned to my daughter:

'He's got an awful lot of pets,' he said in awe.

When a Mrs Definitely-Disgusting visited an 'istoric house recently there was a frightful squawking match because she refused to pay to go on the little train which ran round the estate, saying,

'We don't have to pay for things like this. We ought to go free. We're the underprivileged.'

BUYING-UP AND DOING-UP

The upper-middle classes, not subscribing to the law of primogeniture and tending to move where their jobs take them, seldom live in the same house for generations. They start off in a flat in London or in some other big town when they get married, then move to a terraced three-bedroom house with the first child, then to a five-bedroom house when the second child arrives, because they need room for an *au pair*, or possibly for a lodger to help with the mortgage. Samantha Upward prefers a student, so she can combine altruism, free baby-sitting and help with Zacharias' maths prep, which will soon—despite workshops—be quite beyond her. To live in a house with more rooms than you have family is regarded by the working classes as a middle-class characteristic.

The major change in the upper-middle-class house over the last twenty-five years has been the kitchen, which used to be an airforce-blue barracks where a sucked-up-to maid sourly banged saucepans. In the 'seventies financial necessity, coupled with the absurd stigma attached to domestic servitude, forced all but those with very young children out to work. The status-conscious upper-middle classes promptly revamped their houses. If Samantha Upward occasionally has to sink to housework or cooking she must do it in congenial surroundings. Kitchens became more and more like drawing-rooms with sofas, low lighting, Welsh dressers covered in ornaments and books, pictures on the walls, and a low pine table for the children to play improving games. As it was essential for the children to play on the ground floor near their parents, the dining-room was also turned into a 'playroom', and in order that Samantha shouldn't miss a word of the intelligent dinner-party conversation, as she was flambéing chicken breasts, or whipping the zabaglione, the kitchen was turned into a dining-room as well. The drawing-room by this time was feeling a bit neglected and was consequently filled up with plants and natural earthy colours until it resembled Kew Gardens. The garden filled up with furniture, reclining chairs with gaudy seed-packet upholstery, stone lions and white wrought-iron chairs and tables. What was once the 'terrace' became the 'patio', or, as Mrs Nouveau-Richards would say, the 'pate-io.'

As stripped pine and William Morris are taken up by the lower-middles, the upper-middles have latched onto rattan and art-deco sofas and chairs, French and English antiques when they can afford them, good Chinese furniture and Laura Ashley itsy-bitsy cottage prints (sort of William Morris Minor). Recently a friend heard a builder showing a plumber over the house they were working on.

'They've got Philip Morris curtains in the lounge,' he said.

A word might be said here about the words 'drawing-room' and 'sitting room'. Both seem to be acceptable except that 'droin' room' is slightly more formal, and 'sitting room' more easy and relaxed. You'd never have a 'droin' room' in a cottage for example. 'Living room', a ghastly modern compromise, is extremely vulgar. So are 'lounge' (except in an hotel), 'front room' and 'parlour'.

In Samantha Upward's house you would find a few antiques and some good china and silver. She thinks repro furniture is very common, and whereas she might put prints or reproductions in the lavatory or the chil-

216

'Zacharias is very creative at the moment.'

dren's room, they wouldn't be allowed in the drawing-room. Nor would a Victorian painting from her parents' house of a four-year-old girl in a boat with a grizzled fisherman entitled 'His Mate' get further than the landing. All her curtains would be on brass rails. Her carpets would be plain but fitted, and relieved by a few rugs, and her counterpane would be distributed evenly over the whole bed, not mill-pond smooth and then edged in a fat sausage under and over the pillows. Since the middle classes discovered sex in the 'seventies, she'd probably have a bidet in the bathroom, next door to Gideon's and her bedroom. The bidet is a constant reproach as Gideon is usually far too tired and too drunk to want sex. Samantha is gradually installing 'continental quilts', as she insists on calling them, in every bedroom; she thinks the word 'duvay' is vulgar. Zacharias's cello is allowed to stay in the drawing-room among the *Spectators* and *New Statesmans* and the clutter of books. Samantha spends a lot of time removing the jackets from books to make them look more read. Dried flowers, or honesty in a pewter mug, gather dust on the window ledge.

In the downstairs lavatory, as a sort of 'bogography', Gideon modestly records his achievements, with photographs of himself in school hockey, rugger and cricket teams. In his dressing room are concealed all the atrocities Zacharias and Thalia have given him and Samantha for Christmas over the years—china poodles, cats wearing bow ties playing the banjo, glazed china flowers and so on. He also has to put up with all rich Aunt Mabel's paintings on the walls which are whipped down to the drawing-room when she comes to stay, and a photograph of Samantha, framed by herself at evening classes, taken 20 years ago when she had a beehive. Samantha waits till the daily woman goes home to loosen up the serried ranks of cushions on the sofa.

Upper-middle-class houses smell of beeswax, drink and sometimes cats. As their owners are always knocking things over when drunk and not being able to afford new ones, they have a lot of Christopher Wray lamps with bites out of them.

On Saturday mornings throughout outer central London—Fulham Clapham, Islington, parts of Hackney—the streets are alive with the sounds of 'gentrification', as coats of paint are slapped on the front of terraced houses, rooms are knocked through and the net curtains of previous occupants are shoved in the rag bag. The upper-middle classes would far rather spend a bit of money knocking a Victorian workman's cottage into shape than move into a modern house where everything worked, so they quite happily rip plywood off doors to reveal the original mouldings, strip banisters and replace aluminium windows with wooden frames as close to the original as possible. Soon follow the French number plate, the brass letter box, the trellis for the honeysuckle from the garden centre and the bay tree which soon gets nicked. Blue tubs, bought cheap from the brewery round the corner, are soon filled up with bulbs or pink geraniums (Samantha thinks red ones are rather common). Vivaldi pours out of the stereo into the street, and balding architects can be seen drawing lines at their desks and drinking coffee out of Sainsbury's mugs.

Having also cottoned onto the fact that they can get £25,000 tax relief for an extension, and with the price of houses being so prohibitive, my dear, and the traffic being so frightful we never get down to the cottage till midnight, the upper-middles are beginning to sell up their 'shacks' in the Isle of Wight or Gloucestershire and build onto their houses instead. Gideon and Zacharias are working at home so much now, they both need a study. And as Samantha so often wants to watch opera and Gideon late night sport, it avoids so many rows if they have two televisions in different rooms, and now that Thalia's getting a bust it's not quite right for her to entertain boys in her bedroom which calls for a second sitting room where they can all play pop music as loudly as possible. As a result £300 worth of clematis and hydrangeas are crushed under foot as an extension is slapped on to the patio.

Another trick of the middle classes is to buy old houses, then form a pressure group to have their street declared a Conservation Area in order to stop the compulsory purchasers touching it or building flats nearby. They then get absolutely livid when the Council rather understandably drags its heels over planning permission for an extra music room or a new bathroom.

DON'T SAY 'PARDON', SAY 'SURREY'.

> 'Merridale is one of those corners of Surrey where the inhabitants rage a relentless battle against the stigma of suburbia. Trees, cajoled and fertilized into being in every front garden, half obscure the poky 'character dwellings' which crouch behind them. The rusticity of the environment is enhanced by the wooden owls that keep guard over the names of the houses, and by crumbling dwarfs indefatigably poised over goldfish ponds. The inhabitants of Merridale Land do not paint their dwarfs, suspecting it to be a suburban vice, nor for the same reason, do they varnish the owls, but wait patiently for the years to endow these treasures with an appearance of weathered antiquity, until one day even the beams in the garage may boast of beetle and woodworm.'
> John le Carré, *Call for the Dead.*

'Oh look,' said a friend as we drove through a rich part of Surrey, 'all those houses have been Weybridged.' This is a practice of the socially aspiring who've made a bit of money and want to shake off the stigma of suburbia by living in Sunningdale, Virginia Water, or any rich dormitory town.

First you buy a modern house, which you refer to as

a 'lovely property', then you age it up to look like a Great West Road pub. Rustic brick with half-timbering and leaded windows are very popular, with a lantern or carriage lamp outside the front door and a name like 'Kenilworth' or 'Decameron' carved on a rustic board. A burglar alarm is discreetly covered by creepers.

An alternative is white pebbledash with a green pantile roof and matching green shutters with cut-out hearts, and the name in wrought-iron treble-clef writing on the front of the house. Wrought iron, in fact, is everywhere.

A few years ago a Weybridged house would have had a chiming doorbell, but, suspecting this to be a bit suburban, the owner has responded to an ad in *Homes and Gardens*:

'No more electric bionic ping pongs... every lover of style can now capture the elegance and tranquillity of less hurried days with a real brass doorbell, complete with mechanism and most attractive pull arm to enhance your doorway.'

The hall, as Anthony Powell once said, looks like the inside of a cigar box, with a parquet floor, panelled walls and a very thin strip of carpet running up the polished stairs. At the top is a round window with a stained glass inset. The Weybridged house smells of self-congratulation and Pears soap.

In the living-room (they've heard 'lounge' is suburban but can't quite bring themselves to say drawing-room) you find wall-to-wall glossies and coffee-table books. On the walls are imitation candle brackets, with fake drips and little red hats, bumpy white and gold mirrors and pictures by real artists from Harrods and Selfridges. The carpet is tufted two-tone, the curtains pinch-pleated, the 'settee' and 'easy chairs' are covered in terracotta velvet Dralon. Repro furniture is inevitable to give a nice 'Ollde Worlde' look: 'period doors', a Queen Anne 'bureau' and Regency Chippendale cabinets to hide the TV, (the upper-middles call it 'the box', the upper class 'the television') and the 'stereo'.

221

Every piece of furniture has mahogany or teak veneer. The Weybridged house suffers from veneerial disease. A Magi-Log fire flames in the repro Adam fireplace—'the ultimate in realism'—with incombustible oak logs knobbly with knotholes and twigs. The alternative might be a 'feature fireplace' in stone. The *Radio Times* is wrapped in a sacking cover with a thatched cottage embroidered on the front. If you came for drinks, you would be offered goblets.

In the dining-room lacquered silver candlesticks sit on the Elizabethan repro table even at lunchtime, and an Ecko hostess trolley keeps the rack of lamb, creamed potatoes and garden peas piping hot. There will be an overhead light, or more bracket lights with fancy lots, and six chairs with oxblood and silver regency stripes.

Howard has a 'den' where he's supposed to work at weekends, but in fact does nothing but read *Penthouse* behind Saturday's *Financial Times* and long to be asked to a wife-swapping party. Poor Howard feels he is not 'ollde' enough for the house; if he plays with himself a lot it might age him too.

The kitchen is usually very pretty and quite indistinguishable from the upper-middle, or even modernized upper-class kitchen. Next door a 'utility' room is filled with expensive machinery—the word 'dishwasher' as opposed to 'washing-up machine' is very Weybridge, so is 'freezer' instead of 'deep freeze' and 'tumble' instead of 'spin dryer'.

In the 'master bedroom' tufted carpeted steps lead up to a dais on which a huge brass four-poster bed swathed in white Norfolk lace sits like a wedding cake. The lampshades match the duvet cover and the wallpaper.

Next month Mrs Weybridge will receive her eighth German porcelain coffee cup and saucer from the 'Collector of the Month Club' special offer and be able to hold her first coffee morning.

The Weybridged house is very 'ollde' and tasteful, as opposed to the Nouveau-Richards' mansion which is very plush, ostentatious, and modern—another great monument to showing off.

Reacting against the working-class over-the-wall familiarity, Mr Nouveau-Richards has high walls built round his house and the whole place is burglar-alarmed to the teeth. Ten-foot-high electric gates protect him from the road. As he arrives in the Rolls he presses a button and the gates open. The drive is lined with toadstools which light up at night. The garage for five cars opens by remote control and, so you don't get wet, a lift takes you up to the hall.

Every room in Mrs Nouveau-Richards' house has a rake for the shag pile. The daily woman's visit is a sort of rake's progress, nor does she much like having to climb into the onyx and sepia marble double bath to clean it, and having to polish up the 22-carat gold mixer taps with headworks of solid onyx. She nearly got her hand chopped off when she was shaking her duster out of one of the electric windows the other day. When she answers the telephone she has to say, 'Mrs Nouveau-Richards' residence'.

In the lounge acrylic pile tiger skins with diamante collars lie on the ebony shag pile. Mrs Nouveau-Richards reclines on the leather chesterfield in front of the heated coffee table, while Mr N-R revolves in his captain's club chair in deep-buttoned hide. The walls are covered with black and silver flocked wallpaper. When the maid in uniform hacks her way through the 'house plants' to bring in 'afternoon tea' she is sent back because the sugar bowl doesn't match the tea cups. A ship's bell summons people to dinner, and the nautical motif is maintained by a bar in the corner with a straw ceiling covered in lobsters. After a few drinks they crawl by themselves. In the bar every drink known to

223

man hangs upside down with right-way-up labels. Mr Nouveau-Richards doesn't drink very much because it makes his face red and his accent slip. Off the lounge are the solarium, the gym and the swimming pool, kept at a constant temperature of eighty degrees by the pool attendant. The stables are built under the lawn, so the horses can look out of their boxes into the pool like Neptune's mares. In Mr N-R's library, all the books in which were bought by the yard, he has eighteenth-century repro library steps. When he presses a button the entire works of Sir Walter Scott slide back to reveal yet another bar. Even the goldfish tank is double-glazed.

Everywhere there are executive games played with clashing chrome balls, and orbs with revolving coloured oils. Mr N-R is very proud of his dimmer switches; in a mellow mood he'll give his guests a *son et lumière* display. In every room musak pours out of speakers, even in the loos, which have musical lavatory paper, fur carpets and chandeliers. The lavatory has a wooden seat. Mr N-R responded to an ad in *House and Garden:*

'After years of mass-produced plastic, feel the warmth of solid mahogany. Each seat is individually sanded and french-polished. Hinges and fittings are made of brass, and we offer as an option at no extra cost a brass plaque recessed into the lid for your personal inscription.' Mr N-R has 'Piss Off' wittily inscribed on his.

In the guest bedroom, as Mrs N-R calls it, everything is upholstered in peach satin, with a peach fur carpet. The master bedroom, however, has a vast suède oval bed, so humming with dials for quadrophonic stereo, radio, dimmer switches, telephones, razors and vibrator (which Mrs N-R uses for massaging her neck) you don't know whether to lie on the thing or hi-jack it.

Such houses are always blissfully comfortable to stay in: 'Chandeliers in the loo and a bidet on every bed,' as my mother put it.

The world is divided into 'Haves' and 'Have-Nets'. The upper classes never had net curtains because, if you live at the end of a long drive, there is no likelihood of being overlooked and, not being worried about other people's opinions, you don't give a damn if anyone sees what's going on anyway.

The upper-middles, aping the upper classes, don't have net curtains either. They traditionally had servants to keep their houses tidy, so it didn't matter anyone seeing in and, as they only had sex at night (unlike the shift worker coming home for lunch), they drew the curtains if they wanted privacy. Samantha Upward wouldn't dream of having net curtains; she wants the whole street to look at the gay primary colours and extra bright drawings and posters in Zacharias's playroom.

The middle classes sometimes have net upstairs. If Eileen Weybridge is changing out of her tennis shorts in the middle of the day, she doesn't want the workman mending the road looking in. If they have nets downstairs, they might explain it by saying they've got an American mother.

The rough and friendly element of the working classes never bother with net at all and have an expression for someone putting on airs: 'Net curtains in the window, nothing on the table.'

It is where the more thin-lipped element of the working classes blends into the lower-middles that net reigns supreme. You can see out and chunter over everyone else's behaviour, and twitch the curtains to indicate extreme disapproval, but they can't see you. Suburban privet hedges and Weybridged latticed windows fulfil the same function.

Jen Teale, however, wanting to priss everything up and shake off the stigma of upper-working class—which is a bit too close for comfort—hangs pink jardinière festoon cross-over drapes which leaves three-quarters of the window clear. This allows space for 'floral decorations' on the window ledge, makes the windows look 'so feminine' and enables the neighbours to see how 'spotless' (a favourite lower-middle word) her house is. Other examples of the lower-middles trying to go one better are ruched nets, putting a row of package-tour curios on the window ledge outside one's nets, or hanging one's curtains so the pattern shows on the outside. Mrs Definitely-Disgusting tried yellow nets once, but they made the whole family look as though they'd got jaundice.

BEHIND THE MAUVE FRONT DOOR

Jen Teale, liking to have everything dainty, wages a constant battle against dust and untidiness. Bryan sits in the lounge with his feet permanently eighteen inches off the ground in case Jen wants to 'vacuum' underneath. In a bedroom, a Dralon button-back headboard joins two single divans with drawers underneath for extra storage, into which Jen might one day tidy Bryan away for ever. Gradually all their furniture—wardrobes, sideboards, cupboards—is replaced by fitted 'units' which slot snugly between ceiling and floor, rather like Lego, and leaves no inch for dust to settle.

As soon as the Teales move into a house the upper-middle process is reversed: all the doors are flattened so the mouldings don't pick up dust any more; the brass fittings are replaced by aluminium, which doesn't need polishing; all the windows and old 'French doors' (as Jen calls French windows) are replaced by double-glazed aluminium picture windows. Being hot on insulation, because they loathe wasting money, the Teales even have sliding double-glazed doors round the porch. Bryan does all this with his Black-and-Decker.

The mauve front door has a rising s᠁ in the bottom left-hand corner of the glass. The doorbell chimes. The house smells of lavender Pledge and Freshaire. In the lounge the fire has a huge gnome's canopy to concentrate the heat and keep smuts at bay. Beside it stands the inevitable Statue-of-Liberty combination of poker, brush and shovel in a thistle motif. On the walls Bryan and his Black-and-Decker have put up storage grids, like vast cat's climbing frames with compartments for the hi-fi, records, scrabble, the odd spotlit bit of Wedgewood or 'vawse' of plastic flowers. ('Fresh' flowers, as Jen would call them, drop petals and paper ones gather dust.) A few years ago the Teales wouldn't have had any books—too much dusting—but as culture seeps downwards, there might be a few book club choices tastefully arranged at an angle to fill up a compartment.

The lounge suite has easy-fit nylon William Morris stretch covers which have interchangeable arms that can be switched from unit to unit or rotate on the same chair to give that straight-from-the-showroom look which is the antitheses of the shabby splendour— 'majestic though in ruin'—of the upper classes. Jen also rather likes the continental habit of offering lounge furniture as a group, comprising three-seater settee, two-seater settee and one armchair, called 'Caliph'. (Down-market furniture invariably has up-market names like 'Eton' and 'Cavendish'.) There is also a Parker Knoll recliner in case an 'elderly relative comes to visit'.

As well as her books Jen also has her Medici prints and her Tretchikoff (under a picture light, to show there's no dust on the frame), and in the dining-room there's a David Shepherd elephant gazing belligerently at Bryan's vintage car etchings. There is no bar because the Teales are tight with drink; Bryan keeps any bottles in another room with measures on. Just as a guest is putting his glass down, a mat with a hunting scene is thrust underneath to stop rings on a nest of tables called 'Henley'.

227

The kitchen is like a laboratory. No ornaments alleviate the bleakness. As the lower-middles disapprove of money spent on luxuries, Jen probably wouldn't have a washing-up machine. She doubts it would get things really clean. She calls washing up 'doing the dishes'. She washes, Bryan 'wipes' with a 'tea towel' rather than a 'drying-up cloth'. (Caroline Stow-Crat would call it a 'clawth'.) Jen also does a lot of 'handwashing' and, as she's very conscious of understains, she 'boils' a lot. Friends say her whites are spotless.

In the bedroom a doll in frills, to show Jen's just a little girl at heart, lies on the millpond smooth candlewick bedspread. (Caroline Stow-Crat has a worn teddy bear). 'Robe units' with motifs and very shiny lacquered brass handles slot into the walls. Jen tidies her make-up away in a vanity case. The only ornament on her white formica-topped vanity unit is a circular plastic magnifying mirror. When she makes up and brushes her hair, she protects her clothes from 'dandruff' with a pink plastic cape. The matching bathroom suite, in sky blue or avacodo, with a basin shaped like a champagne glass, has a matching toilet cover, toilet surround and bathmat in washable sky-blue nylon fur.

A Spanish 'dolly' with Carmen skirts discreetly conceals the toilet tissue (pronounced 'tiss-u' not 'tishu' as Samantha Upward would pronounce it). Jen, being obsessed by unpleasant odours, has Airwick, potpourri and a pomander on top of the cistern, and a deodorant block hanging like a sloth inside. In the toilet there is bright blue water. Bryan and Jen prefer showers to baths; they waste less water and are easier to clean up after. Jen calls a bathcap a 'shower cap'.

Although she keeps her house like a new pin, Jen always does housework in tights and a skirt rather than trousers. Her whole attitude is summed up by her feather duster, which keeps dirt at a distance.

There was an advertisement recently in a magazine called *Home Buying* offering 'Modern houses in Wood Green, the ideal site for those who want a convenient rung on the home-ownership ladder'. Among the other attractions was 'garage with space for work bench'.

This was aimed at the spiralist who is continually buying houses, doing them up, selling them at a profit and moving on to a better part, which means a safer suburb, with a nicer class of child, more amusing parents at the P.T.A. and no danger of coloureds (although a black diplomat is O.K.) Usually the process is to start with a flat, then move to a terraced house, then to a large 'period semi', where you let off the top flat to pay the mortgage. Then, as soon as the house is done up, you buy a cheap flat for the sitting tenant, put it on the market and look for an even bigger house. The process is basically the same as that of the upper-middle-class couple, except that the spiralist moves as soon as he's got the house together, while the upper-middles wait until they've run out of room.

Spiralists like anonymous furniture—chrome, glass, and unit sofas and chairs—because they can be shifted around to fit into any size of house. Just as they often adopt a phoney American accent to hide the Cockney or the Yorkshire, they also embrace American terminology: 'trash cans', 'garbage', 'closets' and 'car ports'. Even in the short time they stay in a place the spiralists are deeply competitive.

The spiralists are likely to buy a three-piece suite in a sale, then put it in a Harrods depository so it can be delivered three weeks later in a Harrods van.

They are the estate agent's nightmare—they never stop arguing and expecting more for a house because of another brick on the night storage heater. Evidently the upper-middles treat the agent like a pro, because they're used to one chap doing one job.

When Mr Definitely-Disgusting thinks of buying a house other than his own council house, he fills in a coupon and goes off and sees a show house on an estate called some grandiose name like 'Northumbria' and puts his name down for it if he likes it. Attractions include 'teak laminated kitchenette, stainless steel sink, coloured bathroom suite with matching vein tiles, veneered doors in the living room, kitchen dinette and shower room'.

Ads in the 'homebuying' press show neighbours looking friendly and helpful in wide-bottomed trousers, so as not to intimidate Mr Definitely-Disgusting. In a comic strip guide to 'homebuying' the solicitor has spectacles and brushed-back hair, and wears a suit and a tie, while the buyer has wide trousers again, an open-

'Well it's the Council's job, innit?'

neck shirt and hair brushed over his ears. His wife has shoulder-length hair swept back from her forehead by a kirby grip, and a skirt on the knees. This is presumably the ideal working-class prototype.

The Definitely-Disgustings hurry now and buy everything from Williams's sale, even the once-famous actor with tired eyes doing the telly commercial. Up to their necks in H.P., they get carried away by the ads and buy three-piece suites in deep-pile uncut moquette and wildly expensive domestic appliances, which go back when they can't keep up the payments. The house-to-house upstaging is as subtle as the spiralists.

'You can't hang your washing out anymore, because everyone'll know you haven't got a tumble dryer,' said one wife.

Mrs Definitely-Disgusting, on the other hand, buys a fridge for the first time and stands at the front door saying, 'I'm worried the kiddies will catch their fingers in the door,' just to show she's got one.

(My favourite advertisement of all time appeared in an Indian magazine and showed a woman and child gazing admiringly up at a huge fridge with the caption: 'Just right for our living room'.)

Mrs Definitely-Disgusting's front room, if she's feeling flush, will be dominated by a black cocktail cabinet with interior lighting, containing every drink known to man, just like the Nouveau-Richards, and a glazed tile fireplace with a gas fire (although councils are beginning to put in what is known as a 'fuel alternative'). Most of the ornaments look as though they have been won at a fair, or bought for his mother by Zacharias Upward: china Alsatians, glazed shire horses, china ladies in poke bonnets and crinolines. Here also are the curios from a hundred package tours—green donkeys with hats and panniers, matadors under cellophane, a mass-produced plastic bull with a piece of the next bull's back attached to its cock, ashtrays barnacled with olives and souvenirs of trips to historic houses. There might be a few very small reproductions: Con-

231

stable's Haywain, Van Gogh's Sunflowers, or the Queen by Annigoni.

The colours are garish, with everything—wallpaper, sofas and chairs—in different patterns. The carpet, a symphony of yellow, nigger brown and orange exploding in circles, doesn't cover the linoleum. On the huge colour television there might be a clock with the works well exposed under a pyrex dome. Mrs D-D's plastic flowers differ from Jen Teale's in that they make no attempt to copy the originals: mauve snapdragons and blue roses, pink primroses and da-glo tulips mass gaudily together in a sharply cut glass vase (to rhyme with praise).

The less respectable element of the working classes would have no ornaments or pictures, having smashed the lot during drunken brawls. The room would be furnished by a huge colour television and biked bean tins.

Miss Definitely-Disgusting's house or flat might smell of cabbage, stale fat or leaky gas, and Jen Teale, wrinkling her retroussé nose, would claim, dirt. One of the ensuing battles in the class war is Samantha Upward, Eileen Weybridge, Jen Teale and Mrs Definitely-Disgusting all accusing each other of being sluts.

The Bronco is hung up with string in the outside lavatory, which is probably shared with several other families. This explains why so many of the working classes suffer from constipation. Only two per cent of the professional classes are overcrowded, compared with over fifty per cent of the working class.

10 GEOGRAPHY

Oh, to be in Great Britain
Now that April's here.

Where you live is just as important as what you live in. I myself keep very quiet about having been born in Hornchurch, always justifying it by saying we were only there temporarily because my father was working at Fords. At the time my parents' friends used to laugh it off by saying: 'Bill and Elaine live in the slums. Ho! Ho! Ho!'

With relief, after two years, we moved back to Ilkley in Yorkshire, where my father was born. Even here the Middleton side of the valley was much smarter than the town side, because it was greener and got the sun all day; but at least Ilkley was smarter than Otley because the inhabitants were richer and because it was further away from the industrial towns of Bradford and Leeds; and Harrogate was much smarter than Bradford and Leeds because it was more rural and nearer the East Riding, which was much smarter than the industrial West Riding, but not as smart as the North Riding. And so it went on.

All over the North, as in the South, there are snob patches, immortalized by John Braine as 'T'Top'. Hoylake is 'T'top' for Liverpool; Cheshire is 'T'top' for Manchester; Ilkley is 'T'top' for Bradford and Leeds. 'You can't get anyone local to char for you,' said a friend who lives there now. 'When people move to Ilkley they think they've arrived.'

Certainly when we lived in Ilkley, which was devoid of anyone one would have thought of as upper-class, the upper-middles (or people who considered they spoke the King's English) stuck together. There were plenty of people we knew well and who came to our parties, but only a handful of them were invited to meet friends who came up from the South, particularly London, because the southerners were so easily bored and so much fussier about Yorkshire accents. One Ilkley woman was described as having 'snobbed her way out of friends', because she never invited any of the locals to meet any of her friends from London. The North think, quite mistakenly, that they're much less snobbish and more open than the South, despising the emollient phrases of the southerner, which they think smack of insincerity.

Fulham, from a class point of view, is an interesting part of London. In the early 'sixties it was principally working-class and considered very unsmart. We lived in Redcliffe Square (which called itself Kensington in those days,) and I remember saying in shocked tones to my solicitor, 'But you can't live in Fulham'. Fifteen years later Fulham is swarming with upper-class and upper-middle young marrieds in their first house, probably before moving to the country. And in estate agents' ads, Redcliffe Square is not described as Kensington any more but as Fulham.

As the Arabs take over Mayfair (they must have access to strip and gambling clubs,) and Saudi Kensington, and as Paddington and Maida Vale are invaded by 'chocos', the upper classes and trendies are tending to move further and further out. In the old days they liked to keep their 'S.W.s' low—one, three, five, and seven being the best, like the Beethoven Symphonies—but now one finds them in Battersea, Clapham, Camberwell and particularly Islington and Canonbury, because the two latter are so convenient for the City.

As birds of a feather traditionally flock together, the B.B.C. wireless people who work in Langham Place, the *New Statesman* readers and the left-wing trendies tend to go north to Hampstead, Highgate and St John's Wood, while the telly-stocracy polarize around Barnes, Putney, Chiswick and even Hammersmith, because it is near the television centre. The richer ones even buy houses along the common in Wimbledon, which was once regarded by the upper classes as somewhere you only visited during the tennis fortnight. Certainly the older generation of the aristocracy still think of North of the Park and South of the River as beyond the pale, regarding anyone who lives there as a taxi-exile. (You can't pick up a taxi in the area and you can't get a taxi to take you out there because they won't get a fare back.)

If you pick up upper-class address books, they are still full of Flaxman, Fremantle, Belgravia, Knightsbridge and Mayfair numbers. And the upper classes still tend to live in places like Cadogan and Eaton Squares, (although even these are getting a bit 'araby') where they set up elaborate systems of one-way streets, which make it impossible for the hoi polloi to find their way around.

But, in spite of their flats or houses in London, the upper classes still live mainly in the country, while the upper-middle classes live in London and have cottages in the country. I know one Mrs Nouveau-Richards who has the only country cottage in the *A-Z*. Despite pleading poverty the middle classes still have a million second houses.

Harry and Caroline Stow-Crat would never be in London at the weekend—which they call 'Friday to Monday'—although Georgie and the younger generation call it 'weekend' and tend to stay up more often.

'You'd never have got this sort of person in Harrods on Saturday in the old days,' a friend overheard one Harrods shop assistant saying to another recently.

Harry Stow-Crat is usually out of England skiing in February, and in Scotland shooting in August. Scotland is always smart, and packed with upper-class English, but the Highlands are smarter than the Lowlands, although Northumberland and the border country is considered pretty grand.

Although you will find upper-class people in all counties, there tend to be more in Yorkshire than in Lancashire. The Midlands are beyond the pale, except for Rutland, Herefordshire and Lincolnshire. Norfolk and Suffolk are much smarter than Cambridgeshire, which is not as grand as Berkshire and Oxfordshire, and of the home counties only Sussex and Kent are tolerable.

Just as the upper-middles in Ilkley stuck together, the grander aristocracy might deign to know some of the people who live in the neighbourhood, but on the whole prefer to go into another county to dine with people they regard as their own level—this presumably is where the expression 'county', to describe the upper classes, came from. Hence you get those interminable forty-mile drives just to go out to dinner.

If they were going to stay with the Tavistocks at Woburn Abbey or the Sitwells at Weston Hall, they would say, 'I'm going to Woburn' or 'Weston', and expect the other person to know where they meant. They always spell out the whole county, i.e. Warwickshire nor Warwicks, and Yorkshire not Yorks on envelopes, writing paper, and in conversation.

It is very lower-middle to talk about 'Great Britain' rather than 'England', and to describe oneself as 'British' rather than 'English', 'Scottish' or 'Welsh'.

In London the richer of the middle classes tend to polarize round greens and commons, and on hills like Hampstead, Harrow-on-the-Hill, Richmond, Kingston and Putney. The exception is the Thames. Water in a city plays a dual role: it repels the rich where there are docks and industry, but attracts them where there are not. As the docks fall into disuse, people are moving in. The former Foreign Secretary for example has a house in Narrow Street, so he can boast on television that he lives in the East End, implying that he's an authority on the slums, like the Duke who said he lived among miners, because his estate flanked some coalfields. Narrow Street, in fact, is a comfortable middle-class enclave on the river's edge, and when pressure got too great, the Foreign Secretary whizzed off to his vicarage in Wiltshire.

The papers a year or two ago quoted a taxi-driver grumbling about the erosion of cockney London by the middle classes, pouring into Hackney, Whitechapel, the Old Kent Road and the Isle of Dogs, wanting a house with a bit of garden for the children and within bicycling distance of the library. Soon the new settlers start action groups to have their own areas barricaded off against the traffic, so it spills into peripheral working-class areas; football is stopped in the streets; prices rocket, and the pubs are full of people called Nigel drinking gin and tonic. The old shops are rapidly replaced by antique shops and expensive delicatessens catering for career couples ('Ossie's Taramasalata is so delicious, it would be crazy to make it myself'). The garish-looking dress shops crammed with skirts and sweaters in da-glo pink and royal blue vanish in favour of ethnic boutiques catering for size twelve upwards.

One of the great urban middle-class movements of the late 'seventies has been the development of community associations. When we were in New York in 1971 a publisher's wife was talking about a block fête she and her friends had organized, and what fun it had been. Didn't we think fêtes were fun?

No we didn't, my husband answered, appalled. They were absolute anathema. One of the best reasons for living in London was to escape from that sort of thing.

'But we met so many nice new middle-class people,' she said.

'Oh Bryan—it must be the great community feeling they told us about.'

Where America leads England usually follows, and now, eight years later, community and conservation societies flourish, and every bit of urban grass has its own horse show, street party, or block community fête to raise money for park benches and shrubs round the churchyard—all organized by the middle classes banding together to protect their own property.

'I may have a large, beautiful garden crammed with climbing frames,' says Samantha, 'but I don't want a hair of the common outside touched by adventure playgrounds and hockey pitches. And don't you dare build houses in the churchyard to pay off your parish debts, or the price of my house will plummet.'

As the authors of *Voices from the Middle Classes* have pointed out, in London you can often tell at a glance whether a street is basically middle or lower-middle class. The latter has narrow, terraced houses, with no room for a front garden. People are cleaning their cars and windows, and painting their houses. Mongrels roam around the streets chasing cats away. An occasional cake tin, painted to look like a burglar alarm, hangs on the wall, and there will be several 'For Sale' signs, as the spiralist, having done up his house, is ready to move on. His aim is the middle-class street, probably only blocks away, which has large houses set back from the road, hidden by a privet hedge and with full-grown trees in the front garden, burglar alarms and cats asleep on the window sills. There is very little do-it-yourself; no one is seen cleaning their cars or their windows. You might even find a couple of horse-boxes parked. There are very few 'For Sale' signs here, because people usually stay until their children leave home, whereupon they retire and move into a smaller house.

The lower-middles tend to colonize in suburbs like Worcester Park, Cheam, Morden and Hendon.

To the spiralist, as we have seen, St George's Hill, Weybridge, East Horsley, Cobham and Sunningdale are social meccas. Here he will meet more people in

Who's Who than in any other county and rub shoulders on the train with more commuters from Social Classes I and II of the Census (stockbrokers, architects, Harley Street specialists and rich businessmen) than anywhere else.

There was recently a programme on television about the inhabitants of Cheam in Surrey, in which they interviewed a lot of spiralists with brushed-forward hair who all talked about the importance of 'competing' and 'living in an upper-class he-ome'. There was great community feeling in Cheam, they said; the 'holl' thing had exploded at the Jubilee Party in 1977 and they all got on because they had the same sense of humour and enjoyed the same sort of hobbies: going 'horse racing and playing for Esher Rugby Club'. The wives had coffee evenings if their husbands had a night down at the Club. They all thought of themselves as living in upper-class he-omes'. These are the kind of people the spiralist regards as 'upper-class'. He doesn't realize that the real upper classes—except for one or two like the Earl of Onslow whose family have lived near Guildford for cen-

'Now do tell me—does one go *up* or *down* to Weybridge?'

turies—wouldn't be seen dead in Surrey.

According to a brilliant book by John Connell called *The End of Tradition*, which explores rural life in central Surrey, there are only two classes left there: the middle-class 'foreigners', i.e. rich commuters who've moved in and bought up the old cottages, doing them up at vast expense, and the villagers who used to live in the cottages but now live on council estates.

Or as Jeffrey Bernard put it a few years ago in the *New Statesman*: 'The place is divided into two halves. At one end it's lavender, medium sherry, the *Daily Telegraph* and what a wonderful job the Conservatives are doing, and at the other end it's baked beans, bicycle clips and what a lousy job Sir Alf Ramsey's doing.'

What is happening in Surrey is that gradually the 'foreigners' are imposing their own middle-class life style at the expense of the council tenants. The middle classes form their own preservation societies, rather like the community associations in London, and reject any improvement as 'smacking of suburbia, and this is one up on suburbia'. John Connell points out the scarcity of bowling greens and football pitches, while there are plenty of tennis courts and rugger, cricket and hockey pitches. Proposals for launderettes, children's playground and more shops are stamped on in case they spoil the beauty and quiet of the 'countryside'. For the same reason the street lighting and bus shelters asked for by the council tenants are rejected. The middle classes, of course, are All Right, Jack. They've got cars to take them shopping at Bentalls, and out to their 'rack of lamb' dinner parties. What does it matter if they run over a few council tenants on the way? They're only spoiling the 'rural' look of the 'countryside'.

The tragedy is that the council-house tenant has no mobility. The man who owns his own house and who doesn't fit into the bridge and golf club set can always move away, but the council tenant is stuck where he's put and with whom he's put. If he doesn't like his next-door neighbour he can't move out until the council says so and then he may be suddenly moved to an estate with higher rent and central heating which has to be paid for. He has no gift of the gab, so he can't air his grievances, no clout and no Surrey Tenants' Association to fight for his rights.

Meanwhile the chasm between house-owner and council tenant grows wider. 'The trouble with Surrey', grumbled one of the foreigners who couldn't get anyone to re-thatch his roof, 'is that there are no real yokels left.' Rather like the earnest woman who said that the trouble with the Third World was that there was no middle-class.

In other parts of England, of course, the class division is much more hierarchical, the upper classes in rural areas getting on much better with the working classes than the middle-class professional man whom they both despise and regard as an upstart.

In any hierarchy, in fact, you are likely to find each class trying to segregate itself from the class below. In Wolverhampton council tenants had to make a three-quarters-of-a-mile detour rather than walk two hundred yards through an owner-occupied estate. 'I don't want them coming through here,' said one house owner, 'playing their radios, dropping ice cream papers, pulling up tulips and our little willows. Someone even stole our pet rabbit.'

Another example was in Dawlish, where the council planned a two-storey housing estate, but was subjected to such an outcry from nearby house owners that they turned them into bungalows. 'I mean,' protested one woman, 'they would have been able to look into our large picture windows and seen us at our meals and in our private life.'

At the bottom of the scale, when some Romney Marsh gypsies were re-housed in a council estate, all the council tenants got up a petition and had them thrown out.

'These people are really not our class. We don't think New Church is the right place for them.'

242

11   GARDENS

Climax into the patio, Maud.

The Englishman traditionally loves his garden. It needs cherishing and tending, but doesn't answer back. It is hardly surprising, therefore, that class distinction should be almost more rampant outside the house than in it. Once again garden centres—like furniture shops—do a roaring trade because of snobbery. People are constantly ripping up the plants and paving stones of previous owners—'Too ghastly, my dear'. I remember being mystified once when a friend came to stay. We were having tea outside, enjoying the sunshine and the quiet (for once the aeroplanes were silent) when suddenly she fixed me with a beady eye and said,

'You know, its frightfully common to have Peace in one's garden.'

It was a few minutes before I realized that she was referring to the beautiful pink and yellow rose next to the magnolia which flowers so gallantly and continually all summer. I can only suppose that she thought it was vulgar because it is so universally popular.

In the same way Caroline Stow-Crat wouldn't touch gladioli, begonias and chrysanthemums, or fuchsias—except in the conservatory. Also on the index would be gaudy bedding plants like petunias, French marigolds, calceolarias, cinerarias, calendulas, salvia, Californian poppies, zinnias, asters and yellow daisies, although Michaelmas daisies and white daisies are all right. Colour is also important: the white and green tobacco plants are much more upper-class than the red or mauve ones and dark red wallflowers better than yellow or mauve. Trails of pale blue lobelia are all right, but Oxford blue is very common, particularly when combined in military rows with white alyssum and scarlet geraniums. Caroline wouldn't be keen on any flower of a different colour to that which nature intended—blue roses, brown irises, pink forget-me-nots or daffodils. Daffodils should be planted in long grass, not in flower beds. She hates regimented tulips. If she had rhododendrons she would have not individual ones, but great clumps lining the drive. A friend once asked a West Country peer how he achieved his magnificent multi-coloured display.

'Oh, I move them around,' said the peer. 'When I want to change the colour scheme, I just get twenty men up from the factory.'

'Yellow and green should never be seen', so Caroline would soon rip out anything variegated such as laurels or, even worse, privet and mother-in-law's tongue.

Some trees are more upper-class than others: one thinks of great flat-bottomed oaks, beeches, limes and chestnuts, that look, as Taine said, as though they'd been tended for hundreds of years like the children of rich parents.

If you discount the cedars planted by Capability Brown, indigenous trees are considered much smarter than foreign ones, which is why the white double cherry scores over the imported pink one, and why the Stow-Crats tend to despise the silver birches and conifers of Surrey. Willow trees are all right growing naturally by a lake or stream, but would be considered the height of vulgarity in the middle of a suburban lawn, particularly if planted in a circle of earth.

The suburbs in spring, with their candy-floss mass of pink and white cherry, dark pink crab-apple, almond, laburnum and lilac, are quite beyond the pale. Pink hawthorn, although considered much more common by the upper classes than white, is for some reason more acceptable in the suburbs.

The names of buildings in the garden are also pronounced differently. Harry Stow-Crat says 'garidge';

Samantha Upward, wanting to show off her French pronunciation, says 'gar-azh; the Weybridges say 'gar-arge' in order to upstage the lower-middles who say 'garidge' like Harry Stow-Crat. Mrs Nouveau-Richards has a carport. Harry has a 'gaz-ee-bo' in his garden. Samantha calls it a 'summerhouse', while Mrs. Nouveau-Richards reclines in her 'gayze-bow'. Harry pronounces 'loggia' 'lodger', but the Weybridges call it a 'lowjea', in case there is any confusion about paying guests when someone says Howard is relaxing on the loggia. A friend says that his very grand grandmother used to refer to ants as 'aunts', saying, 'There's an aunt-heap in the garden', which sounds like a great fleshy pyramid of maiden ladies.

The point about the upper-class garden is that it should look as 'natural' as possible—great sweeps of mown grass leading down to the lake, huge trees with new little saplings always being planted and nurtured, trout streams, parks full of deer, and cows swishing their tales knee deep in the buttercups. Away from the house there might be a series of flower gardens, divided by walls, or hedges of box or yew, a conservatory full of nectarines, peaches and the oldest vine in Europe, a herb garden and a huge vegetable garden. Around the house, plants will grow in genuine Versailles pots, which are made of wood, are square and topped with balls. 'Everything to do with balls is very U,' says Harry Stow-Crat.

But everything would be mellowed and weather-beaten, the walls and roof of the house 'stained by time and many-coloured lichens, and overgrown with creeper to a richly variegated greyish red'. The drive would be made of stone chippings or gravel—not black tarmac or concrete like the M.1.

The Stow-Crats are very keen on vistas (Mr Nouveau-Richards thinks they're something to do with chicken curries). Through a gap in a wood you might see a temple of Flora, a folly or a bend in the river. But it must look natural.

The great gardens, in fact, show the ideal blending of classic and romantic. At Sissinghurst, Nigel Nicolson attributes the firm perspective of the vistas, the careful siting of an urn of a statue, the division of the garden into a series of small separate gardens to his father's classical influence.

But, in the overflowing clematis (Howard Weybridge would call it clematis) figs, vines and wistaria, in the rejection of violent colours or anything too tame and orderly, one discovered his mother's romanticism: 'Wild flowers were allowed to invade the garden. If plants strayed over the path they must not be cut back. Rhododendrons must be banished in favour of their tender cousin the azalea, roses must not electrify, they must seduce.'

Once again the secret is sweet disorder and faded Beatrix Potter colours. Weeds in moderation don't matter, because the plants are so closely massed they don't show the earth beneath. A dearth of earth is very upper class.

Sissinghurst, too, is the elder sister of the cottage garden—a law unto itself with all the flowers the Stow-Crats love jockeying for position: rosemary, drifts of lavender, ramparts of honeysuckle, an ancient wistaria, sweet peas, hollyhocks, lupins, delphiniums, pinks and mignonettes, love-in-the-mist and cornflowers, clove carnations, pansies, sweet william, white stocks and phlox, Canterbury bells and lilies; moss and plants instead of cement fill the cracks in the flagstones.

Percy Lubbock, writing about the easy abundance of a particular upper-class garden, realizes that it's not the plants themselves but the way they are planted that matters: 'Lobelia stripes, for example, and those marigold patches, which might have looked harsh and hard, (one knows how smartly odious they can look in a well-kept garden) all rejoiced together, rambling and crowding in liberal exuberance. The gardener might wreak his worst will, but the free soul of the garden escaped him and bloomed tumultuously.'

A garden like that, however, requires not just money and genius ('Planted 400 bulbs in the orchard this afternoon,' wrote Vita Sackville-West to Harold Nicolson) but also gardeners you can bully.

In the old days gardeners used to wash all the vegetables and take the thorns off the roses before they were sent up to the house. An eighteenth-century handbook advised them to look clean and neat: 'Your employer will not wish to look on a dirty, ragged, uncouth, grinning or conceited bi-ped in his garden.' They were also instructed to 'put the manure on the flower beds early in the morning, so the putrescent vapours may not prove offensive to the owner of the garden and his friends.'

But as costs get higher and gardeners get scarcer, it is becoming increasingly difficult to keep up a large and beautiful garden. In the country, gardens tend to get smaller and smaller, and the orchards bigger and bigger. Donkeys are becoming increasingly popular for keeping the lawn down. That mixture of concern and self-interest which always colours the master-servant relationship was neatly summed up by a woman I met at a party the other day who said:

'Our darling old gardener died last week—isn't it *maddening*!'

In Harry Stow-Crat's London garden you find a few bulbs in window boxes, followed by pink geraniums and ivy, followed by irises and Albertine, a pale pink rose which stops flowering in June. After that the upper classes are always out of London so it doesn't matter what their gardens look like.

In the country the upper-middles tend to have beautiful gardens, with shrubberies and herbaceous borders more related to the house and not set aside in separate gardens, although the vegetable garden will be separate. Plants and flowers grow round the house and on

the terrace you might see imitation plaster Versailles
pots by Julian Jenkinson, an Old Etonian who copied
them very successfully from genuine pots at Lord Har-
court's house. The lawn will be well tended, but there
will be more brown patches on the lawn because upper-
middle-class dogs are less likely to pee in the house
than upper-class dogs. As manure is seldom available
all the time, there will also be greater interest in com-
post. The roses and dahlias will be very fine and the
colours slightly brighter than in the upper-class garden. As we go down the social scale gardens tend to
become neater and gaudier.

Samantha Upward is very proud of her green fingers, particularly as she lives in London. She reads
Wordsworth to her potted plants, rushes out with a
shovel every time the police horses go by and, by feed-
ing Zacharias' daffodil with John Innes and Liquinure,
she won him first prize in his form's flower-growing
competition. But, alas, the herb garden she planted so
she could have all the ingredients in Elizabeth David's
recipes has been turned into a cats' lavatory by visiting
toms. She knows, too, that plastic flower pots and plastic hanging baskets are frightfully common, but such
is the greenness of her fingers that she couldn't possibly
afford pottery flower pots for all her plants. She's also
far too soft-hearted to rip out that variegated horror
donated by a neighbour that time she had shingles, or
the rose that looked the palest pink in the catalogue,
but turned out bright crimson and clashes horribly
with the da-glo orange rose beside it. She knows, too,
that dear funny Sir John Betjeman said that every time
he looked at a rhododendron he thought of a stockbroker, so she moved her two mauve ones under the
catalpa, but, alas, they're doing *terribly* well. At least
she hasn't descended to crocuses in a wheelbarrow, or
a plastic Venus de Milo like the one on the patio next
door which melted at their last barbecue party.

Her garden would really be quite lovely if only she
could stop the gardener, who comes two hours a week,

planting tulip bulbs in serried ranks like the ones outside Buckingham Palace. But if she checks him she's
terrified he'll take offence and not turn up next week.

Gideon and Samantha sit in their garden on a Sunday morning, swilling back the chilled wine saying,
'This is the life!' and watching the half-leg of lamb
rotating jerkily on the barbecue, wafting intimations
of garlic, rosemary and envy into the nearby council
estate.

THE SUBURBS

> 'Ewbank'd inside and Atco'd out, the English
> suburban residence and the garden which is
> an integral part of it stand trim and lovingly
> cared for in the mild sunshine. Everything
> is in it's place. The leaves of the virginia
> creeper which climbs the rough-cast wall just
> below the best bedroom hardly stir.
>
> J.M. Richards
> The Castles on the Ground

Nothing has really changed in the suburbs. When we
lived in a working-class part of Fulham no one minded
that we never bothered with our garden. A few neighbours grew vegetables and fought a losing battle with
visiting tom cats, but the rest of us let the weeds flourish and chucked our beer cans and spare-rib bones over
each other's fences when we ran out of dustbin space.
Only when we moved to Putney, a Madam Butterfly
land of cherry trees and flowering shrubs, and inherited a beautifully kept garden which we promptly let
go to rack and ruin, did we discover that gardening
here was taken very seriously indeed. Soon the whole
street were clicking their tongues over our hayfield of
a lawn and making cracks about calling in the Forestry
Commission to deal with the weeds. Finally a kindly
neighbour could bear it no longer and found a gardener

to come in three hours a week and sort us out.

More recently the local Conservation Association, which howls with protest if so much as a harebell is touched on the common, produced stern proposals, which were circularized round the district, for tidying up the garden of the only house along the common that happened to be owned by the council. This, they felt, was letting down the tone of the road by the number of weeds. At any minute one expected the dandelion detector van to be policing the streets bleeping noisily outside offending gardens. My husband suggested it would be far cheaper to declare the garden in question an Area of Outstanding Natural Beauty; then the weeds and wild flowers could riot unimpeded.

Though Putney is more upper-middle than suburban, the idea of not letting down the street is shared by the suburbs further out. Few people there are dedicated gardeners in the winter. Unlike the upper classes, they stay inside in bad weather. But, come the first temperate weekend, suburban man peers out of his window at his colourless plot and thunders off to the garden centre to load up the Volvo with bags of John Innes, bedding plants, do-it-yourself cucumber kits, and a plaster fig-leafless cherub to upstage the plastic Dolphin regurgitating blue water on the patio next door.

For the suburban gardener is deeply competitive: he doesn't want anyone else to let down the street, so that his own glory may be greater when his garden is the best. Rivalry is particularly fierce over roses. Hybrid teas and floribundas mass in clashing colours above a totally weedless flower bed. You can't get a lie-in at weekends either; it's like the pits at Silverstone with the roar of all the mowers revving up, interspersed by the excruciating, teeth-grating rattle as they drive over the crazy pavement.

The patio is also a focal point, a mosaic of Italian titles, covered with plastic urns filled with striped petunias, deckchairs with foot-rests, canopies and seed-packet upholstery, and sun umbrellas bought with Green Shield stamps.

The Weybridged house has a circular gravel drive bordered by 'rhodos', 'in' and 'out' entrances with no gates, an up-and-over garage door, a swimming pool which, despite its barrage balloon cover, is filled in winter with dead leaves and sparrows, and a dog yard for the terriers to dry off in. Having gone one step up from the suburban garden with its high laurel hedges, Weybridged houses are often open-plan with no dividing fences at all, although there might be a hedge of conifers to shelter the roses from the wind, or interlaced larch fencing around the vegetable garden. Here Howard and Eileen sit in their summer house admiring the well-tended lawn with its crazy-paving stepping stones, the conifers and golden willow in their little circles of earth, the beautifully kept shrubberies full of pampas grass and bamboo, and the thrushes pecking at the rack-of-lamb bone, which hangs from the dovecote (pronounced dovecoat: Harry Stow-Crat says dovec't). A heavily ferned stream flows under a wooden, willow-pattern bridge and over a waterfall by the heaths in the rock garden. Heather, except on the moors, is considered very vulgar by Harry Stow-Crat. Even its Latin name, *erica*, sounds frightfully common.

On Monday, aping the upper classes, Eileen Weybridge feels it her duty to pick up the litter dropped by trippers in the nearby beechwoods before she goes out to bridge or a Conservative coffee morning.

Believing that upper-class women spend their leisure hours doing the flowers, the Weybridges are heavily into flower arrangement by numbers, ramming salmon-pink 'glads' into green foam blocks, so that they stand up in the plastic 'dole-phin' vase and pick up the apricot décor in the lounge.

Yellow 'chrysanths' and button dahlias have always been a talking point too, when arranged in the white basket held by a naked cupid on the dining-room table when Howard's business associates come to dinner. While the orchids Howard raised in the '*con*serve-a-tory' (the Stow-Crats say 'c'n*serv*'tri') look so well in driftwood in the vestibule. The expression 'fresh flowers', to distinguish them from dried or plastic flowers, is also very Weybridge.

Although Jen Teale lives in a house with a number, she has re-named it 'JenBry' which combines both her and Bryan's names; she puts it in inverted commas on her notepaper. This drives the postman crackers. Her wrought-iron gate also incorporates the name. On either side Bryan has built a bright yellow wall, shaped like a doily. A plastic flowerpot container, filled with purple and shocking pink petunias, hangs by the mauve front door. Jen remembers to remove the dead heads night and morning. There are no creepers up the house. Jen doesn't want earwigs in the bath. Most of the back and front gardens have been crazy-paved by

252

Bryan because it looks so much neater, but there are a few crescent-shaped flower beds which might have been dug out by a pastry cutter. Here in neat rows in the spring stand military lines of blue grape hyacinths, yellow 'daffs' and scarlet tulips. In the summer these are replaced by white alyssum, French marigolds, Oxford blue lobelia and scarlet geraniums, or, by way of a change, calceolarias and salvias. Jen loves bedding plants because, once they've finished flowering, they can be thrown away. There is not a weed in sight. The garden is oblong, regular and compact like a park garden. When Bryan is not in his toolshed, he tends his 'chrysanths' and his 'toms' in the greenhouse. It's better than being hoovered under. Occasionally on summer afternoons Jen and the family sit out on tubular steel picnic chairs that can fold away neatly afterwards.

'For God's sake pull the plug out!'

There was a nasty moment once when an 'elderly relative come to visit' got stuck in the couch hammock with aluminium frames. Harry Stow-Crat ties hammocks to trees.

As a first-generation gardener, Mr Nouveau-Richards pulls out all the stops. Apart from lighting up his tarmac drive and technicolour lawn with toadstools, he has all his flowerbeds floodlit and coolie-hat lamps stationed like street lights round the garden.

Weeding, watering and edging is all done by electricity, which also keeps the earth warm under the cloches. In the propagating frames all-night fluorescent lighting forces tulips into bloom in November, and vast strawberries to ripen in time for Christmas. Plastic grass lines the outdoor swimming pool which is constantly kept at 80° like the indoor one.

Mr. N-R reclines on the underfloor-heated 'pate-io' and plays with a computerized mowing machine, a new toy just imported from Texas. He has just mixed a mint julep from his portable drinks trolley which glides over tiles and shag-pile and was described in the catalogue as 'the ultimate way to enjoy a cocktail on the patio, an aperitif by the pool, or those after-dinner drinks in the lounge'.

Mr Definitely-Disgusting hasn't got a garden, but he grows tomatoes and geraniums on his balcony, and he also has an allotment, which means a lot to him. It is illegal to sell 'produce' (a very Jen Teale word) from one's allotment, but at least he can grow vegetables for all the family. Here stand neat furrows of potatoes, curtains of runner beans, rows of lettuces and 'collys' and, at the end, a blaze of annuals and bedding plants in primary colours to rival Samantha Upward's playroom. When Mr D-D pulls up a lettuce he calls it 'picking a salad'.

12 FOOD

LET THEM EAT GÂTEAU

> 'When a woman asks for back, I call her
> "madam",' said a grocer. 'When she asks for
> streaky I call her "dear". You can always tell
> the gentry,' he went on, 'by their knowledge
> of cheese. They don't have trouble saying the
> foreign names.'

The food you eat often indicates what class you are.
The way you eat it, namely your table manners, does
so almost more. The upper classes, for example, don't
have any middle-class inhibitions about waiting until
everyone else is served: they start eating the moment
food is put in front of them. This stems from the days
when they all dined at long refectory tables and if you
waited for fifty other people to be served, your wild
boar would be stone cold. Nor would Harry Stow-Crat
comment on the food at a dinner party, because one
doesn't congratulate one's hostess on something one
expects to be done perfectly in any case.

The ritual of table napkins is interesting. The working-class man tucked a handkerchief under his chin to
protect his shirt and waistcoat (he would never eat in
a coat.) The lower-middles, daintily thinking 'napkin'
sounded too much like babies' nappies and wanting to
show off their knowledge of French, called it a serviette.
The middle classes, wanting to go one up, talked about
napkins, but, being frugal, also wanted them to last a
few days, so they introduced napkin rings. The upper
classes, who had plenty of people to do the laundry
(Harry Stow-Crat's mother calls it 'larndry'), had clean
napkins at every meal and regarded napkin rings as
the height of vulgarity. One peer, when presented with

a pair in a velvet box, had to ask the mayor what they were for before embarking on his speech of thanks. Even today Caroline Stow-Crat would rather use paper napkins than napkin rings. Mrs Nouveau-Richards, having read in some etiquette book that the word 'serviette' is common, calls them "s-napkins'. In the same way, she only just remembers in time that dinner in the middle of the day is called lunch, and talks about 'd'lunch', which sounds faintly West Indian. Harry Stow-Crat's mother still calls it luncheon.

Both Harry and Gideon Upward would lunch from one o'clock onwards, have tea around four and dinner at eight to eight-thirty in the evening. The Teales would breakfast very early because they don't like to be rushed, so would the Definitely-Disgustings because Mr D-D has to get to work early. Both Bryan and Mr D-D probably have a cheese roll or a bar of chocolate at nine-thirty, followed by 'dinner' at twelve and 'tea' the moment they get home from work about six to six-thirty.

The worst thing about the lower classes, complains Caroline Stow-Crat, is that they never know when to leave. If she asks them round for a quick pre-dinner drink, they've always had their tea first and are all set to carry on drinking until midnight. Samantha Upward gets round the problem by asking Mrs Nouveau-Richards at seven, then lies and says she's frightfully sorry but she and Gideon have got to go out to dinner at eight-thirty. Unfortunately Mrs N-R spoils everything by asking if she can see the kitchen and discovers three large baked potatoes and a casserole cooking in the oven. Samantha stands on one leg and says:

'The au pair has the most enormous appetite.'

Then there's a whole new ball game about what to call the courses. Caroline Stow-Crat never uses expressions like 'starter', except in quotes, or 'the soup'. She would talk about the 'meat' or 'main' course or 'cold cuts', but never 'the entrée' or 'the roast'. (The middle classes say 'joint'.) Nor would she refer to chicken or grouse as 'the bird' or 'poultry', although if Harry were farming he might use the word in that sense. Howard Weybridge says 'polltry' and 'casseroll' with a short 'o'. Everything from lemon water ice to jam roly-poly Caroline would call 'pudding': she would never say 'sweet' or 'dessert'. Cheese would be served after pudding, never before. Then, to muddle everyone, this might be followed by dessert, which is fruit, even bananas, eaten with fruit knives and forks.

A few months ago I went to the annual general meeting of the 'Istoric Houses Association, a gathering bristling with members of the aristocracy and the henchmen who organize the people who see over their houses. Having been gossiping in the bar, I arrived late for lunch and found a fat henchwoman sitting by herself, the rest of the table having gone off to help themselves to pudding.

'It would never 'ave bloody well 'appened, Ricardo, if you'd 'eld yer knife proper.'

'Who else is sitting here?' I asked, 'anyone exciting?'

'Well ay don't think they were ducal folk,' she said, 'Because they were holdin' their knives like pencils.'

Indeed she was right.

One of the great class divides, along with living in a 'bought house' and saying pardon, is the way you hold your knife. The lower echelons hold them like pencils, the upper and upper-middles to a man putting their first finger (the one Mr D-D uses to read with) on the knife where the handle joins the blade. Harry would also turn his fork over to eat his peas if he felt like it, and pick a bone—behaviour that would horrify Jen Teale.

Michael Nelson, in *Nobs and Snobs*, tells a story to illustrate what a gentleman his grandfather was. When sitting next to his hostess, he saw a slug on his lettuce. Rather than embarrass her, he shut his eyes and ate it. 'And my grandfather,' the story ends, 'managed not to be sick until after dinner.'

While it is a touching story, I think this was the act of a gentleman, but not necessarily of an aristocrat—the two are not synonymous. Harry Stow-Crat wouldn't swallow a slug, nor eat anything he didn't like. Nor would he ever resort to the lengths of a Jen Teale who dropped in on my brother and his wife and was asked to stay for lunch. To eke out the sausages and mash my sister-in-law fried three kidneys, which this Jen Teale was too polite to say she couldn't eat. In silent glee my brother watched her whip it off her plate, when she thought no one was looking, and hold it in her hand all through lunch. Afterwards she sidled inch by inch towards the fire and, choosing a moment when she thought my sister-in-law was pouring out coffee, flicked the kidney discreetly with a brisk backhand into the flames, whereupon it let out a prolonged and noisy hiss.

If someone else was paying for lunch in a restaurant and the food wasn't up to scratch, Mr Nouveau-Richards would complain noisily to the waiter; Harry, however, would keep his trap shut. If, on the other hand, *he* was paying, he would never be too embarrassed to complain, like Gerald Lascelles lunching at the Ritz, who sent a trout back because it was too small. Or the crusty old baronet who peered into the communion cup at early service and, because it was only a quarter full, bellowed, 'That's not enough'.

If you stayed with the Stow-Crats you would go in to dinner at eight on the dot because it's inconsiderate to keep the servants waiting, and you wouldn't sit around the table swilling brandy until midnight, because the servants want to clear away. But the men would stay behind with the port and grumble about estate duty, while the women would go into the drawing-room and probably grumble about constipation.

Things are changing, however. You now find far more upper-class people telling the hostess her food was lovely, because she's probably cooked it herself—and if you've spent two days slaving over a dinner party you want a bit of praise. In London fewer and fewer men wear dinner jackets, although the upper classes and upper-middles tend to in the country, while many of the women still stick to their horse-blanket long skirts and frilly shirts. With the inroads of women's lib, however, upper-middle women are less and less often shunted off to drink coffee by themselves after dinner, the merrytocracy in particular believing in a port in every girl, and as the husband often cooks the dinner he's the one who needs to go upstairs and tone down his flushed face.

The other great change in the upper-middle-class life-style is the swing back to traditional English food. In the 'fifties and 'sixties, on those three-week holidays to various costas, the wives picked up tips for five-course dinners. If you put garlic and green peppers in everything it showed you'd travelled. Samantha Upward even used the same plate for all courses, so you could still taste the squid vinaigrette and the boeuf-provençale when you were eating your *Poire Belle Helène*.

As a reaction to all this, the trend now is for simple cooking designed to bring out the flavour of good food instead of concealing it in a cordon blur of cream and wine sauce with grated cheese and breadcrumbs on top. At dinner parties Samantha now serves fish pie, pink beef and, particularly, English lamb. And for puddings it's treacle tart, jam roly-poly and bread and butter pudding, which in a time of insecurity remind Samantha of nanny, childhood and security.

Meanwhile other trends move downwards. The patrician habit of not commenting on the food, for example, is reaching the suburban spiralist belt.

'Dinner gets more elaborate,' said a wife on a neo-Georgian estate, 'but people pretend not to notice. It's all passed over to prove we're used to avocado pears and brandy in everything.'

Although the Surrey commuters are still wafting out garlic like dragon's breath—a sort of last gaspachio—the return to traditional food is just reaching the Weybridge set. Determined not to let the Chancellor ruin their 'wholl new fun lifestyle', they are into communal dinner parties with one wife cooking each course, and all keeping a stern watch on anyone getting too elaborate and putting in too much cream.

The foreign food bug has just filtered down to Jen Teale; Colman's Cook 'n Sauce is the best thing that has ever happened to her. She has also started tarting up the Oxo stew with package Hungarian goulash, and finds that Chicken Marengo Mix gingered up with garlic salt makes a nice change from an 'assorted platter of cold meats', and all these mixes do save bothering with messy ingredients. Packaged *Boeuf Trogignon* was a smash hit, too, the time Bryan's boss came to dinner. Bryan's boss's wife also admired Jen's table. Pink paper napkins in the glasses, matching pink doily in the basket under the slices of 'crusty bread', pink flowers in the centre of the table, and pink needle-dick candles casting a lovely light. Jen, who believes that things that look good taste good, has decorated everything with radish flowerets and cucumber hearts. And her new tupperware Jel 'n' Serve bowl set the orange mousse in a rose shape, and Jen garnished it so prettily with piped cream and mandarin segments. The one bottle of table wane looked so attractive in its basket too. In the old days Bryan used to decant it, so people wouldn't see the V.P. label. And Jen made sure no one got tiddly by serving little glass bowls of crisps and nuts with the Bristol Cream before dinner.

Jen's knives have stainless steel handles and resemble fish knives. The forks look like tridents and have long thin handles to keep you further away from messy food. Jen never 'cooks': she calls it 'preparing a meal'. After she's been to a 'resteront', she expects the waiter to ask, 'Enjoyed your meal?'. The word 'meal' is a convenient cop-out when you don't know whether to call it lunch, dinner or tea. Bryan's Rotarian father says 'repast'.

The Nouveau-Richards still over-do their dinner parties—smoked salmon and caviar soufflé to start with, sole flamed in brandy with a Pernod cream sauce, *boeuf en kraut* and a moated sugar castle for pudding, followed by After Ape mints. 'Chá-o bŏ-elled' wine flows throughout. Afterwards all the guests are sick.

The Definitely-Disgustings don't give dinner parties. Everything is geared towards Sunday dinner. In the old days you were paid on Saturday night, rushed off to the pawn shop, got out your Sunday suit and then hurried down to the late-night market to buy food for 'dinner' the following day. The warmth and friendliness of the pub often proved too seductive for the wage earner, and his wife would try to drag him out before he blued all his earnings. When there wasn't enough money to pay for dinner, Charlie Chaplin remembers his brother and he being told to sit down at a bare table and clash their knives and forks together so that the neighbours wouldn't realize they were going short.

Today the tradition continues. Mr D-D starts Sunday with a good breakfast—fried egg, bacon, beef sausages, because they're cheaper than pork, and fried bread. At twelve he goes to the pub and is dragged home at two-thirty for the 'roast and two veg', followed by apple pie and custard, or, as a treat in the summer, tinned peaches and cream. Having slept off the excesses, he would then have whelks and two slices of 'ovis for tea, this being the only roughage he has during the whole week.

GROWING, SHOPPING AND COOKING

Like Mr Definitely-Disgusting, Harry Stow-Crat has always liked plain unmessed-about food, the Costa Brava/Elizabeth David revolution having hardly touched him. Harking back to the old days, when mediaeval barons had to take care of themselves, the upper-class estate has always been self-sufficient. The Stow-Crats kept their own cows and sheep, shot their own game, caught their own salmon and trout, picked their own fruit and vegetables, and stalked their own deer (which Harry calls 'ven'son').

Harry also likes food that is tricky to eat and holds pitfalls for the socially uninitiated, such as oysters, asparagus and artichokes. The first week a London girlfriend went to live in the country, someone asked her if she could 'draw a mallard'. No one flickered when she said she'd always been frightful at art.

The upper classes tend to be unimaginative in their tastes. Lord Lucan used to lunch at his gambling club every day off cutlets in winter and cutlets *en gelée* in summer. I have a friend whose father always has Stilton and rice pudding for lunch. Lord Ampthill, who is in charge of the food at the House of Lords, has tried and failed to get tapioca taken off the menu.

As has been pointed out, lack of servants has only recently prompted the upper classes to take an interest in cooking. Lord Montagu may get up early and cook woodcock or snipe for his guests' breakfast on Sunday, but more characteristic is a story told by Nancy Mitford about the evening her maid went out and left her some macaroni cheese to put in the oven for three-quarters of an hour. After the alloted time she took it out and was surprised to find it stone cold. It had not occurred to her to turn on the oven.

In Harry Stow-Crat's house an eternal battle rages between the cook, who keeps asking for tiny young carrots and potatoes because they're more tender, and the gardener who wants them to grow to horticultural-show size.

Conversely in street markets you can't sell tiny potatoes, tomatoes or sprouts to Mrs Definitely-Disgusting because they appear to be a bad bargain. Many working-class eating habits are based on eking things out further. Sandwiches are left with the crusts on, lettuce is served with Heinz salad cream, so you need only use as much as you want, rather than wasting the whole thing by drenching it in French dressing. Mrs D-D's cabbages always seem over-cooked because she uses everything and by the time the stalk and tough outer leaves are tender the inner leaves are overdone. Jen Teale calls them greens. As late as 1973 only 37 per cent of the working classes in Britain had refrigerators, which explains why they ate so much out of tins, and why so many things—beetroot, onions, herrings, cockles and whelks—are stored in vinegar to make them last.

Because Mr Definitely-Disgusting likes frozen and marrow fat peas, Jen Teale would refer even to peas that came out of a field in Norfolk as 'garden peas'. Mrs D-D in return would take the mickey out of Jen by saying he wouldn't touch any of 'them petty poys'. Jen would ask for 'green' beans, to distinguish them from the Cockney 'biked' beans, while Samantha Upward would say 'French' or 'runner' beans. Jen would talk about 'creamed potatoes' because it was one up on the working-class 'mash', not realizing that the upper-middles and uppers talk about mashed potatoes as well. She'd also call baked potatoes 'jacket' potatoes, which she'd cut in half horizontally, spread out like two halves of an Easter egg on a separate plate, and fill with sour cream. Jen thinks chips are very common. If she had to eat them she'd say 'French fries', but she'd rather have sauté potatoes, which Samantha calls 'fried potatoes'.

And so it goes on, the endless one-upping and upstaging between the classes. Another lower-middle expression, attempting to put down the Definitely-Disgustings, is 'fresh fruit' or 'fresh cream', to distinguish it from tinned fruit or cream. The classes above would just say fruit or cream; nor would they talk about 'real coffee' or 'instant', calling it just 'coffee' or 'Nescaffi'—the Weybridge set say 'Nescaff-*ay*'. Trying to disguise their lack of class by using transatlantic expressions, they would also talk about 'burgers', 'crispbreads' and 'crackers' instead of biscuits.

Fish holds numerous pitfalls for the socially unwary. After John Betjeman's poem 'How to get on in Society' received wide circulation when *Noblesse Oblige* was published in 1956, the antique shops were flooded with fish knives, and the upper-middle and some of the upper classes sat solemnly at breakfast trying to bone kippers with forks.

Mr Definitely-Disgusting thinks fresh salmon is utterly tasteless and prefers it out of a tin. He likes pilchard salad too, and cockles, roll mops, eels either jellied or in a pie which he calls pie and mash, and eats with a viscous green sauce. Other favourites include rock salmon, skate, coley and chips, and 'ollibut and 'addick. But the working-class Northerner wouldn't touch mackerel, regarding it as the scavenger of the seas. 'If my missus gave me mackerel for tea,' said one fishmonger, 'I'd go to a Marriage Guidance Council.'

If Mr Definitely-Disgusting went to a 'resteront' he'd probably start off with prawn cocktail, as an acceptable way to eat neat tomato ketchup mixed with salad cream with a few bits of rubber thrown in. Jen Teale talks about tuna instead of tunny fish; she rhymes the first syllable of scallops with 'pal' (Samantha rhymes it with 'doll') and stresses the second syllable of anchovy, while Caroline Stow-Crat emphasizes the first. The Weybridge set are particularly fond of scampi in the basket, which they think is both dainty and ollde-fashioned, but which is really a corruption of it being deep-fried like chicken in a wire basket.

Another fashion that has moved downwards is the quiche, which was once called bacon-and-egg pie, until it got tarted up with peppers, onions, mushrooms and corrugated pastry, and was produced every time Caroline Stow-Crat had to provide something for a charity luncheon or Samantha had a buffet party. The merrytocracy also found it much cheaper than china to hurl at each other at the end of drunken evenings: 'And then I shut her wild, wild eyes with quiches four.' The Weybridges produce it for rugger and cricket teas, and the trend has finally filtered down to Mrs Definitely-Disgusting who calls it a 'qwitch'.

I think the popularity of quiche may be explained by the fact that people no longer feel easy about using the word 'tart'. Treacle tart and apple tart sound all right, but expressions like savoury tartlets, or 'My son says I make a good tart,' usually get a snigger. 'Queer' and 'gay' have gone the same way. Only Mrs Definitely-Disgusting could still get away with saying:

'I turned queer in the night. It must have been the prawns.'

Mrs Definitely-Disgusting tends to buy meat from the less attractive part of a pig or a cow because it's cheaper: black pudding, tripe and onions, pigs' trotters, belly of pork and faggots. Then she drenches everything in tomato ketchup and H.P. sauce to take the taste away. Mrs Definitely-Disgusting's mother, being a widow and an old-age pensioner, (or, as Jen Teale would say, a 'senior citizen') is so poor that when she goes to the butcher she asks for bones for the dog. She has no dog, but at least the bones will make soup. Sometimes she asks the fishmonger for pussies' pieces, even though she has no cat. As some compensation, if she lives in the Borough of Camden on her own she is entitled to a free budgerigar. Mr D-D, who is not very keen on his mother-in-law, says the old cow will probably boil that for soup as well.

As one moves through the day the class indicators come thick and fast. The upper classes have coffee or China tea for breakfast, the lower classes Indian tea, which they drink very strong and very sweet. Jen Teale says she doesn't 'favour' a 'cooked breakfast' or a 'continental breakfast', and instead has 'just a drink in the morning', meaning tea. (When Gideon or Harry use the word drink they mean alcohol.) Jen sometimes has 'segments' instead of 'cereal', which means tinned grapefruit pigs. Caroline Stow-Crat has Oxford marmalade on her toast. So does Samantha; she doesn't like it very much but she read somewhere that Golden Shred was common. Mr Definitely-Disgusting has 'two a drip, a chuck a bubble, and a cup of bug,' which, when translated, means two slices of bread and dripping, a plate of bubble and squeak and a cup of tea (which rhymes with flea, hence bug). Jen thinks the word chuck has a nasty derivation so she says 'portion', Samantha says 'helping'.

On to luncheon, at which no gentleman, according to Harry Stow-Crat, has soup—presumably because the upper classes were always out slaughtering wildlife, and soup is difficult to eat when crawling through bracken or sitting on a horse. Jen Teale, knowing the importance of eating a proper lunch, has frozen cod in cheese sauce boiled in a cellophane bag, which is indistinguishable from the dishcloths and tea towels she is always simmering on the hob. 'On the weekend' she and Bryan sometimes have 'an assorted platter of cold meats followed by the cheese board'. As a first-generation 'restront' goer, Bryan has picked up some of the ghastly terminology—'bill o'fare', 'sweet n' sour' and 'turkey and all the trimmings' (which means a teaspoon of cardboard stuffing and one burnt chipolata). He's very partial, too, to duck 'allaronge' which is a piece of burnt duck covered with mandarin segments with a spoonful of sugar in the gravy. Jen, being a great reader of women's magazines, is fond of adjectives like tasty, beefy, crusty, crispy, garlicky and chewy. Along with the vast majority of her class, she is slowly poisoning her family with convenience foods, television dinners, Vesta beef birianis, cake mixes and instant whips—a sort of national Chemi-kazi.

On to tea, which for the unwary is also full of pitfalls. It is very common to call it 'afternoon tea' to distinguish it from 'high tea'. Now that people of all classes use tea bags, everyone puts the milk in second, so this is no longer an upper-class indicator. The upper classes drink China tea out of china teacups, 'but it's awfully difficult drinking out of hand-painted cups,' said one spiralist's wife, 'so we have mugs when we're alone, and porc-ell-*aine* when we have guests.' (Caroline Stow-Crat calls it 'porsl'n'.)

Jen Teale's tea is a symphony of doilies under pastries and gâteaux, cake forks and scones (with a long 'o'). She provides paper napkins and a knife even if you're only eating sandwiches, which she pronounces 'sand-witch' like 'spin-itch'. Caroline Stow-Crat says 'samwidge' and 'spin-idge'.

Mrs Definitely-Disgusting says 'butty' or 'booty' if she lives in the north.

Jen would be shocked by Mrs D-D's milk bottle and bloater paste on the table, by the way she holds the bread in the palm of her left hand and spreads it with the right, and dips her biscuit in her tea because of her sore teeth. Caroline has Earl Grey or China tea the colour of washing-up water (just the colour Mr D-D likes his coffee), home-made cake and cucumber sandwiches. White sliced bread is particularly lower-middle because of its lack of roughage.

A fellow journalist tells a wicked story of the time

he interviewed a famous romantic novelist who was also a passionate health food freak. During the interview he was subjected to a long lecture on the merits of wholemeal home-made bread. Just as he was leaving, a little Sunblest van came jauntily up the drive.

'Surely,' said the journalist in mock horror, 'you're not buying sliced bread?'

'That, darling,' said the lady novelist airily, 'is for the servants.'

'Don't! It must be decanted!'

13 DRINK

Say 'Cheers' to me only with thy peepholes.

I was talking to a man in a pub the other day who'd
done very well for himself, and we got on to the subject
of class. 'I was born working-class,' he said, 'but I must
be middle-class now because I'm drinking wine.'

This is reminiscent of the working-class father who
sneered at his son-in-law every time he produced a
bottle of wine for lunch. But if drinking wine has come
to be a middle-class indicator, it wasn't always so.

Angus Wilson says that at Oxford just before the
war only the richest of his middle-class friends were
used to drinking wine regularly at home, and goes on:

'I think this lack of regular wine drinking was much
more common in middle-class homes in the inter-war
years, not only now but than it had been in late Victorian times.'

Certainly my own mother, being a vicar's daughter,
remembers the horrors of having a completely dry wedding in the 'twenties; and right up to the end of the
'fifties I remember that my parents hardly ever drank
wine at home. They sometimes had dry martinis before
dinner, and, if they were having a dinner party, occasionally a bottle of claret between eight guests. Then
there would be whisky and soda at the end of the evening to tell the guests it was time to go home. There
was a set in Ilkley who drank a lot whom I regarded
as rather exciting, but whom my mother considered
fast and very jumped-up.

The wine-drinking habit seems to have caught on
in the late 'fifties and early 'sixties when bistros started
replacing coffee bars, and the middle classes went to

Spain, Italy and France, and discovered, along with all those ideas for their dinner parties, the pleasure of drinking the local wine. Soon the husbands were enjoying Sauternes with watery sprouts at cricket dinners, and showing off in restaurants— 'Let it breathe, Luigi'.

Wine-drinking spread rapidly, particularly in the 'seventies when the middle-classes, believing they were being slowly squeezed out of existence, started drinking themselves insensible. During the austerity years of the middle 'seventies, the merrytocracy gave up their foreign holidays, but not their booze.

The middle classes also have totally dislocated values about drink. Every time a T.U.C. leader entertains a few foreign union leaders in a smart restaurant there is a sanctimonious uproar in the popular Tory press over the price of every item on the bill. No wonder Wedgwood-Benn and Jim Callaghan are teetotal.

The Stow-Crats have had cellars filled with excellent wine for generations, so Harry's always drunk it, but not to excess. Because it's there he doesn't feel the need to swill it round the clock. Before dinner he would probably offer guests a glass of dry sherry or white wine —nothing to rot up the palate, unless he were an alcoholic whereupon he would keep topping up everyone's drinks, to the frenzy of his wife who is longing to go in to dinner.

Harry doesn't taste wines in restaurants to see if it's all right; he just swings his nose back and forth over the glass to make sure it's not corked. He tends to drink at home rather than in pubs, because if he goes into the local all the tenants want to buy him a drink. Mr Nouveau-Richards finds himself picking up the bill far more often, both in 'resteronts' and bars. Tightness with drink isn't entirely to do with class, although the working classes are invariably generous. So too are the merrytocracy because they want an excuse to fill their own glasses.

The lower-middles, who enjoy dressing up in hired

dinner jackets and 'taking wane' with each other at Rotarian ladies nights, are given to euphemisms like 'partaking of liquid refreshment', 'imbibing potations' and 'just a wee dram'. Howard Weybridge is very up on bar terminology, he has 'snorters', 'snifters', 'ones for the road', and 'a few jars'.

The Weybridges are also very keen on barbecue parties. Samantha tried them and gave up. It just meant midge bites, charred pork chops in the flower beds, everyone losing their glasses in the dark when they were half-full and wanting new full ones, so she had to spend the evening frenziedly washing up, and her face got so covered in smuts from the barbecue that she looked like a token black.

Among the working classes, the great divide between the rough and respectable is summed up in two words: the drink. One of the reasons for the heavy drinking of the poor was that drink took away the misery and the appetite, and gin and beer were much cheaper than food. It was Nathaniel Hawthorne's opinion that the poor in England could only maintain their animal heat by means of alcohol, without which the harsh climate would destroy them. The great struggle for the wives was to get their husbands out of the pub before they drank all the wages.

Today, gin being so prohibitively expensive, Mr Definitely-Disgusting drinks beer because television advertisements, extolling the male cameraderie and virility that will stem from it, tell him to.

14 APPEARANCE

CLOTHES

Whenas in Crimplene my Julia says cheerio.

In the past fifteen years we've been through a complete
sartorial revolution. There was the self-expressionism
of the late 'sixties when everyone did their own thing,
followed by unisex and jeans for all classes and all
sexes, followed by the punk revolt of the late 'seventies.
And now, as Christopher Sykes has pointed out, after
the age of turmoil an age of conservative consolidation
has set in. As a result it is almost impossible to tell
what class the young are from their appearance.

On the one hand you have the tear-away from Eton
wearing polyester trousers and shirts with key motifs
to irritate the establishment, on the other the working-
class undergraduate, determined to identify himself
with the establishment, who smothers himself in college regalia. The hacking jacket has just about filtered
down the class system to Sharon Definitely-Disgusting,
while Fiona Stow-Crat turns up at a party with bright
purple hair, wearing a leopardskin rayon jump suit and
gold stiletto-heeled boots. Although the upper classes
usually settle down sartorially with marriage, I did
meet an extremely grand, much divorced old lady recently wearing orange satin drainpipes and a white T-
shirt with 'I AM A VIRGIN' printed across the bust.
Meanwhile the majority of parvenu Tory ladies in Weybridge, terrified of betraying their origins by putting
a foot wrong, dress exactly like the Queen.

Recently I went to a lunch party in a middle-class
house where some Americans had been invited to meet
a duke's daughter. The daughter of the house, herself
apprehensive about meeting a member of the aristoc-

racy, wore a tweed coat and skirt, flat shoes, a pale blue cashmere jersey and pearls. The duke's daughter roared up on a motor bike wearing a leather skirt, fishnet stockings, a tight black sweater and punk eye make-up. The Americans, who arrived just after her, made a justifiable mistake.

One comfort is that even the grandest people worry about what to wear. That scourge of the middle classes, Nancy Mitford, was thrown into total panic by a last-minute invitation to dine with Edward VIII.

I was told a rather touching story by one of the Queen's dressmakers. The Queen was visiting his shop and admired a very beautiful evening dress, glittering with crystal and rhinestones. When both the dressmaker and her lady-in-waiting urged her to buy it, she shook her head wistfully saying, wasn't it a pity, but really she hadn't got anywhere smart enough to wear it.

What she probably meant was that it was too ostentatious.

Traditionally the aristocracy survived because they were the wiliest of the tribe and knew when to lie low. Let the *nouveau riche* swagger around in their finery, showing off their wealth and getting their heads chopped off by royalty, or later by revolutionaries. Harry Stow-Crat's ancestors were prepared to dress up in their robes when the King commanded it; otherwise they camouflaged themselves and blended in with their surroundings. Thus today Harry is only copying his forebears when he wears a dark suit in the grey of London, and green, dung-coloured or brown clothes in the country. There was an additional reason for this. Harry's ancestors lived on what they shot, hunted and fished. It is easier to land your prey, whether it be a girl in London or a salmon on the Tay, if you blend with your background.

If there is one single class indicator where clothes are concerned it is colour. The upper classes tend not to wear crude, garish, clashing colours. Not for them the da-glo oranges or reds, the jarring lime greens and citrus yellows, the royal blues, mauves and cyclamen pinks. One thinks of the aristocrat dismissing the rating officer, coming out shooting 'in his dinky little blue suit', or a friend who was witheringly written orf as 'the sort of girl who wears shocking pink in the country'. Mrs Nouveau-Richards can pore over *The Tatler* and Jennifer's Diary, and find out exactly when and in what styles different clothes should be worn, but while the photographs go on being printed in black and white she'll never get the colours quite right.

Traditionally, too, because the upper classes believe in supporting their own industries, they regard anything that's lived—wool, leather, silk, cotton—as all right, but anything man-made—crimplene, polyester or plastic—as decidedly vulgar.

At a meeting of the Historic Houses Association, Clive Jenkins and Lord Montagu, the departing president, wore identical clothes—dark blue suits, slightly lighter blue plain shirts, and dark blue ties with red spots; the difference was that Clive Jenkins was dressed in man-made fibres. He looked somehow much shinier and less substantial.

The upper classes, as Michael Fish has said, also believe it is morally wrong to buy more clothes than you have to. So as clothes have to last they have to be conservative and of decent stuff. It is a point of pride for Harry at forty to be able to get into the same coat and trousers he wore at Eton.

The higher up the social scale you go, the taller and more finely boned people tend to be, because of diet, work patterns and extra vitamins over the years. Harry has no bum, Caroline no bum or bust; both are tall and thin, so their clothes, which have the advantage of being very well cut, tend to look good on them, and set them apart. Leanness, as Mrs Gaskell pointed out, is a great aid to gentility. Even if Georgie horrifies his father by buying an orf-the-peg suit, his etiolated figure and self-confidence will allow him to get away with it. Aristocrats, even if they live in London and have little opportunity to take exercise, seldom allow themselves to put on weight.

Harry Stow-Crat is therefore very conservative in his dress. But from the way he describes what he's wearing— 'black tie' for a dinner party, 'white tie' for an official occasion, or a 'morning coat' for a wedding— you'd think he was going about half-naked. One aristocrat I know got caught out very badly in this way. He was going to spend a weekend at a very grand house in the country and asked his batman to pack his dinner jacket. It was only when he was dressing for dinner that he discovered his batman had taken him at his word and only put in the coat. In the end he was reduced to borrowing a pair of trousers from his host, which were midnight blue, half his size, and about three times too large in the waist. No one made any comment at dinner or afterwards.

Harry Stow-Crat's dinner jacket is almost green with age. He would never call it a 'dinner suit' or have one in midnight blue, particularly in terylene with braiding. Georgie, however, might wear a different-coloured velvet tie, but not a waterfall of duck-egg blue frills like Jison Richards.

Harry, as we have said, would wear a dark suit in London, but he wouldn't call it a 'lounge suit' or a 'three-piece suit' or a 'business suit'. The buttons on the sleeve would undo, and there would be a real buttonhole for a carnation in the lapel, which he could do up in bad weather on a button hidden under the lapel on the other side. He might still wear fly buttons rather than zips, to protect his member for carrying on the line, but Georgie would probably have a zip, just as he might easily wear a leather belt to hold up his trousers. Harry would wear braces, which he would take off before removing his coat. His shirts would be striped, checked, or plain coloured, and never have pictures or initials on them—initials on clothes are considered very vulgar. Harry would never wear a striped tie with a dark suit, but he might wear a Guards tie with a tweed coat in the country. Georgie probably wouldn't bother to wear a tie at all, but it is interesting to observe that when the tieless fashion was at its height in the late 'seventies, girls started one-upping each other by wearing the old school, club and regimental ties their fathers and brothers had jettisoned.

Harry would wear one 'han'k'rchif' (not 'hand-kercheef') in his trouser pocket and another in his breast pocket—not up his sleeve. But it would not match his tie, and it would be casually arranged just to show a tip of a corner and a bit of fold. It would not be folded across in a white rectangle as though, as someone bitchily said, 'You'd forgotten to post your pools coupon' (although Prince Philip wears it this way), nor in a neat right angle, nor in a made-up mountain range on a piece of cardboard like Bryan Teale. Mr Definitely-Disgusting wears a handkerchief on his head at the seaside.

Pottering about at home, Harry would probably wear old corduroy (pronounced 'cord'roy') or whipcord trousers, and a tweed jacket, which he would refer to as a tweed coat, or, as he called it at Eton, a 'change coat'. He would never use the expression 'sports jacket'. He would call a blazer a boating jacket and tells Georgie he would have been thrown out of the Guards for saying 'blazer'. He might occasionally wear a polo-neck sweater, but never in pastel colours or in white, and always in wool. He would call it a 'polo-neck jersey' because the upper classes think the words 'jumper', 'sweater', 'pullover', 'slipover', 'woolie' and particularly 'cardi' extremely vulgar. He would never wear a mackintosh in London, nor call it a 'raincoat' or, even worse, a 'showerproof'. He would never carry an umbrella in the country (only vicars are allowed this privilege) except at point-to-points or anywhere where women might be dressed up and need cover—on the moors they can drown. The umbrella would be black and without a tassel. He would wear gum boots in green or black, but never call them 'wellington boots' or, even worse, 'wellies'. If he wore an overcoat he would refer to it as a 'coat', or a 'covert coat' (pronounced 'cover' to fox the unwary).

If Georgie wore just a shirt and trousers, he would take off his tie, undo the top button and roll his sleeves up to below the elbow. Mr D-D would do the same except that he'd roll the sleeve above the elbow. Bryan Teale would leave his tie on and his shirt sleeves buttoned up. (What does it matter if his cuffs get dirty? Jen can drip-dry them in a trice tonight.)

If Harry wore a signet ring, which would not be *de rigeur* as he doesn't need status props, it would have a crest and be on the little finger of his left hand. Georgie might wear a wedding ring merely to irritate the upper-middles who all wear signet rings with crests on their little fingers and think it's awful to have rings, particularly with initials, on any other fingers.

Harry would probably still decant his cigarettes into a cigarette case, although Georgie wouldn't bother. Not long ago an officer in the Guards got bawled out for offering the Duke of Gloucester a cigarette in a packet. 'You're not in the garage now,' said his Adjutant in a sarcastic aside.

Mr D-D smokes his Woodbines between finger and thum to eke them out, and curled in the palm of the hand to hide them from the foreman. Howard Weybridge and Colonel Upward smoke pipes; Mr Nouveau-Richards smokes very expensive cigars and leaves the label on, like a signet ring; Georgie Stow-Crat would certainly smoke in the street if he felt like it. His mother would not. Harry Stow-Crat keeps his money in a 'notecase', not a 'wallet'.

Gideon Upward, trying to be trendy but slightly out of date, would still be squeezing himself into jeans. He might wear a blazer but not with a badge, more likely a corduroy or a velvet coat, or last year's denim which Samantha bought him; it has four buttons and a high neck and makes him feel slightly silly. Since Zacharias

278

and Thalia went to boarding school he can't afford to buy suits, so all his Christmas presents are chosen by Samantha, usually sweaters from Marks and Spencer, in colours which suit her and which she wears during the week, so they have two bumps in the front when he puts them on at the weekend. He has reluctantly started to wear part-nylon socks, because Samantha shrinks his wool ones to Action Man size in a few weeks. He knows that shirt collars ought always to be worn inside a coat and a sweater, and he never wears a hat, although when he goes shooting occasionally his grander friends force him into a cap, saying, 'You'll be frightfully cold, Gideon.'

Howard Weybridge dresses straighter than straight, not unlike Colonel Upward. He wears regimental ties, golf-club ties, the Hurlingham Club tie and an old school tie if he's got one. Occasionally he wears a paisley scarf, which he refers to as a 'cravat', with a brass scarf ring. At the pub he wears a very clean blazer with an Esher Rugby Club badge, and slightly too new cavalry-twill trousers, although the nearest he's got to the cavalry is an hour's horse ride through the pine trees in Oxshott woods. He has never gone in for wide trousers, but his suede ankle boots are slightly too ginger. When he goes to Twickerham he wears a sheepskin coat, often with brown fur, and an assortment of hats, Russian fur, flat caps, and deerstalkers.

A hat designed for shooting Scottish deer
Though Haywards be the only Heath he's near
wrote Paul Jennings.

He wears huge riding macs, and his spectacles have no bottom rims to them. In bed he wears a red wool nightshirt from Bentalls, grandiosely called a 'sleep coat'.

Mr. Nouveau-Richards wears too much jewellery—huge gold cuff-links, a large diamond ring and a huge gold watch. He likes wearing bow ties so he can show

'I am your demon lover in my new red sleep coat.'

glittering studs on his shirts, but if he wears a tie he
puts on a huge gold tie pin. In his early working-class
days, like Mr Definitely-Disgusting, he wore a tie clip
and sleeve garters. He wears a camelhair coat with a
belt, and in the evening changes into a burgundy velvet
smoking jacket, with his initials in gold on the breast
pocket.

Jison Richards, as a member of the telly-stocracy,
wears three-piece suits in white with a black shirt and
no tie, or very light blue suits with the jackets so waisted and with such long slits at the back that they look
like miniskirts. He used to wear very fat, flamboyant
ties borrowed from Wardrobe at the B.B.C. but the knot
is getting slimmer. He often leaves his make-up on
after a programme when he goes to the pub to remind
people he's a telly star.

The spiralist who is climbing very fast, but hasn't got the same kind of money as Jison, studies the fashion magazines slavishly and co-ordinates carefully. He might select a neat check jacket to go with plain beige slacks, and a 'wesket' to match the slacks; the whole ensemble can double up as a business suit during the week. He's also very keen on herring-bone suits, which, worn with a sporty cravat, will double up as a sports suit for leisure wear. He likes British accessories—a jaunty check cap matching the check insets of his high-button jacket or a Donegal tweed hat with the brim turned down worn with a matching coat and 'holld-all'. He's also heavily into luggage. Last year's gold plastic bag on a coathanger has been replaced this year by a 'travel robe' in tartan which has a handle to enable him to carry all his co-ordinates vertical. Nattiness reigns.

Bryan Teale is dressed from top to toe in drip-dry clothes. Sometimes Bryan thinks Jen might put him through the washing machine under the setting for 'whites lightly soiled'. Bryan wears burgundy crimplene slacks (which never fit because Jen brought them by mail order in the *Daily Mail*), rust cable-stitch cardigans and cavalry-twill-style trousers in brown/black/navy/lovat/fawn in 100% washable polyester. He wears his rotary badge on his lapel. Instead of pants he wears tartan jockey shorts. He wears striped ties which the shop categorizes as a 'Club tie'. Bryan also has a whole robe unit in the bedroom for his car wear, woolly hats, zip-up car coats, fake sheepskin coats for cold days, overalls to save his good clothes when he's lying under the car, and driving gloves with holes in the back.

Gideon changes out of a suit into old clothes when he gets home or at the weekends. Mr D-D changes out of old clothes into one of Gideon's old suits that Mrs D-D bought at a jumble sale. It is a bit shiny but still has plenty of wear in it. She likes a good fight at the jumble on the weekend. Indoors Mr D-D always removes his coat and sits in a waistcoat and collarless

shirt; any shoes he wears inside the house will be called
slippers. His bedroom slippers he calls 'carpet slippers'.
If he wears a shirt with a collar with a coat, he arranges
the collar neatly outside the jacket. He always keeps his
hat on in the pub.

Apart from the fact that Caroline Stow-Crat never
wears man-made fibres except for stockings, it is far
more difficult to tell the difference between her clothes
and those of Mrs Weybridge. It is even more difficult to
distinguish Fiona Stow-Crat from Sharon Definitely-
Disgusting. Aware of the cruelty involved, Caroline
reluctantly no longer wears her fur coat, which was a
marvellous standby for London and in the evenings.
Since sheepskin coats have sunk down the scale, the
upper classes of both sexes wear a hideous quilted
rubber coat called a 'husky', not unlike Mrs D-D's
dressing gown, except it is nylon and green or blue.
Soon we can expect 'husky knickers' to keep out the
cold. They sound as though they ought to be white and
furry and matted with arctic snow, but actually turn out
to be overtrousers.

Caroline tends to underdress. Except for a watch or a
small brooch, nothing but pearls before sundown is her
maxim. Her pearls have little knots between each pearl.
(The world is divided into have-knots and have-nets.) At
night she wears some very good, inherited jewellery,
which adds a lot of light to her face; she would never
wear modern jewellery, and particularly never refer to
it as 'costume jewellery'. After she'd been through her
wild deb stage, and certainly after she was married, she
wouldn't show cleavages, or wear mini-skirts, whatever
the fashion; nor would she wear see-through shirts. (She
thinks the word blouse is very common).

Caroline would prefer the expression 'coat and skirt',
and although Fiona might say 'suit', neither of them
would ever say 'two-piece' or 'costume' or 'skirt suit'.
Caroline wears trousers, but never very tight, and never
a trouser suit. Her shoes would be plain and never
too high or brightly-coloured or decorated with bows or

with peep toes. Wedge heels and platform heels and coloured boots, particularly drum majorette white boots, would also be out. She used to prefer the word 'frock' to 'dress', but since Samantha's taken up 'frock' as being more old-fashioned and Kate Greenaway, Caroline's swinging back to 'dress' again. Other expressions she doesn't use are 'ball gown', 'hostess gown', 'evening gown', 'house coat' and 'bathrobe' instead of 'dressing gown'. As she has very good legs, she doesn't need the flattery of dark stockings, but if she did she'd wear navy blue with blue shoes, rather than black which she thinks a bit tarty.

Samantha is much more untidy in appearance. She is just emerging from her Third World ethnic phase and still has a sloppy, bra-less, long-straight-haired, intellectual earth-mother look. She's not as good at staying on diets or as naturally thin as Caroline and found those kaftans and peasant dresses almost better than Gideon's sweaters for covering up a multitude of tums.

At dinner parties she's weighed down with ethnic jewellery picked up from various Oxfam or African project shops, which is the nearest she gets to abroad, now they're so poor. The difference between the upper-middle classes and the lower-middle is admirably illustrated by Shirley Williams and Margaret Thatcher. As Rebecca West pointed out, Mrs Thatcher has one great disadvantage—she is a daughter of the people and looks trim as daughters of the people desire to be. Shirley Williams has such an advantage over her because she's a member of the upper-middle classes and can achieve that distraught kitchen sink, revolting look that one cannot get unless one's been to a really good school. The upper-middles tend to be untidy not only because they are more secure than the lower middles but because they like to look vaguely intellectual and because, unlike Caroline Stow-Crat, they don't feel they need to set an example to anyone.

The middle-middles try to dress just like Mrs

Thatcher, the Queen and Grace Kelly, very upper classical. Eileen Weybridge shops at Dickins and Jones, Peter Jones or Bentalls of Kingston. She wears velvet jackets over a shirtwaister pleated dress, or a blouse with a pussy-cat tie bow and a pleated skirt. When it rains she puts on a scarf decorated with snaffles and horses' heads, which she thinks give it a very nice country look. She wears a camelhair coat with saddle stitching in slightly too dark a shade, and a brown melusine bowler hat for shopping. Her shoes are in slightly too orange a tan and she spends days and days finding a matching 'handbag' as she calls it. She rather lets the side down by buying an emerald-green trouser suit with a matching peaked cap for Twickenham. In the evening she wears a polyester floral shirtwaister bang on the knee. She would never show bare arms after thirty-five.

Mrs Nouveau-Richards, coming from working-class origins, likes to dress up whenever she goes out, even to the shops. In the evening she wears white or silver fox furs and a great deal of very flash modern jewellery, particularly diamonds. On her dresses she has lots of spangles and sequins, and her figure is as heavily corsetted as her ve-owell sounds but inclined to break out above and below her stays to give her a cleavage like the Grand Canyon and makes her straight skirts 'rade' up. She wears long coloured gloves and invariably very high-heeled shoes with straps round the ankles, and a spangled butterfly or a flower in her hair, which is peroxide blonde like Diana Dors.

Jen Teale, like Bryan, lives in drip-dry co-ordinates—little terylene tops which she's always pulling down over the derrière of her terylene slacks when she is doing anything strenuous. (Mrs Nouveau-Richards talks about 'botties'.) As she hates untidy hair she puts on one of those scarves with a fitted pleated centre for tying at the nape of the neck. She wears rain hats which match her raincoat and carries a plastic transparent concertina hood in her bag in case it rains.

Everything is washed after one wearing and she never buys from jumble sales—'You don't know who's worn it'—or wears clothes bought in a sale until she's 'hand-washed' them first. She always wears a bra and panti-girdle, not only to keep Bryan and others out but to make her figure as anonymous as possible. She's very keen on capes, because they don't reveal a single out-line, and yet look neat. Mrs Whitehouse wore one re-cently when flying to America and was described in the *Daily Mirror* as 'The Caped Crusader'. If Jen wears a transparent shirt, she always wears a full-length pet-ticoat and a bra underneath, so all you see is rigging. Even when she relaxes in the evening her primrose brushed nylon housecoat is worn over all her under-clothes. Although she's not a catholic, she wears a gold cross round her neck to remind people she's a 'nice girl'. For weddings her 'outfit' is a navy crimplene two-piece trimmed with lemon, bought from the Littlewood's catalogue. Her uniform with a summer dress is a long white orlon cardigan.

Mrs Definitely-Disgusting only started wearing trousers a few years ago when she was cleaning Sa-mantha's house. Normally she does housework in a skirt, tights and bedroom slippers. Like Caroline Stow-Crat she always wears a scarf outside, but hers is in shiny rayon and made in Hong Kong. Like Jen Teale she buys by mail order—it's the only post she gets—filling in coupons in the *T.V. Times* while Mr D-D watches Match of the Day. When she tried it on in the privacy of her own home, she finds 'the princess-line dress in dusky pink/African violet two-tone floral, in uncrushable polyester 100% washable with figure-flat-tering panels' doesn't look nearly as good as it did in the *Daily Mirror*. The stretch waist band for comfort seems to be stretched to its utmost. Like Harry Stow-Crat, Mrs D-D has a change coat, in new French navy with a nylon fur collar. She needed it to cheer her up: her old burgundy barathea clashed with her 'ot flushes.

How men wear their hair is an invaluable social lit-
mus—less so with women. Although there are exceptions (Lord Weymouth may wear his hair long and in
a million pigtails; Lord Lichfield, at least in his photographs, looks like a hairdresser). Most of the aristocracy if they're over thirty-five brush their hair backwards, with the parting directly north of the outer
corner of the eye, two wings above the ears and cut just
above the collar. Harry Stow-Crat wears his hair very
shiny, probably as a result of Nanny's hundred brushes
a night, and because he doesn't have much stress worrying about himself like the middle classes, or tend to
work so hard, he seldom goes bald. If he did, however,
he would never brush his hair forward to cover a receding hairline, or in strands over a bald patch, or part
the hair above the ears and brush all the remaining
hair over his bald cranium like anchovies over a hard-
boiled egg.

Aristocrats seldom wear their hair over their ears.
Mr Heath dropped a class or two visually when, instead
of brushing his wings back, he trained them forward
in two tendrils over his ears. Nor would Harry Stow-
Crat cut his hair short in front so it fell in a cow's lick
like Dr Owen, or in a serpentine ripple like Lord Man-
croft, or in a just-breaking fall-over wave like Peter
Jay and David Steel. His sideboards would stop level
with the entrance to the eardrum. Neither he nor Georgie ever comb their hair in public.

Georgie Stow-Crat might well have a fringe, not to
hide a receding hair line but because it was trendy, but
he would start off brushing his hair back, and letting
it fall forward, and it would be so well cut, and his
features so lean and finely drawn, that the effect would
never be like the lacquered thatched roof on top of a
cottage-loaf of the spiralist. At the moment there seems
to be a trend towards the Edward Fox short-back-and-

sides look, so soon, no doubt, Georgie will be looking just like Harry again.

Harry has his hair cut at least once a month at Trumpers, which shows how often he stays in his Chelsea flat. He refers to the man who cuts his hair as his 'hairdresser' and asks him to 'wash', never to 'shampoo', his hair. He occasionally buys a bottle of Bay Rum which has a nozzle on it like Angostura bitters in cocktail bars. His hairdresser clips the hair out of his nostrils, but not his ears.

Gideon Upward's hair is still longer and more straggly than Zacharias's, because that used to be trendy in the late 'sixties; but it's getting shorter. He goes to the barber when he finds that his shirt collars are getting dirty on both sides. The barber is Cypriot and near the office. After the perfunctory snipping and primping Gideon is asked if he wants anything else, which means French letters, always prominently displayed alongside metal combs, razor blades and various cheap male toiletries. Gideon secretly admires Michael Heseltine who claims only to have his golden mane cut on quarter days. Occasionally in the privacy of his own bathroom Gideon brushes his hair forward like Melvyn Bragg, screws up his eyes, and wonders when he'll ever get an opportunity to use one of those French letters.

The only men left clinging to long straggly hair are middle-class left-wing trendies. As a reaction the rightwing Howard Weybridge has his hair cut short. So does Mr Nouveau-Richards, but, having spent so much of his youth working hard to get to the top, he tries to stay young with Grecian 2000. Jison Richards, now he's a member of the telly-stocracy, brushes his blond, tinted locks firmly forward to hide any incipient wrinkles across his 'fawhead' and round the eyes. He has it cut at Smiles, and washes and blow-dries it himself before television appearances. He keeps it in place with all sorts of toiletries. If he is not pulling a bird, he might even sleep in a hair net. He ages ten years in a high wind.

Mr Definitely-Disgusting's hair is seldom cut and seldom washed. It falls out early and what remains is coiled in oily strands inside some sort of headdress. He wears it very short.

Dive Definitely-Disgusting has a perm like a footballer. When it's just been done he looks like a Tory lady. He always combs his hair in public.

Mrs D-D is coiffure mad. Not only does she help in Mario's salon next to the chip shop on the weekend, but most Fridays goes spangled peroxide blonde and bouffant so that she and Mr D-D can be seen in all their glory at the pub music night on Friday evening. This bouffant remains till the end of the week, when it looks like a haystack ravaged by gales. I once heard a hairdresser claim that she has on occasions demolished such edifices to find them full of maggots which feed on the lacquer. If Mrs D-D is not bouffant she wears curlers around the house and in the street, because it's cheaper than drying it by the gas fire and because Mr D-D's on night shift and sleeps during the day. This, however, is going out with affluence.

Jen Teale cuts Bryan's hair to save money—likewise the kiddies, who are all drenched in Vosene to ward off the dreaded dandruff (Caroline Stow-Crat calls it 'scurf'). Bryan has a shower every day which flattens and brushes his hair forward automatically. If he is a rep and goes to conferences he has a razor cut. Jen wears her hair short because it's more hygienic and so much cooler in summer. She has a curly fringe halfway down her 'fawhead' and the side bits swept behind her ears, a style Caroline Stow-Crat would think very common. Once a year when she's feeling skittish she scrapes her hair into two bunches above her ears.

Eileen Weybridge has hair exactly like the Queen, so does her mother, with an additional blue rinse on her grey hair. Samantha's mother has hair like the Queen but slightly looser, more like Mrs Thatcher, and

'Well if you 'aven't got time for the wash, bleach and perm
we can just give it a spray of this.'

she thinks blue rinses are very vulgar.

Samantha has a fringe on the eyebrows and wears
her hair long, straight and mousy to match her dirndl
skirt. She doesn't wash it more than once a week because it would destroy the natural oils. Occasionally
she puts on a henna rinse, which Gideon is supposed
to admire when she stands under the light. Now she's
got bored with the women's movement she shaves her
legs with Gideon's razor, which she leaves clogged in
the bathroom. She shaves under the arms too, but
smells like a polecat when excited, because she wants
to be natural and not use those horrible deodorants.

Caroline Stow-Crat's hair is worn with flick-ups and
sometimes an Alice band. Like Harry she has the sort
of bone structure that can take hair worn orf the face—
she doesn't need to have a forelock to pull to anyone.
Recently she has taken to wearing a quarter fringe on
either side, and Harry hasn't grumbled about it. She
has her hair done quite often, partly for something to

do and partly to catch up on back numbers of *The Tatler* and *Harper's*. Her hair is never in very good condition, as it spends too much time under a headscarf or a hat. A few years ago she would never have dreamt of dyeing her hair, but streaking looks so natural and it does mean at least seven hours at the hairdressers looking at *The Tatler* and *Harper's*. Her hair often smells of cigarette smoke from going to too many yocktail parties given by the Deputy-Lieutenant. She will go grey suddenly.

Fiona Stow-Crat washes her collar-bone-length hair every day, so it always looks slightly untidy, and brushes it back in two wings like Harry. She has been known to dye it extraordinary colours.

On the whole the aristocracy's hair is a sort of light brown, upper-class mouse. If Harry said one of his friends had brought a 'blonde' to a party, the expression would be slightly dismissive because if she was anyone Harry would know her anyway. He would talk about 'a pretty girl with dark hair'; the expression 'an attractive brunette' is very common. And if a girl had red hair, he'd call it red; he wouldn't have any truck with expressions like 'auburn' or 'copper'.

FACES

The upper classes, as has already been pointed out, are tall and thin and have narrow stoats' heads with very few bumps on them. Their faces therefore tend to be narrow, with the skin more finely drawn over the nose and jawbone. Their eyes turn down rather than up at the corners, and although not very large, tend to be bigger than their mouths which look not unlike the private parts of a female ferret. Often these hang open because they're not ashamed of their teeth. Big rubber-tyre mouths and large rolling eyes give a face a very plebeian look. Used to very cold houses, and an outdoor life, Harry Stow-Crat has the kind of delicate pink and white skin, which flushes up at parties and in hot restaurants. From lack of stress, he tends to age more slowly than the other classes. Because he has a poker face you are less aware of his wrinkles. At fifty, he may look thirty-five, but when he laughs or gets angry his face suddenly breaks into hundreds of lines like a dried-up river bed. Harry and Caroline both have very long thin feet.

As you go down the classes people tend to be bulkier in the face, particularly round the jaw and chin. Mrs Definitely-Disgusting's mouth disappears altogether once she's lost her teeth.

15 VOICES

*'The men of Gilead said unto him, Art thou
an Ephramite? If he said Nay, then said they
unto him, Say now Shibboleth and he said
Sibboleth: for he could not frame to pronounce it right. Then they took him and slew
him'.*

Judges, Ch 12, vv 5,6.

When people talk about class barriers they often mean
sound barriers. The story of the poor Ephramite is one
of the saddest in the Bible, but such a universal one
that the word shibboleth has passed into the English
language and has come to mean, among other things,
the criterion or catchword of a social group. Thus Jen
Teale would have a little eye-meet with Bryan if they
heard Mr D-D talking about an ' 'orse', and Samantha
and Gideon Upward would immediately identify a
lower caste if they heard Eileen Weybridge talking
about 'zebras' with a short 'e' or asking for 'a portion
of gâteau'. Your pronunciation and the words you use
are so crucial in determining your class that the subject
has been already touched on on numerous occasions.
For despite the egalitarian revolution and the em-
bracing of crypto-working-class accents by a few of the
upper and middle classes, a person is still mocked because of the way he speaks. The other day, shouting
across the road to an old colonel, I reduced two youths
in anoraks to fits of laughter. I could hear them mimicking me all the way up the street. As Bernard Shaw
said in the preface to *Pygmalion*, 'It is impossible for

an Englishman to open his mouth without making some other Englishman despise him'.

Things have certainly improved, however. Thirty years ago the announcers at the B.B.C. solemnly put on dinner jackets every night to read the nine o'clock news and spoke with an accent called 'B.B.C. English', which was actually upper-middle—they enunciated far too well for the upper classes—and every young actor who wanted to get on ironed out his accent and tried to talk just the same. Pitmans agreed with them, so every secretary learning shorthand discovered that 'bath' and 'class' were pronounced with a long 'a', because the squiggles depicting them went on the line rather than above it as they would have done if the 'a' had been short.

Then came the revolution of the 'sixties as a result of which English as spoken by the B.B.C. has dropped to somewhere between middle and lower middle, with dozens of Regional Bosanquets being matey and calling everyone 'luv', and female interviewers with flat voices talking about 'Ufrica' and 'bunk bulunces'.

What has also happened in the last twenty-five years is that people no longer despise you if you have an accent as long as you're successful and amusing. Everyone adores Twiggy and the Campari girl. Zandra Rhodes and Janet Street Porter are asked everywhere. As Geoffrey Gorer says:

'The young now like to call themselves upper-working-class. Twenty years ago the bright young of working-class origin with intellectual gifts or talents would have been likely to acquire a B.B.C. accent and pass as upper-middle-class. Today they feel no need to hide their accent. They are the new trendsetters.'

Maybe. But if these trendsetters were not successful I doubt if Caroline Stow-Crat or Samantha Upward (and certainly not Eileen Weybridge) would ask them to dinner, and I suspect that as the country swings back and becomes more reactionary, not only Janet Street Porter and Zandra Rhodes, but all those upper and middle classes with their flat 'a's, may begin to sound a bit dated.

What people still object to, however, is people changing their voices, as poor Mr Heath and Mrs Thatcher learnt to their cost. Everyone knows that politicians are dishonest but when they have 'dishonest' voices as well they are doubly suspect. Whenever they appear on television, all classes sit listening to the ironed-out vowel sounds and the slow, low delivery (so that every word can be enunciated carefully) and gleefully wait for the first slip. Mr Heath's 'e-out' and Mrs Thatcher's 'invole-ved' must have lost them thousands of votes. But if people shrink from affected gentility, they also shrink from deliberate anti-gentility. Bringing your voice down is considered just as silly—like the girl in the 'sixties who had elocution lessons to try and get her accent made less patrician so she would be accepted at demos or Lord Stansgate calling himself Tony Benn and 'yer know-ing' folksily all over the electorate like Doctor Dale.

'Don't call me sir, my good man,' he was heard telling some unfortunate Labour supporter in a pub. One is reminded of Aldous Huxley, who once admitted that he had tried but failed to communicate with a working-class audience.

But of course the whole subject is relative. Everyone dismisses upper-class shibboleths they don't use themselves as out-dated, and any word they consider vulgar as barbarous. Thus I think the word 'luncheon' is pedantic, but the word 'phone' is vulgar, whereas my children probably think 'telephone' is pedantic.

In a recent survey fifty per cent of the people interviewed said they didn't have *any* accent, a statement with which the classes above and below would certainly have disagreed. In fact everyone has an accent, from the Queen downwards. It may not be regional, but there are certainly upper-class, upper-middle and middle-class accents, all of which are quite different.

The trouble with the upper classes is that they're

inclined to change their vocabulary just to outsmart the middle classes. Now that the word 'loo' has sifted down and been taken up by *Daily Mirror* readers, the uppers have reverted to 'lavatory' again. And you could feel the horrified frisson among the upper-middles when Princess Anne said 'ee-ther' on television. They'd studied *Noblesse Oblige*; they *knew* the upper classes said 'eye-ther'. It was really too bad.

If you go abroad, of course, your accent matters far less. Ironed-out English cockney doesn't upset the Americans at all, and no one minds Irish and Scottish accents half so much as Birmingham or South London ones. The Welsh are particularly good at acquiring upper-class accents; they have deep, liltingly attractive voices, coupled with a very good ear. Richard Burton and Roy Jenkins are two good examples.

If the B.B.C. wants a voice to represent the people, however, they go north and use Colin Welland.

'I seem,' he said recently, 'to have cornered the market in the Common Touch.'

But if accent does make the heart grow fonder, there are still a lot of people trying to get rid of theirs. One thinks of all the spiralists talking mid-atlantic, and the union leaders learning all those long words (surely 'indoostrial action' is the greatest euphemism of them all). Men promoted from the shop floor, egged on by their wives, are often sent by the management to elocution lessons. There was a piece in *The Sunday Times* recently about a cockney girl called Shelley who was trying to eradicate her cockney accent. It hadn't mattered when she'd had a backroom job in the bank, but now she was a receptionist at a ballet school and meeting people all the time, she decided she needed a new voice. 'It's nice to improve,' she said. 'You're stepping upwards not backwards. It'll be useful for the rest of my life.'

Rather like the schoolmistress who felt all her lower-middle vowels spilling out when she got angry in class, and the bank manager who felt his voice thicken when he had to talk to people about their overdrafts. We all know how our mouths seem to fill with marbles when we try to sound grander than we really are. Most people are bilingual, of course: telephonists, curates talking about carnal know-ledge with a long 'o', airline pilots ('This is your Captain speaking'), demonstrators and women who tell you your train times over the tannoy all have special put-on voices.

Ironing out an accent can, of course, cut you off from your background. It didn't matter to Shelley because her parents were both dead, but the schoolmistress admitted that she was ashamed of her parents:

'They have every awful pseudo-refinement of the lower-middle classes.'

Harry Stow-Crat has a very distinctive accent. Because of his poker face he only uses vowels that will hardly move his face at all. You open your mouth far less if you say 'hice' rather than 'house', and 'aw' rather than the short 'o'. Thus Harry automatically says 'orf', 'corsts', 'gorn', 'clorth' and 'lorst'. This of course is old pronunciation: 'Ride a cock horse to Banbury Crorse'. Harry also manages to move his face less by clipping his words: hence 'Lond'ndri' and 'mag'str't' instead of 'Londonderry' and 'magis-trate'. He often uses a short 'e' for 'ay', like the man who went into the village shop and asked for some pepper.

'Red or black pepper, sir?' asked the shopkeeper.

'Don't be ridiculous.' snapped the man, 'lavatory pepper.'

The upper-class accent may alter, but they are united in their absence of euphemism or circumlocution. They don't say 'pleased to meet you' because they don't know if they are, and anyway wouldn't feel the need to resort to such flattery. They are not arch. They never talk about 'botties' or the 'little girl's room', or ask, as Howard Weybridge might, if they can go and 'point Percy at the porcelain'.

'If "loo" is out now, there's "bathroom", "gents", "ladies", "convenience", "lav", "water-closet", "WC", "bog", "john", "can", "heads", "latrines", "privy", "little girls' room", "smallest room", "powder room", "khasi", "rears"....There must be *something* we can call it....'

Samantha Upward enunciates more clearly than Caroline. Her features are more mobile, she smiles more, her voice is less clipped. She is also less direct, talking about 'having help' in the house rather than 'servants', and saying, 'How's your glass' rather than 'Would you like another drink?' Because she is slightly unsure of herself she will probably cling to words like 'wireless' and 'children' long after the upper classes are saying 'radio' and 'kids'. On the other hand she clips her words far more than Eileen Weybridge—saying ''dmire' rather than '*ad*-mire', 's'cessful' rather than '*suck*-sessful' and 'c'm*pete*' rather than '*com*-pete'. She doesn't say 'lorst' or 'corst' but she would say 'sawlt' and 'awlter'. She keeps forgetting to say 'knave' rather than 'jack' when she plays cards and to call Gideon's 'wallet' a 'notecase'. Dive Definitely-Disgusting couldn't distinguish Samantha's voice from Caroline Stow-Crat's, but he would think Caroline sounded more commanding, and Samantha more hearty and jolly hockeysticks.

If you meet Howard Weybridge you probably won't be able to tell immediately what part of the world he comes from; he will be very careful not to let his voice slip—a sort of Colonel Bogus. Mrs Weybridge articulates far more than Samantha—she talks about 'coff-*ee*' and 'syst-*im*', like Mr Healey, who is very Weybridge and probably says 'higgledee-piggledee' between each word.

There was a Howard Weybridge living in Yorkshire who had a marvellously haw-haw voice, but slipped once at a dance when a fat teenager doing the Dashing White Sergeant with much vigour stepped back on to his foot and induced him to let out a most uncharacteristic yell of 'Booger'.

Enough has been said about Jen Teale's refinement. Many of the lower-middle genteelisms—commence, pardon, serviette, perfume, gâteau, toilet—probably became currency to show off the speaker's familiarity with French. When it comes to 'o' sounds though, one might have thought that the English language had been deliberately invented to fox the Teales and the Nouveau-Richards. I defy anyone to say the following list of words very fast three times without slipping: 'Dolphin, dolt, doldrums, revolving, revolting, involved, holiday, hold, holly, holm, whole, golf, gold.' Class is a sort of sadistic *Histoire d'0*.

Mr Nouveau-Richards packs Mrs N-R and all his children off to elocution lessons when he becomes mayor and takes a W.E.A. course in public speaking. Mrs N-R, opening the Bring and Buy, exhorts everyone to 'give generously like what I have done'.

Mr N-R ticks Jison off for talking too posh in the factory; it alienates the lads. 'Sorry Dad', said Jison, 'You shouldn't have sent me to such a good school.'

Mrs Definitely-Disgusting has a directness of speech not unlike Harry Stow-Crat. She says 'definitely' instead of 'yes'; Harry says 'absolutely'. She speaks in very short unfinished sentences, with a total disregard for syntax, and makes great use of conjunctions like

299

'so' and 'but' and 'like I said'. Sentences are often left unfinished. She uses very few subordinate clauses, and punctuates with words like 'shame', 'just fancy', 'only natural, innit' and 'do you mind'. Statement and answer are often the same.

'I told you to hold on tight,' she says.

'Why,' asks Dive.

'I told you to hold on tight, din' I?'

Dive often changes the first consonant and the final one—'I've fort a' somefink'—and drops the middle one, as in 'me-al' for 'metal'. Because the working classes tend to be inarticulate, they also rely very largely on facial and bodily gestures—shrugging their shoulders, waving their hands, jerking their heads, rolling their eyes, and raising them to heaven, just like Old Steptoe.

Mrs D-D is full of malapropisms. She's always wanting to get up a 'partition' or 'fumigating' with anger. She also uses adjectives instead of adverbs: he cooks lovely, she dresses fantastic. Because of her limited vocabulary she is likely to latch onto a new adjective and flog it to death. The ghastly 'caring' is becoming a great favourite, with Express Dairies running a competition now to find your 'caring' milkman. Because Mrs D-D has received so many lectures from lefties on the dignity of the individual, however lowly, she's quite keen on the word 'dignified' as the opposite of 'vulgar'.

When a working-class girl played truant last April and posed naked on a horse in the middle of Coventry, her mother said afterwards,

'Louise made a very dignified Godiva. We are not ashamed of her showing her breasts. We are liberated parents.' One would have thought it was more Louise's breasts that were liberated.

16 THE ARTS

The creative writing is on the wall

Of all élite, the two that mix most easily are the aristocracy and the arts—Hamlet and the players—traditionally perhaps because they have the same bohemian disregard for other people's opinion and the same streak of exhibitionism. In the past, as we shall see later in this chapter, artists have been tragically dependent on the caprice of their rich patrons, but things have changed in the last century. Now successful writers, actors and singers no longer struggle, but are often far richer than the aristocrats. Mick Jagger now dines with Princess Margaret and has Patrick Lichfield as his best man. Jack Hedley and Margaret Drabble have lunch at Buckingham Palace. Elton John keeps his flat cap on throughout Prince Michael's speech because of a hair transplant he didn't want anyone to see. And you even have a group of Etonians coming out of a punk concert nearly in tears saying, 'We put safety pins in our ears, but they *still* don't like us.'

The Royal family have over the years been consistently resistant to the arts. George I hated all 'boets and bainters'. 'Was there ever such stuff as Shakespeare?' asked George III, although he did have a massive crush on Handel, and even re-wrote one of Dr. Burney's reviews of a Handel concert because it wasn't favourable enough. Even today one has only to watch the jaws of the Royal Family absolutely dislocated with trying not to yawn at gala performances at Covent Garden. If you go to an investiture at Buckingham Palace, you find red flock wallpaper like in an Indian restaurant, pictures that need cleaning and a band playing gems from *South Pacific* and *White Horse Inn*. It is at this stage that someone always leaps to their defence and starts talking about Prince Charles's cello and Princess Margaret being a good mimic.

On the other hand, when one thinks of Lady Diana Cooper, Nigel Nicolson, Caroline Blackwood, Lord Ravensdale who, as Nicholas Mosley, writes brilliant novels, Lord Anglesey's military history, Lord Weymouth's murals and novels, the Sitwells, the Pakenhams, the Mitfords and many others one realizes that for a section of society that is statistically negligible the aristocracy have done pretty well for the arts.

The upper-classes were traditionally patrons of the arts, but because they have had their libraries, their old masters and minstrels in their galleries for so long they tend to take the arts for granted—unlike the middle classes who today make up the audiences at the theatre, ballet and the opera and who tend to regard a knowledge of the arts and literature as a symbol of having got on.

In the same way the lower-middles who want to get on equate culture with upper-class, and promptly start acquiring books, pictures and records. In the furnishing trade bookshelves and record cabinets are actually categorized as 'furniture for the better home'. The more upmarket a newspaper or magazine is, the more comprehensive the coverage of the arts.

ART

Put not your trust in prints.

Crossing the threshold of Sotheby's, one feels that sacred frisson, that special reverence evoked when great works of art and vast sums of money are changing hands. Of all the arts painting is the smartest, because it involves the best-dressed people and the most money. Private views are far more frequently covered by the glossies than first nights (which Jen Teale calls 'preemiaires'), publishing parties or concerts. This may be because the best galleries are situated around Bond Street and Knightsbridge, not far from the offices of *The Tatler*, and because all the elegant, aesthetic young men, with their greyhound figures and Harvey and Hudson shirts, who work in them, look aristocratic even if they are not.

Caroline Stow-Crat often goes to private views when she's in London. It's nice to have a free drink and meet one's chums after an exhausting day at Harrods, and she likes bumping into all those old schoolfriends of Harry's who, in spite of being devastatingly handsome, somehow never got married. The upper classes, too, are very good at looking at paintings. They are able to keep their traps shut and whiz round galleries very fast. Samantha Upward, brought up to fill gaps with conversation, can't repress a stream of 'How lovelies'.

What of the social standing of the painter himself? Andy Warhol and David Hockney are asked to the best parties—but they are not restricted by wives. 'Society is so constituted in England,' wrote Samuel Rogers, 'that it is useless for celebrated artists to think of bringing their families into the highest circle when they themselves are only admitted on account of their genius.'

But even genius has to be tempered with charm. No one asked Hogarth to dine, because he was the son of a tradesman. Reynolds on the other hand was taken up by society because he was urbane, intelligent and a gentleman. Sir Alfred Munnings, when he went to Eaton Hall to paint the Duchess of Westminster, was not invited to eat with the Duke and Duchess.

Despite upper-class philistinism, it has always been a status symbol to have one's portrait painted to provide ancestors to be shown off by future generations. Elizabeth I epitomized the Royal attitude. 'There is no evidence that she had much taste for painting,' said Horace Walpole drily, 'but she loved portraits of herself.' Once a portrait painter became fashionable he

'"Dejeuner sur l'herbe"?—Looks more like tea and crumpet
to me!'

went from one stately home to another, sucking up to duchesses—a sort of Toady at Toad Hall.

'I don't want to become a portrait manufacturer,' sighed Hogarth. While Millais, succumbing to the inevitable tedium, admitted that the best bit was putting the shine on his subject's boots.

Harry Stow-Crat doesn't buy paintings—he inherits them. Various ancestors were painted by Romney, Gainsborough, Lely and Van Dyck. Peter Greenham, however, has just finished painting Caroline. It was so successful that he will probably do Georgie and Fiona in the holidays. Harry has also commissioned a new painting of the house, taking in the vista of Gorilla Island, Flamingo Lake and the amusement park.

Mr Nouveau-Richards now thinks it was rather a mistake to commission Francis Bacon to do Tracey-Diane's por-trait (which he rhymes with gate; the Stow-Crats say 'portr't'), but at least Mrs Nouveau-Richards has learnt to say 'Trechicorf'.

Jeremy Maas, of the Maas Gallery, has a theory that art historians despise Victorian paintings and concentrate on Romneys and Gainsboroughs because this gives them access to grand houses, whereas the Victorian paintings are mostly owned by wool and steel manufacturers in the industrial north who are far less amusing to stay with.

BALLET

'I do not know anything about ballet except that in the interval the ballerinas stink like horses,' wrote Chekhov. Since then ballet has been prissying itself up and has become a very lower-middle-class art, intensified by all those layers of tulle and the ballerinas walking around on tiptoe. Jen Teale loves 'the ballet' as she calls it: all those good tunes and something undemanding to look at. Except for *Eugene Onegin* Tschaikovsky is an irredeemably lower-middle-class composer.

Occasionally Covent Garden have gala nights, which

305

Jen Teale pronounces 'gay-la', presumably because of the number of homosexuals present. The effeminate appearance of the men puts off Harry Stow-Crat and the Definitely-Disgustings alike. 'Pouffe's football' Old Steptoe called ballet dismissively.

A recent survey of ballet audiences broke them down as 61 per cent upper-middle-class males, 19 per cent middle-class, 15 per cent lower-middles and only 5 per cent working-class, who presumably are the rough trade accompanying the upper-middle homosexuals.

'Have we come for the dancing or the singing?' Mr Nouveau-Richards was overheard saying to his wife as they arrived at Covent Garden.

ACTORS

Until recently Thespians were not considered respectable. A gentleman might go to bed with an actress and shower her with presents, but he did not make an honest woman of her, and, although a few aristocrats married Gaiety Girls, the parental opposition was stiff enough to discourage most Mrs Worthingtons from putting their daughters on the stage.

Since the advent of the talkies, and even more so of television, things have changed. Acting is one of the most popular professions for girls from public schools. Actors and actresses get lionized out of proportion to any other profession. (When Kurt Jurgens gets half a million for a coffee commercial it's hard to ignore him.)

Caroline Stow-Crat, however, still regards the show-business world with a mixture of excitement and horror. I remember a debs' mums' lunch at which they were discussing whether they could entice Georgia Brown or David Essex to sing at some charity ball:

'Anyway, Elizabeth can look after whoever it is,' said the chairman. 'She's *so* good with those sort of people.'

The upper-middle classes, who apart from homosexuals, tourists and the coach trade, are the only consistent patrons, tend to go to the theatre for a good sleep, but sometimes they manage to wake up for the last scene. At a production of *Vivat Regina* at Chichester some years ago, when Elizabeth and Mary stalk out of opposite corners of the stage at the end, Mary to be beheaded, one Tory lady was heard saying to another, 'That's *exactly* what happened to Monica.'

Actors and actresses, although the good ones can adjust their accents to cross most class barriers, seldom appear upper-class because they are too self-conscious, too theatrical, too expansive of gesture and mobile of feature. Their diction is also far too good—the upper-classes would never say 'yee-eers' or 'how-ers' for 'years' and 'hours'. Actresses do this to make their parts longer.

Mrs Nouveau-Richards loves 'to do a show in town', and rustles a box of milk chocolates through the entire performance.

LITERATURE

Like the actor, the professional writer wasn't always socially acceptable. The Elizabethans considered poetry, dancing and playing an instrument the sort of accomplishment, rather like sex, that you did in the privacy of your own home, but never for money.

Lady Mary Wortley Montagu said that it was contemptible to write for money, and even in the nineteenth century Flaubert attacked the practice—though admittedly from the security of a large private income.

It was only in the middle of the nineteenth century, as Frank Muir pointed out, that the habit of reading spread down the classes and became fashionable, in a very minor way like television today.

Reviewers, bitterly opposed to emergent lower-middle-class writers, savagely attacked Keats for not being a gentleman, and belonging, with Leigh Hunt, to what was derisively called the 'Cockney school'. Cockney in those days didn't mean working class but 'genteel suburban'. It is hardly surprising that Byron and Shelley, as very nouveau aristocracy (Byron inherited the title from a great-uncle; Shelley's grandfather managed to marry two heiresses), should initially have attacked Keats's poetry, not only because he was beneath them socially but, more dangerous, he looked suspiciously like a far greater poet. Once Keats was dead he was no more competition, and it was much easier for Byron to leap to his defence with *Who Killed John Keats* and for Shelley to write *Adonais*.

Recently a reviewer expressed amazement that Hardy could be simultaneously such a towering genius and such a raging mean-minded snob. This seems quite logical. Any English novelist, if he is to draw characters with any accuracy, must be aware of the minutest social nuance. Many English writers have been frightful snobs. Shakespeare's heroes and heroines, except for the middle class Merry Wives, are upper-class; working-class characters are only introduced to provide comic relief.

Pope always pretended to be related to the Earl of Down. Jane Austen was probably so obsessed with class because on one side she was related to an earl, but on the other side to a haberdasher.

Even today, a critic grumbled, the thing wrong with English writers is that they'd rather dine with a duke than with other writers, a sentiment echoed by Nancy Mitford's comment on Evelyn Waugh:

'I feel he is all right with duchesses. It is the middle-class intellectuals who come in for the full bloodyness of his invective.'

It is significant that the only poet to achieve best-seller status in the last twenty-five years (apart from the Pam Ayres/Mary Wilson Tea-Cosy school) is Sir John Betjeman, who is totally obsessed with class and whose genius is that he can be tender and wickedly funny at the same time about every rung on the social ladder.

'If you stay with the Queen at Sandringham,' according to Robert Lacey, 'you will find an electric fire with three bars in your room, a fitted carpet, naval paintings on the wall and huge bookcases filled with regimental histories and army lists. But there are also more contemporary books put out for guests—Hornblower yarns and Nancy Mitford—all with the same simple book plate inside, "The Queen's Book" in flowing white script which stands out of a black background.' If an author goes to Windsor, he is likely after dinner to see his latest book laid out on a table in the library on a blue satin cushion. The Queen Mother is a Dick Francis addict, and is always presented with a copy on publication day.

Harry Stow-Crat reads *The Times*, the *Sporting Life* and the *Daily Express*: he has a soft spot for that Rook Woman. Caroline reads *The Tatler*, whose book reviews epitomize upper-class taste: a recent issue included a Standard Guide to Pure Breed Dogs, a book on heraldry, a history of the Isle of Orkney and a biography of the pekinese.

Samantha Upward is a great reader; she also feels it her duty to buy books. She is very guilty about reading popular novels and thinks biographies are somehow more worthwhile. Virginia Woolf's letters (in fact anything about the Bloomsbury group) are ideal because they combine sex and culture. Samantha knows that literature is all about disadvantaged people struggling to make ends meet, so she would never admit to anyone that she finds Bertold Brecht a king-sized yawn. She always refers to 'Maupassant' because she knows saying 'De Maupassant' is considered common in France, and she always talks about Willy Maugham rather than Somerset, and Jay Reid rather than Piers Paul, to show she's in the 'know'. She always asks 'creative writers', as she calls them, what they are 'working on', but she'd *never* make the mistake of telling them she'd love to write a book if only she had the time. The Weybridge set buy 'real coffee'-table books.

Jen Teale prefers to read home-improvement books, which she always wraps in brown paper, so the cover won't get 'soiled'. Bryan's home-library of do-it-yourself manuals and Reader's Digest condensed books are practically pushing the carved wise-owl bookends off the colour telly. Samantha thinks Mrs Definitely-Disgusting's habit of licking her finger to turn the page more easily is absolutely 'rev-ollting'. Sharon Definitely-Disgusting reads *Jackie* and *True Romances* which she calls books.

Mrs Nouveau-Richards is struggling with the first volume of 'Prowst'. Copying upper-class French mothers, she has stopped going upstairs every evening to kiss Tracey-Diane goodnight.

A Mr Nouveau-Richards rang me the other day.

'Darling', he said, 'I've just bid a fortune for two first editions'.

'What are they?' I asked.

'I'll just go and look,' he said.

They were Shelley and Keats.

MUSIC

There was one peer who only employed butlers who could play the piano in the key of C. He didn't give a damn if they could buttle; he merely wanted someone to accompany him when he played on the mouth-organ. He, however, was the exception. Although Harry Stow-Crat sets a good example by singing loudly in church on Sundays, he is actually tone-deaf. His children sometimes learn an instrument at school, which is called extras, and grumbled about when it appears on the bill.

Occasionally *The Tatler* cover a concert, but it's invariably for charity, some flaring-nostrilled Peruvian playing Chopin in aid of Father Mantua's mission in the East End, and all the audience surreptitiously looking at their watches, and wishing the still fat wad of pages the pianist still has to strum through would suddenly get thinner. Audiences, however, are much better mannered than they used to be. In the past musi-

310

cians or minstrels just provided wallpaper music, a kind of musak against which the audience laughed and talked. A good minstrel, of course, was part of an aristocratic household. Frank Muir suggests that William the Conqueror was so fond of his bard Taillefeau that he allowed him to strike the first blow at the Battle of Hastings. According to legend Taillefeau advanced up the beach singing ballads about Charlemagne, and was promptly struck dead by an enemy arrow. One suspects that if William had been that keen on his carolling, he wouldn't have exposed him to such danger.

Later of course there were fashionable musicians like Paganini who were very well paid and fawned on by aristocratic groupies. Liszt, in fact, was the first Beatle: society women brought special tweezers so they could pluck out his hair, and after a concert would fight for a fragment of the cushion he'd sat on. Kreisler was once asked to play by a fashionable but *nouveau-riche* American hostess. She would pay him 750 dollars she said but after the concert she didn't want him to mingle with her guests, in case he lowered the tone.

'In that case,' replied Kreisler gravely, 'the bill will only be 500 dollars.'

In England music was only respected if it was imported, and Italian castrati charged a fortune in the eighteenth century to give concerts to the rich and noble. The middle classes, it seems, had to make do with a lady from the local opera house.

'I detest these scented rooms,' wrote Coleridge, 'where to a gaudy throng, the proud harlot heaves her distended breasts in intricacies of laborious song.'

Opera, it appears, was something to be endured. The audience played draughts during the recitatives, and merely looked in for one act to be seen, to show off their jewels, and gossip. When a very grand but garrulous hostess asked Charles Haas, Proust's model for Swann, to sit in her box, he replied:

'I'd love to. I've never heard you in *Faust*.'

Today the upper-middle classes, liking their opera

sugar-coated, regard Glyndebourne as the smart thing to go to. They particularly enjoy picnicking with other middle-class people and writing down the names of the more attractive herbaceous plants in the garden on their programme. Today the only people who can afford Covent Garden are foreign diplomats, homosexuals and Samantha Upward's maiden aunts with plaits round their heads, referring to the singers by their surnames like prep school boys: 'Isn't Sutherland too marvellously in voice?' There is a mile-long queue for the loo in the interval, while all those who pretend to know the opera backwards mug up on the synopsis for the next act.

Mozart, Haydn, Vivaldi and Purcell are upper-class composers. Brahms, Mahler, Schubert and Beethoven are upper-middle. Tschaikovsky, Grieg and Mendelssohn are lower-middle.

Samantha would simply love to sing in the Bach Choir. Her mother adores Gilbert and Sullivan. Howard Weybridge has a few classical records: *Peer Gynt*, the Moonlight Sonata and 'Cav-and-Pack-them-in'. He is also 'very active' in amateur operatics. Jen Teale enjoys *Down Your Way* and *Your Hundred Best Tunes*.

Mr Nouveau-Richards likes the cuckoo in the Pastoral Symphony and claps between movements. Tracey-Diane sways from side to side when she plays 'The Lost Chord' on the pianola. Mrs Definitely-Disgusting likes Mantovani and Ron Goodwin, and thinks Verdi's Requiem is a 'resteront'.

In a recent survey it was discovered that people who own their houses prefer classical music, but people in council houses prefer pop. One suspects that the house-owners claimed to prefer classical music because they felt they ought to, because it seems more upper-classical than pop. After all the announcers do talk in 'posh' voices on Radio Three while the disk jockeys on Radio One and Capital all sounds like yobbos.

The Radio Three voice is not in fact upper-class at all, it is Marghanita Laski/Patricia Hughes sens-it-ive,

312

which involves speaking very slowly and deliberately to eradicate any trace of a regional accent, with all the vowel sounds, particularly the 'o's, emphasized: 'vi-oh-lins', 'pee-ar-*noes*', 'Vivald-ee', 'ball-*ay*'. The pronunciation of foreign composers and musical terms is also far too good. The upper classes have frightful accents when they talk in a foreign language. As Harry Stow-Crat's mother once admonished him: 'Speak French fluently, darling, but not like them.'

17   TELEVISION

*Why did you choose such a backward time
and such a strange land?
If you'd come today, you'd have reached a
whole nation.
Israel in 4 B.C. had no mass communication.*
                              Jesus Christ Superstar

Light years above everyone else are the telly-stocracy.
The man in the street is far more impressed by Esther
Rantzen than by Princess Anne. 'When I go to the country,' said Reginald Bosanquet a year or two ago, 'I am
more revered than the Queen.' Our own local telly-
stocrat, David Dimbleby, is particularly impressive.
With a famous television father, he is second-genera-
tion telly and looks like founding a dynasty:

'Once in Royal David's Putney,' sing the children in
the street.

To show the influence these people have, a couple
I know were watching Angela Rippon read the news
one evening when the wife admired her dress.

'Why not see if they've got one like it in Bentalls?'
said her husband.

So off she went next day and found something very
similar.

'Every time Angela appears on television,' confided
the sales girl, 'we get people pouring in here trying to
buy what she was wearing.'

It's not just the telly-stocracy. Everyone who appears
on television is somehow sanctified, albeit temporarily,
with a square halo. It doesn't matter how inept one is,
credit improves dramatically in the High Street. If ever

A member of the telly-stocracy

I appear, my enemies in a nearby council estate, who usually shake their fists at me because of my cat chasing dogs, start waving and saying, 'Saw you last night. What's Eamonn really like?'

Our particular part of Putney is known locally as Media Gulch because so many television stars, actors and journalists live here. One can only keep one's end up if one has the television vans outside one's house at least once every two months, plus a gutted bus where all the crew break every couple of hours for something to eat and hordes of men with prematurely grey hair and he-tan are draping plastic virginia creeper over the porch to give an illusion of spring.

But apart from creating a telly-stocracy, the looming presence of television has done more to change our social habits than anyone realizes. When commercial television appeared in the 'sixties, it was hailed by Lord Thomson as the great leveller. As a new and thrilling medium, it seemed to epitomize the change from a rigid class system. In fact it has reinforced it. Every day 23 million eyes stay glued to the commercial television screen. Advertising in particular makes people dissatisfied with life. The initial effect is to encourage them to go out and buy consumer goods, formerly enjoyed only by their social superiors. As they acquire these, and feel themselves to be going up in the world, television becomes their social adviser. It tells them where to go on their hols, what car they should own, which wines to order, what fuel to burn, what furniture to buy. 'Win Ernie Wise's living room,' screams the *T.V. Times*, 'Win Ian Ogilvy's bedroom'—nearer, my God, to thee! In fact, it is most unlikely that Ernie Wise or Ian Ogilvy has anything to do with those rooms; they took their cheques and left the furnishing to some lower-middle-class advertising stylist with a penchant for repro tat. (Someone once unkindly described Bruce Forsyth's house as being filled with the sort of things people couldn't remember on the conveyor belt of The Generation Game.)

317

Even more pernicious, television gives lots of advice on attitude and behaviour. Mrs Definitely-Disgusting doesn't hit the roof any more every time Dive and Sharon come charging in with mud all over their newly washed jeans. She gives a crooked smile and reaches for the Daz. She feels guilty if her kitchen isn't spotless, and discontented if it isn't a modern one. If a horde of children drop in she doesn't tell them to bugger off, she fills them up with beefburgers. Mr D-D knows now not to talk about 'Cock-burn's port' and to pronounce Rosé as Ros-*ay*.

Television, too, has created a new type of plastic family: smiling, squeezy mums, woolly-hatted Dads playing football and crumbling Oxo cubes, plastic dogs leaping in the air, plastic children stuffing baked beans, lovable plastic grans who are befriended by pretty air-hostesses but are never sick. 'Why aren't we as happy as they are?' asks Mrs Definitely-Disgusting. 'It isn't fair.'

Television increases aspiration but underlines the differences, and has thereby produced strong 'Them' and 'Us' polarization. Mr D-D can pile up goods till he's blue in the face, but it's still difficult for him to improve his status, cross the great manual/non-manual divide and join the Martini set.

Television has created a battered victim, rendered insensible by a ceaseless bombardment of mindless hypocrisy. It is hardly surprising that so many children can't read or write, that few people can be seen in the streets of towns or villages after dark. The nation is plugged in. They are watching Big Brother.

Television forms the basis of nearly all conversations in offices and pubs. (A friend spent a week at Butlins on advertising research and said people talked permanently in television jingles, one person beginning one, the next ending it.) Worse still is the effect on debate and argument, because of the law that requires television to be politically fair, all arguments end in compromises not in conclusions.

318

'You have the highest quality television in the world,' said an American to Professor Halsey who wrote the recent Reith lectures on class, 'but *I Claudius* would be impossible in midstream America. Nowhere else in the Western World does the élite have the confidence both to indulge its own cultural tastes and also believe these should be imposed on the masses.'

Not surprising too that the Annan Committee on Broadcasting expressed concern, after months of research, that people were being brainwashed by middle-class values. Too many characters talk in non-working-class accents. There are not enough working-class heroes on the screen.

The report also complained that various kinds of upper-class characters—royalty, aristocracy, jet set, etc—occurred in 22 per cent of all programmes, almost always in significant roles. Middle-class characters occurred in 56 per cent of the programmes and 76 per cent of them were significant to the plot. But the working-classes only occurred in 41 per cent of the programmes and in only 71 per cent were significant. In terms of their occurrence, in relation to the population at large, middle-class, and even more, upper-class individuals are over-represented on television drama, and when they appear, they are likely to appear in important and attractive roles. This creates envy.

T.V. Times and *The Radio Times* (to a lesser extent) are also obsessed with class. In every interview a person's character is analysed in relation to his background. In one issue of the *T.V. Times* alone we are told that Tessa Wyatt loathes publicity and doesn't want to strip in films because of her inhibited, middle-class background, that John Conteh 'the fourth born of a family of ten from a yellow painted council house' has risen by working-class guts, and is now a rich man with 'a waterfall in the garden of his luxury Bushey (Hertfordshire) home'. And when Katie Stewart visited Emmerdale Farm, she found them 'gathered for dinner—that's what most people who live in the north of

England call the midday meal'.

The Queen, Robert Lacey tells us, watches television to find out about her subjects. One suspects she's an addict like the rest of us.

Princess Margaret also watches it the whole time. A friend went to dinner when she was married to Lord Snowdon and the television stayed on the whole time before dinner, was carried into the dining-room and placed on the table on which they were eating, then carried back into the drawing-room immediately they'd finished.

Evidently the whole Royal family was livid about the spate of royal sagas, particularly *Edward and Mrs Simpson*, not because the events portrayed were so near the knuckle but because the actors playing them or their relations were, they considered, so common. The Queen Mother was evidently most upset by the girl who played her.

'Oh that reminds me, Bryan. Christine's just had her first understain.'

But half the fun of television is looking for the slip-ups. The supposedly upper-middle-class mother in the *House of Caradus* talking about 'when your father was in active service' or Christina in *Flambards* saying 'Pardon' and 'Ever so'. Recently when Thames serialized one of my novels they got the classes quite cock-eyed. It was supposed to be about the Scottish upper classes, but almost the first shot was of a wedding cake with a plastic bride and groom on top. The hero kept calling the heroine 'woman'; the heroine returned from her honeymoon landing on a Western Isle wearing a hat and high heels, and everyone waved their arms frantically in the air during reels at a ball.

Rebecca, on B.B.C. 2 recently, almost got it right. The only time they appeared to slip was when Maxim talked about 'Cook', and when some very unpatrician extras appeared in the ball.

'It's impossible to make extras behave with any authority,' said one of the cast. 'They always look as though they'd got their costumes from Moss Bros.'

The young in particular have been so brain-washed by the egalitarian revolution that, according to one casting director, it's impossible to find an actor in his thirties who can convincingly play upper-middle to upper-class Englishmen of half a century ago. They lack the assurance, the bearing, the tone of voice. Recently a duke's daughter auditioned for a part in Thames Television's dramatization of a Nancy Mitford novel. Not having a clue who she was, the director passed her over. 'What was wrong with her?' asked the producer afterwards. 'She was too middle-class,' replied the director.

Viewing patterns of course vary from class to class. Mr and Mrs Definitely-Disgusting stay plugged in to I.T.V. whatever's on. They are such telly junkies that if it breaks down they nick another one. The only time Mr D-D switches over is for *Match of the Day*, *Miss World* and *That's Life* (Esther's so good at getting at

'Them'). They much prefer serials and variety to current affairs. And they believe implicitly everything they're told in the ads. Mr D-D admires Twiggy and the Campari girl, although they're both a bit skinny.

Jen Teale enjoys *Come Dancing* and 'ice skating' as she calls it, but she only watches television if she's sewing or knitting. Bryan grumbles that there's not nearly enough 'motor sport'. He doesn't enjoy current affairs, general knowledge programmes or even quizzes very much, but he finds it a 'social asset' to have opinions when he talks to colleagues at work.

Eileen Weybridge admires Angela Rippon, and has a soft spot for Julie Andrews because she comes from nearby Walton-on-Thames. Howard watches *Rugby Special* and *Panorama*. They are much less influenced by commercial television than the D-Ds.

Samantha and Gideon firmly try to restrict Zacharias and Thalia's viewing. They think *Play School, Blue Peter* and general knowledge programmes are all right. When they go out, Zacharias bribes the *au pair* to let him watch *Target* and *The Sweeney*. Samantha insists on watching all the cultural programmes which send poor Gideon to sleep. She actively disbelieves everything the ads tell her.

Mrs Nouveau-Richards naturally has a video tape. 'Hubby and I go out so much, but all our show-business friends would be so disappointed if we missed their programmes.'

Harry Stow-Crat turns the television on as soon as he gets home from shooting and sleeps peacefully through it until the little white dot appears. He might wake up for Anna Ford, whom he prefers to Angela Rippon. So does Mr Callaghan who referred to her with typically lower-middle caution as 'rather an attractive character'. Harry also watches racing and may have a bet if he's ever home in the afternoon.

Finally, a brief word about the ads themselves. Most of them are deliberately aimed at Mr Definitely-Disgusting because he and Mrs D-D belong to the largest class and are more prepared to splash out than any of the other classes at the moment. Generally speaking, said an ad man recently, social mobility pulls don't work on the C.2s, which is how the advertising world catagorizes Mr D-D. The idea of doing something because Lady X or the vicar does it, wouldn't appeal to Mr D-D. He's read the *News of the World*; he knows all about vicars. Success figures like Twiggy, David Niven, Nyree Dawn Porter and Frank Muir are therefore used rather than class figures in ads.

According to Charles Plouviez, chairman of Everetts, who has written a brilliant paper on 'Class and Advertising':

'When Americans are planning a campaign and deciding how to reach the people most likely to buy the product, the main considerations are age and sex. In England they are age, sex and *class*. The advertiser must not offend class susceptibilities.

'The disaster is not in showing affluent or upper-class characters (brands with quality or high-class images require this, and this is accepted) but rather in the tone of the voice (not necessarily accent) in which the situations are portrayed. Jokes at the expense of women or working-class stereotypes, and situations involving master-servant relationships are widely resented.'

The newspapers are luckier. *The Times*, *Guardian* and *Telegraph*, the *Mail* and *Express*, the *Mirror* and the *Sun*, all cater for a slightly different class of reader. But on television the advertiser must avoid giving offence to all classes. All commercials are built round the classic telly family. 'Rural and Scottish accents,' according to Mr Plouviez, are always acceptable, 'but the really rough urban accents are avoided, and "posh" accents, which used to be the rule on radio and T.V. in the days of the B.B.C. monopoly, are only used for commercials when they are being sent up. The voice over or unseen voice which delivers the selling message, presents the greatest difficulty because if it is too posh it offends the viewer and if it is too common it offends the client.'

18 WORLD OF SPORT

O Skipper! my Skipper! our fearful excursion is executed.

In the last fifty years there has been a complete revolution in sport throughout the world. This is particularly noticeable in England and can be directly attributed to the influence of two world wars, and more generally to the advent of wireless and television. More evenly distributed wealth has created more time for 'leisure', and, while we have become more a nation of spectators than participants, less fashionable games and pastimes have, through their exposure on the media, led to a much more varied participating pattern across society.

The aristocracy seldom indulged in such games as football, cricket or hockey. Sport to them has always been either closely linked to survival—hunting, shooting and fishing—or to gambling, hence their traditional addiction to racing.

It was left to the middle classes, working through the medium of the public schools, aided and abetted by the Church which thought that violent athletic activity took boys' minds off masturbation, to champion 'organized games' and the noble art of self-defence. It should not be forgotten that one of the first Association Football clubs founded in this country was the Corinthians, a team of gentlemen. They even won the F.A. cup. Team games which emphasized manly virtues and social solidarity led naturally to the creation of exclusive clubs—almost a defensive movement. This sort of coagulation has always been peculiar to the English. Look at the regimental system in the army, which, although it goes back much further, pays homage to the same code of values. Never let the man next to you see you are afraid; never let the side down; 'Play up and play the game'.

The social history of cricket is very complicated. It began as a peasant pastime, was only later taken up by the gentry and, today, with all the posturing and cuddling at the fall of a wicket that occurs during a Test match, is fast going back to the peasants again. Exactly the opposite happened with rugger, which began as an upper-middle-class pursuit, was then taken up by grammar and then comprehensive schools and ended with the ultimate peasant adaptation of Rugby League.

One only needs to go to the Varsity Match or any home international at Twickenham, 'the last fortress of the Forsyths', as Christopher Laidlaw called it, to see the English middle classes in all their glory and to realize that when the crowd howls for England they are really howling for the middle classes and the survival of middle-class values.

Today the only really smart game left is real tennis, possibly because there are so few courts. Hunting is no longer smart but bristling with Mr Nouveau-Richards and television stars. The Welsh miner in a red coat is no longer an isolated phenomenon.

Fishing is not really a sport, although many of the lower classes who indulge in coarse fishing would argue that it was. Harry Stow-Crat has a beat on the Tay, but the fishing on either side is now rented by Arabs and stockbrokers. Samantha goes to the fishmongers, the Cousteau-Richards go deep-sea fishing off Looe. Mr Definitely-Disgusting sits all day under a green umbrella on the edge of a gravel pit catching inch-long roach and throwing them back.

Harry doesn't take much exercise. He plays billiards (not a sport), backgammon (bridge is too difficult), and might have rowed at school. He seldom rows after leaving Cambridge. That is left to the working-class clubs such as Poplar and Blackwell, and Thames Tradesmen. He sometimes hunts, and takes a packet of pheasant sandwiches. He played fives at school and perhaps raquets, and nowadays occasionally has a game of tennis or croquet (which he pronounces *croky*, not cro-*kay* as Howard Weybridge would.) He wouldn't dream of joining a tennis club. Nor would he use expressions like 'lawn tennis' or 'partner' (for 'play with'). He would never be seen dead on a golf (which he pronounces 'goff') course, and would soon be dead in a squash court. He would never, never jog.

Gideon plays squash, tennis, cricket, rugger until he is thirty, but never hockey which he regards as common and only played by minor public schools, Indians and fat-bottomed female clerks from Barclays Bank, and fat-breasted female clerks from Lloyds Bank.

'No we're *not* staying and having a bloody drink with the others. Get the children into the car.'

Howard Weybridge has a 'Support Surrey Rugby' sticker in the back of his car and enjoys 'a few jars' at Esher Rugby Club. He also plays 'gole-f' if he can find room at Moore Place or Burhill alongside all the bank managers playing against other bank managers, and spiralists playing with their bosses and letting them win after a tough fight.

Although they now allow the pro to drink in the bar, it is evidently still quite difficult to get into the Royal Berkshire and Sunningdale Golf Clubs. You have to be proposed and seconded by members who've known you for a considerable time, fill in a form stating your profession and where you went to school, and then get letters of approval from between six and eight members saying you're the right sort of person. At Sunningdale you actually have to play in front of the management committee to prove you're good enough.

'What happens if a nice bricklayer wants to join the club?' I asked the secretary at the Royal Berkshire.

'Well it would be most unlikely,' he said. 'How could he possibly know six of our members?'

Bryan Teale is too busy with home improvements and tinkering with the Volkswagen to play with anything but himself. His father plays bowls.

Mr Definitely-Disgusting never does anything much out of doors except kick a ball against the factory wall during tea breaks, and watch television all the time when he's not going to the dogs or football matches on Saturday afternoon, filling in football coupons or having a bet. At the pub Mr D-D plays darts, snooker and dominoes.

Mr D-D's brother, who's a miner, races pigeons. He also owns a lurcher. Coursing has a strong cloth-cap following. When Harold Wilson wanted to give government backing to a bill banning stag hunting and hare coursing, Richard Crossman directed his acute political antennae in that direction:

'He [Harold] thinks this is an election winner, and hundreds and thousands of people who read the *Daily*

Mirror will love this idea. Deer hunting is probably very unpopular, but hare coursing is a very proletarian sport, people in the North enjoy it. I didn't think we should jump into this without a much more careful analysis of the minority who oppose it.'

Mr D-D hates athletics because of all them soap-dodgers. Athletics is now the sole province of the black community who in the days of empire were so used to running from place to place with messages in cleft sticks, as well as running after their dinner, that they developed a talent for long-distance running which brings them medal after medal. They also got used to sprinting away from Lee-Enfields and Gatlings, hence their great speed over short distances.

Ping-pong (now called table tennis) is a game only played by young Conservatives or in the games room of decrepit boarding houses in Grange-over-Sands. Swimming is only O.K. if it's done in one's own swimming pool or in the sea. Public swimming baths are out because the working classes use them as lavatories. Caroline Stow-Crat talks about bathing and wears a bathing suit. Samantha gets round the problem by saying 'bikini'. Jen Teale says 'swimsuit' or 'swimming costume'.

The best and only sport the English were ever any good at was war, which all classes could have a go at, but even that is only now on television.

HORSES

God save our gracious Quorn.

The horse was one of the first status symbols. Like the car, it gave it's owner mobility. Originally the upper classes were the only people who could afford horses, and a number of words with aristocratic associations come from riding, the French *'chevalier'* for example, the German *'ritter'*, meaning rider, and the English 'cavalier'. Sitting on a horse enables you to look down on your fellow men. Horsy people invariably have that deadpan look one associates with the aristocracy.

Horses have always been a good way to climb the social ladder, as Mark Phillips showed us. In the nineteenth century the Rothschilds were accepted into the grandest Victorian society because the Prince of Wales was at Cambridge with Nathaniel Rothschild and shared his interest in racing.

Today show-jumping stars like David Broome and Alan Oliver get asked to Princess Anne's pre-wedding ball and the livery stables are full of expensive horses acquired as status symbols by pop stars and actors who are too frightened to ride them. Douglas Bunn, a butcher's son, is referred to by himself and the press as the Master of Hickstead.

Mr Nouveau-Richards buys polo ponies, takes up hunting, slaps point-to-point stickers on the back window of his car and, even if he doesn't ride himself, struts around at local gymkhanas in breeches, having frightful rows with the collecting ring stewards and the judges when they don't put Tracey-Diane first.

Samantha Upward's father, like many another retired army Colonel or Brigadier, often finds an interest in running the local pony club and bossing about nubile little girls. Competition is as fierce between the little girls as it is between the guns out shooting. There was fearsome grumbling at the local Putney show a few years ago because they all thought the jump in the Working Pony Class had been specially lowered for Princess Alexandra's daughter.

Harry Stow-Crat has his breeches made for him and pays about £600 for black leather boots, which have a garter strap which attaches to buttons on his breeches and keeps the boots up and the breeches down. Georgie Stow-Crat, however, is feeling the pinch and has bought a pair of rubber boots so well made as to be indistinguishable from leather ones. Even he wouldn't resort to the stretch nylon breeches worn by Mr Nouveau-Richards. Georgie wears brown boots for polo and laced boots if he's in the cavalry.

It used to be considered extremely vulgar to have buckles on your reins, they had to be sewn on. But now, except for showing, most people have studs which fasten on the inside. Coloured brow-bands are beyond the pale. It is permissible to wear a white hunting tie or a stock with coloured spots. But Harry Stow-Crat considers it very nouveau to wear a coloured stock with white spots.

When Mr Nouveau-Richards goes out hunting he wears an ordinary white tie instead of a stock with his unauthorized red coat—like the show jumpers do on television—and carries his hunting whip upside down without a thong. Tracey-Diane looks like an advertisement on the back pages of a riding magazine. She wears thick eye make-up, dangling earrings, and her loose blonde locks stream out from her black cap. Mr N-R tells everyone she is a marvellous 'horsewoman'. Harry would say 'a very good rider'. Howard Weybridge calls it 'horse-back riding'.

Samantha Upward carefully talks about 'hounds with their "waving sterns", and "pink" coats'. She is rather shocked when Harry refers to his 'red' coat. Far too many *nouveaus* have started talking about 'pink', so the uppers have reverted to 'red'.

Harry says his horse is lame, whereas Howard Weybridge says 'his mount is limping'.

Howard says, 'I was thrown from the horse which was very frisky.'

Harry says, 'My horse was too fresh and bucked me off/gave me a fall/I fell off.'

Howard says his horse 'jibbed at a hedge'. Harry would put it 'put in a stop' or 'refused at a fence'.

Howard's horse 'gets the bit between the teeth'. Harry would say, 'It took off with me', or 'ran away', or 'I was carted'.

Howard's horse 'keeps rearing'; Harry's horse 'goes up with him'.

'Hunting,' wrote Bishop Latimer in 1820, 'is a good exercise for men of rank, and shooting an amusement equally lawful and proper for inferior persons.' Yet three-quarters of a century later shooting was the way in which the great landowners entertained their guests throughout the winter months.

'The railway helped,' as Jonathan Ruffer points out in *The Big Shots*, 'so did technical improvements of the gun ... you combined the opportunities of a Vimy Ridge machine-gunner with an infinitely better lunch.'

And finally, because Edward VII was too fat to hunt, he channelled all his enthusiasms into shooting. 'It was natural that society should exert itself in pursuits which its champion made fashionable.'

A friend once asked the Macnab of Macnab, who is a brilliant shot, whether he really needed a secretary three days a week. 'Of course I do,' replied the Macnab indignantly. 'Every day I have to write letters saying: "Dear Charles, Thank you for asking me to shoot on the fourth, I'm afraid I can't make it," or "Dear Henry, Thank you very much for asking me to shoot on the 18th, I should be happy to accept."'

All through the winter in Scotland and the North of England, in anticipation of the coming season, white plumes rise like smoke signals from various hills, where the heather is being burned. It's all anyone talks about at upper-class dinner parties. If you're not careful you can burn a whole moor. (Harry Stow-Crat pronounces it 'maw', the middle classes call it 'maw-er').

'At Sandringham and Balmoral,' Robert Lacey wrote in *Majesty*, 'day-long shooting sorties take on the character of a military manoeuvre, with shooting brakes, vans full of beaters drawn by a tractor, and Land-Rovers which you clamber into, possibly to find the Queen sitting next to you.'

Prince Philip is one of the best shots in the country, which means the world. Prince Charles, it seems, is all set to overtake him, and is already the best fisherman in the family.

As soon as people start doing well in business they take up shooting, and photographs of themselves knee-deep in the bracken beside a grinning labrador with its mouth full of feathers are placed on top of the piano.

But the pitfalls are great for the unwary. Mr Nouveau-Richards has no idea what to tip the keeper, and keeps shooting his host's grouse, rather like poor Charles Clore asking the late Duke of Marlborough if his loader could join them for lunch.

'Whatever for?' asked the Duke sarcastically. 'Is he teaching you to eat as well?'

It is very smart to drink sloe gin at lunchtime but social death to turn up in gold boots and a shocking pink fun fur and talk throughout every drive like Mrs Nouveau-Richards.

Despite the Freudian terminology of shooting handbooks—all that talk about 'pricked birds', 'cocks only' days, and 'premature gun mounting'—women are expected to keep very much in the background. Their duty is to provide a good lunch, keep an eye on the dogs and occasionally load. 'After August 12th,' sighed one Edwardian beauty, 'wives and mistresses don't exist.'

The exception was a Spanish prince who turned up to shoot in Yorkshire with a ravishing mistress, and missed everything he shot at on the first two drives. Bumping along in the Land-Rover to the third drive the keeper heard scufflings and, looking round, saw the prince and his mistress humping away on a mattress of slaughtered grouse. After that he shot brilliantly.

19 DOGS

The pooch it was that passed away.

'I can get on perfectly well with the people my children marry,' said one aristocratic old woman. 'What I find difficult is dogs-in-law.' She was talking about the troops of Tibetan spaniels, dachshunds and fat irascible terriers who join the family circle with a new daughter-in-law.

The upper classes, of course, adore their dogs. In the country they usually have at least five, like Catholics, and have grilles in the back of their cars to stop them being bothered by the children. The dogs coat the furniture with dogs hairs, wipe their faces on the chair covers, and most of them sleep in the bedroom. (Sir Sacheverell Sitwell's Cavalier King Charles spaniels have a turquoise drinking bowl to match the bedroom wallpaper.) Their portraits hang under picture lights. Most of them are incontinent but no one seems to mind very much. Randolph Churchill was once heard balling out one of his dogs for peeing on the sofa.

'Get down, Boycott, you know you're meant to do that on the carpet.'

There was an old duke who was absolutely devoted to a foul terrier called Spot, who was rotund, blind, incontinent, bit everyone and was over twenty. Finally, under extreme family pressure, the duke agreed to take the dog out and shoot it. Tears pouring down his face, he and Spot set out into the twilight. The family waited in anticipation and jumped out of their skins when, ten minutes later, there was a feeble clawing on the door. It was Spot wanting to be let in. At the prospect of having to kill him the Duke had had a heart attack.

Spot lived on for several years.

Walk through the garden of any upper-class house and, in a quiet, shady corner, you will find a lot of little crosses. This is the dogs' graveyard. One I know in Lancashire includes a favourite parrot buried in a cake tin. A small tombstone at Sandringham bears the inscription 'To The Queen's Faithful Friend, Susan'.

On the whole the upper classes prefer what they call working dogs—labradors to 'shoot over' (they never shoot 'with' them) and Jack Russells, Norfolk or hunt terriers to dig 'Charlie' (as they call the fox) out, although they never get that far. Black labradors are much grander than yellow, and are quite often invited without their owners to shoot in Scotland and travel up quite happily on the train. Another labrador came all the way down to London from Northumberland to be mated. The owner of the bitch booked a room at the Turf Club (presumably in the name of 'Mr and Mrs Smith'). The dogs screwed away merrily all night and produced eight puppies. The owner of one stately home told me he had terrible trouble when members of the visiting public were stretched out asleep on the grass in summer, because his labrador always went and lifted his leg on any bald head.

King Charles spaniels are very upper-class dogs, so are whippets, springer spaniels and corgis. Hounds are never kept as pets, but 'walked' as puppies in the summer. Upper-class dogs often have two addresses on their collars: one for London and another for the country. On the label should be engraved the owner's surname, address and telephone number. It is very vulgar to put the dog's name in inverted commas, and to have anything other than brown leather collars. Tartan collars for Scotties or West Highland terriers and diamanté for poodles are also out. So are red bows on long-haired dogs, or topiary on poodles.

Upper-class dogs only have one meal a day and are therefore quite thin, like their owners. Snipe Stow-Crat is so well trained he doesn't need a collar or lead at all. (Jen Teale would say 'leash'. Mr Definitely-Disgusting uses string, and calls his puppy a 'pup'. He also talks about 'pooches'.)

It is very lower-middle to be frightened of dogs, or to go into queeny hysterics whenever a dog lifts its leg on your garden fence.

Upper-middle dog owners are almost keener on them than the aristocracy. They don't have so many, so the affection is not divided and they don't keep them for working but to talk to and through. Colonel and Mrs Upward address each other through their dalmatian. Samantha has an evening bag lined with congealed fat from bringing home chops and bits of steak for Blücher, her English setter.

Dogs belonging to the upper-middle merry-tocracy always reek of garlic from having doggy-bag pork chops or chicken à la Kiev posted through the door to stop

'Howard—did you remember to give Petal her pill?'

337

them barking and waking the nanny when their owners return from restaurants too drunk to find their keys.

Dalmatians, English setters, cairns, golden retrievers, are upper-middle-class dogs. The upper-middles have also recently taken to foreign breeds—Weimaraners, and rotweillers—because the classes below can't pronounce them. Old English sheepdogs used to be upper-middle but have lost caste since they appeared so often on television advertising paint.

Howard Weybridge likes airedales and rough-haired terriers, great danes and Irish wolfhounds. They look so heraldic loping through the pinewoods of Surrey. He also likes red setters and cocker spaniels.

Mrs Nouveau Richards loves Yorkshire terriers and poodles and all the show-off cruising-partner dogs like collies and Afghans.

Bryan Teale likes dobermanns and boxers because they don't shed hairs. Jen hates all dogs because they're so smelly.

Mr D-D belongs to the *Daily Mirror* Pets Club and loves all 'pooches'. But he's particularly partial to 'Westies' as he calls West Highlands and Alsatians because they're such good guard dogs (and some of his rougher friends might try to get him one day). And of course you can't beat a good mongrel (though he frequently does). Mongrels (which Mr D-D pronounces to rhyme with 'long' and Harry Stow-Crat to rhyme with 'dung') are sometimes called 'street dogs', or 'butcher's dogs' because they used to follow the butcher's van.

Nigel Dempster, in a recent piece on 'In and Out' trends, said that mongrels from Battersea were very 'In'. But on the whole the upper classes don't approve of mongrels. I always pretend mine are lurchers when I go anywhere smart. Caroline Stow-Crat would swallow, then cover up her disapproval by saying, 'But they're supposed to be awfully intelligent and loyal.'

It is pretty unsmart to show your dogs—rather like going in for a beauty contest—and also to enter your

338

guard dog for what is called 'O-bedience tests'. Field trials, however, are all right.

Jen Teale talks about 'veterinary surgeons' instead of 'vets', and 'lady dogs' instead of 'bitches'. Mrs Nouveau-Richards talks about 'doggies' and 'pups'.

Mr Nouveau-Richards recently paid £100 for what he thought was a pedigree labrador puppy for Tracey-Diane. It turned out to be a hamster.

Upper-class dogs have simple names like Badger, Ranger and Bertie. The middle class, however, are madly into the Victorian names which the upper-middles were calling their children ten years ago: Emma, Jessica, Fanny, Cassandra, Sophie, Jason, and funny-ha-ha names like Wellington, Melchester, or Ugly for a pug.

The working classes either name their dogs according to their appearance—Spot, Blackie, Patch, Snowy— or try and upgrade them with names like Lady and Duchess. On Eel Brook Common at night it sounds like a mediaeval roll-call, with cries of 'Rex', 'Prince', 'Duke' echoing plaintively through the darkening mist.

The upper classes don't like cats as much as dogs, and tend only to keep them in the stables to keep the rats down. The more well-bred a cat, usually the commoner the owner.

Mrs D-D refers to her cat as 'Pussy': 'A neighbour took Pussy when I went on holiday.'

20 CLUBS

If the Englishman's home is his castle, the English gentleman's bolthole is his club. I don't mean the kind of club like Esher R.F.C. or Hurlingham (which is not a club, but a place where foreigners go when Harrods is closed) or the M.C.C. which people join to meet people and play games with their 'own sort', but the sort of club that a man joins to avoid meeting people—not least members of his own club. A club is a useful place for a gentleman to remain incommunicado, particularly from his wife. The porter will always put up a smokescreen.

Although a lot of London clubs now allow women in as guests, this has been done grudgingly. At the Army and Navy there's a separate dining room for them. At the Naval and Military there's a special entrance. At the Garrick they are not allowed to use the main staircase before 7 p.m. and are bundled into a side room at lunchtime, where they are forgotten for long periods by the staff. In the rule book it says that no lady visitor be introduced more than ten times within the same year, except members of the family of the member—which presumably keeps mistresses at bay.

There used to be a famous ladies' club called the Cowdray, of which my mother-in-law was a member and which described itself, rather wildly, as a club 'for professional women'. One of the oldest members was a Miss Eardley Wilmot, who wrote the words for 'My Little Grey Home in the West'. Miss Wilmot once met my father-in-law on the landing (men were allowed to stay with their wives towards the end of the Cowdray's existence).

'Oh dear,' she said, 'a man,' and fainted away.

341

I always like the story about the Athenaeum, the august haunt of bishops and dons. It is said that a notice appeared in one of the papers saying: 'The Athenaeum re-opened today after the annual cleaning, and members were replaced in their original positions.'

Harry Stow-Crat would probably belong to White's. If not White's, Boodle's, Brooks's, Buck's or the Turf. He would never be seen in the RAC (The Chauffeurs' Arms) or the Junior Carlton. He would have been lunched at the Garrick probably by his lawyer, but never wants to be asked back there because he saw Robin Day in the dining room.

Colonel Upward is a member of the Army and Navy, which he calls the Rag; his brother, Commander Upward, goes to the Naval and Military, known as the In and Out, but both of them know little places somewhere else called 'Clubs' where you can drink in faintly louche surroundings for longer hours.

All but the very smart London clubs have allowed the spiralists to become members in order to boost membership; uneasy-looking goosenecks with brushed-forward hair in High Street suitings can be seen looking bewildered by the unfamiliar surroundings, wondering which fork to use and desperately trying to stop their gooseneck guests pulling out sheafs of papers and talking shop in whining, nasal voices. Clubs may *not* be used for business purposes or used as a business address.

Clubs Harry would never be seen in include the Savage, the National Liberal, the East India and Sports and the Gresham Club in the city. The Reform is also way down the list now. It is interesting that when Mr Thorpe took Norman Scott there for a drink he used to pretend that Mr Scott was a constituent he was helping with some family problem. He felt Mr Scott was too 'suburban' (his very words) to be introduced as a friend.

Bryan Teale joins the Rotary Club, prompted by Jen who thinks it might advance his career, and belongs to a social club at work. Mr and Mrs Definitely-Dis-

342

gusting go to the working men's clubs on Fridays and have a whale of a time watching high-class variety acts and filling themselves with beer. The working men's club, in fact, is the lynch-pin of working-class culture. Ironically, they were started as temperance clubs by a vicar in 1862 to add a bit of colour to the dismal life of the working man. Later Lord Rosebery introduced drinking and smoking. Some of the clubs are colossal. The one at Batley in Yorkshire is now closed but could hold 15,000 people, big enough to attract such names as Frank Sinatra, who might by-pass London on his way. Even Mr Definitely-Disgusting laughs at Charlie Williams, the famous black comedian who made his name in working men's clubs. Evidently part of his turn is to mop his face and say,

'My God, it won't come off. If thee don't laugh, I'll come and live next door to thee.'

'Yes, but why White's for goodness sake?'

He deals with problems familiar to the working classes: rents, unemployment, mothers-in-law, class ('our lodger's such a naice young man').

One of his favourite jokes is Enoch Powell going up to the pearly gates and a voice says, 'Who Dat out Dere?'

'No,' said Enoch. 'Forget it.'

There was once a very rich financier who wanted to join a smart London club. Anxious to find out how his election had gone, he despatched a sycophantic minion to find out the result. The minion returned sometime later, looking uneasy.

'How did it go?' said the financier.

'Pure caviare, I fear,' said the minion.

21 THE SERVICES

The origins of most of the oldest families in England
are military and feudal. When William the Conqueror
was establishing himself in this country he offered his
henchmen pieces of land if they would provide him with
a certain number of soldiers for a specified number of
days a year. The henchmen who produced the most
men got the most land. By Henry V's reign things had
got a bit out of hand, with everyone calling himself
'knight' or 'esquire', regardless of right. Henry therefore ordered that coats of arms would only be granted
to people who had fought at Agincourt or who could
show ancestral right. Even so several hundred people
were granted arms in the fifteenth century, and in the
sixteenth century many more, an increase that has no
parallel in any continental country. It has also always
been the practice of monarchs to reward their great
soldiers with titles, hence the Dukes of Marlborough
and Wellington, or, more recently Earl Alexander, Viscount Montgomery and Lord Portal.

Once upon a time the army was very smart. 'An
officer', wrote Lord Stanley in the nineteenth century,
'shall still be the son of a gentleman. A gentleman is
understood to mean a man who has plenty of money,
and does not exercise any retail trade or any mechan-
ical profession. If you find a horse dealer or a shopkeeper's son, you may be certain that the rule has been
relaxed because his father has contrived to ingratiate
himself with the class above his own, and not on account of the personal merit of the candidate.'

Because of the last two wars and National Service
there is hardly a family in the land which has not at
one time had some military experience. There are those

who would argue that this did more to break down social barriers than any other single influence during the last century. Certainly the First World War taught young gentlemen from country houses that little men from Durham were not just hairy, illiterate dwarfs who lived and worked underground, but sensitive, loyal, and often fantastically brave human beings. Equally the Durham miners and the Somerset yokels discovered that, far from being aloof, etoliated drips, their officers loved and cared for them, and died for them in what they believed to be the cause of right. This and succeeding wars formed a mutual bond which began to alter the whole social scene, but the Trade Unions and the Labour party in the last few years have done their best to recreate the social divisions that existed in the early 1900s.

Today, sadly, the army has lost caste, as their numbers are cut, their regiments merged, and the cost of living outstrips their pay.

'Colonels used to impress', Heather Jenner told me, 'but today there is a completely different attitude to them. It's a devil of a job to get them married'.

But although it may no longer be a repository for chinless wonders or second sons of noble houses with nothing better to do, the army has, regardless, a rigid social structure.

There are still smart regiments and not so smart regiments. At the top are the Cavalry, still so called, and the Foot Guards (part of the Household Brigade.) There are the Greenjackets, light infantry, line regiments, Scottish regiments and, last and certainly least, the Corps who tend to have even fiercer snobbery and larger chips than their superiors and betters. All Gunners, according to my husband, are boring and most of them are stone deaf.

Of the Cavalry regiments, the Blues and Royals, the Greys, the 17/21st Lancers and, until recently, the 11th Hussars, could claim to be the élite; but when the 11th joined the 10th, they claimed to have been dragged down, just as the Blues have been by the Royals. It used to be smarter to be in armoured cars than tanks, which gave an edge to the 13th/18th, KDGs, Royals, 15th/19th, 11th Hussars and 12th Lancers. Nowadays they chop and charge.

The Scots, Welsh and Irish Guards are looked down on by the Coldstream and the Grenadiers, but all except the latter unite in regarding the Grenadiers as the stupidest.

The Green Jackets (formerly the Rifle Brigade and the King's Royal Rifle Corps, and now including the Oxford and Buckinghamshire Light Infantry) are the soundest socially. They look down on Regiments of the Line. You can't get much lower than The Royal Corps of Transport and The Royal Army Ordnance Corps, unless you are part of an Amalgamated Regiment like the Royal Anglians. The Army Catering Corps is not even Royal yet. The WRAC is staffed almost wholly by

'It's quite simple really: the tenth were shiny; the eleventh wore red trousers; the fifth skins wore green trousers; the seventh turn-ups and crossbelts; and all tank men have dirty finger nails'.

lesbians, incipient traffic wardens and lady brigadiers who become dames.

Harry Stow-Crat probably served in the Coldstream during the war, as had many of his family in earlier wars. He would say 'hurt' rather than 'wounded'; he would never talk about 'the C.O.' or 'mufti', and he would never say, 'When I was an officer in the Coldstream', because he would assume everyone would know he was.

Gideon Upward did his National Service in the 7th Hussars, a not-so-smart cavalry regiment which his father, the Colonel, pulled a great many strings to get him into. He remembers all the working-class boys blubbing on their first night, because they'd never been away from home before. Later he went to Hong Kong for a year.

After National Service in the Signals, Howard Weybridge joined what he considered was a smart Territorial Army unit and went away on long drinking weekends on Salisbury Plain, pretending to be a gentleman and growing a small clipped moustache. Once in the H.A.C., he would begin by going back to non-commissioned rank, and have to work his way up. This mystifies Dive Definitely-Disgusting when he too joins the Reserve Army, and occasionally goes on joint exercises with the H.A.C. Afterwards he describes Howard and his mob, as 'not a bad lot of fuckers but why do they talk so funny?' On one occasion he sidled up to Howard Weybridge saying: 'Tell me Bombadier, aren't most of your lot, ex-officers?'

'Well quite a few,' Howard admits modestly.

'Well what the 'ell did you get busted for?' asks Dive.

Eileen Weybridge hopes that her nephew might join the army to knock him into shape. When asked what regiment, she says vaguely, 'Oh, he's going into the Greens'. Just as Jen impressed Gideon Upward at a P.T.A. meeting by telling him she had a brother in the Brigade. She meant the Fire Brigade.

Bryan Teale did his National Service as a clerk in

the Pay Corps, and spent two years in Bedford looking after the R.H.Q. of a once famous, now defunct, county regiment. He always refers to the adjutant as the 'adj'. Jen Teale nearly joined the Wrens but thought the black stockings would give people ideas.

Mr D-D was a driver in the R.A.S.C. (The Jam Stealers) during the war and had a good time getting the clap twice in Benghazi, and entering Berlin five days after the end of the war, where he briefly became a black-market baron. He reckons his army days were the happiest of his life. He is now a member of the British Legion, because the beer is cheaper.

A last word of warning. Beware of those who use ranks below colonel in civilian life. Colonels and above are usually sound, but it is not safe to ask what they were in. My father-in-law once queried a brigadier too fiercely and extracted the information that he had served in the A.R.P. in India in 1939.

Socially the Air Force is of little interest—no one knows anyone in it, or rather no one admits to knowing anyone in it. The days of blue-eyed boys with silk scarves, heavy limps and labradors vanished years ago leaving behind them a flotsam of sub-astronauts with social chips and nothing to do—they don't have any aeroplanes either. To say you were in the 'Raff' rather than the Air Force is very Bryan Teale.

The Navy are difficult to categorize socially; they are often away for a long time, presumably at sea. As far as I can discover, there are not many of them left. There must be more retired naval people than there are serving, particularly admirals. However, the Navy are a game lot with exquisite manners and a romantic image—probably because one sees them so seldom. They're also quite bright: you can't get in unless you have five Os and three A-levels.

Harry Stow-Crat had a great-great-great-uncle who fought at Trafalgar and there is a battered portrait of him in the ballroom with a hole in it where some young blood threw an ashtray during a hunt ball. There is a rusting sextant which belonged to another uncle who was in Clippers in the downstairs lavatory. Harry also had an aunt in the Wrens.

Gideon Upward's grandfather fought at Jutland, but no one knows what became of him after the *Queen Mary* sank. It was rumoured that he survived and went to Australia. The Nouveau-Richards' connections with the Navy were restricted to a cruise to Bermuda where they were asked to 'cocktails' in the wardroom of H.M.S. something-or-other that was over there showing the flag.

It is very vulgar to call the Navy the 'Royal Navy'. The upper classes wouldn't be in anything else, and regard the Merchant Navy as beyond the pale.

Occasionally hand-picked officers in the Navy are selected to sail in *Britannia* and thereafter keep albums filled with glued-in concert programmes and photographs of princes in grass skirts being ducked at the equator.

Dive Definitely-Disgusting joined the sea scouts because you could smoke more easily in a whaler or a rusty M.T.B. than you could in a scout hut where you spent most of your time running around trying to avoid the clutches of the scoutmaster.

22 RELIGION

Frequent church-going becomes markedly less likely as one goes down the social scale. The upper classes regard it as a patriotic duty to set an example and go every Sunday, quite often to their own church where they have their own pew. As Douglas Sutherland has pointed out, the English Gentleman knows that God believes in him and sees it as his duty to return the compliment. He often reads the lesson, sings loudly but out of tune, and tells the vicar to speak up if he can't hear the sermon. In return his church expects financial support. The Queen always gives £1 to the collection. The local vicar was ludicrously cross recently when the Marquess of Tavistock only sent him £25 for mending the church roof.

The Church of England is predominantly the church of the upper and middle classes. You find that the middle classes hog all the places on the parish council and act as sidesmen and churchwardens, while their wives, with their large well-stocked gardens, are responsible for the church flowers, church fêtes and jumble sales. The working classes feel intimidated and left out.

It's very vulgar to call a vicar 'Vicar' to his face, rather like 'Doctor' and 'Teacher'; you should call him 'Mr Upward' or whatever his surname is. If he is a canon you could call him 'Canon Stow-Crat'. On letters he should be addressed as 'The Rev. Francis Stow-Crat', never 'Rev. Francis Stow-Crat' or 'The Rev. Stow-Crat'.

Despite keeping the working classes at arm's length the Anglican Church, since the introduction of the New English Bible, is getting more folksy and vulgar every day. We now have 'Mother's Day' instead of 'Mothering Sunday', to get it as far away from a church ritual as

351

possible, and instead of 'Harvest Festival' we have 'Harvest Home' or 'Harvest Supper'. In the towns they have plastic fruit, and lots of children arriving with apples on plastic trays. My sister-in-law in the country was asked to 'bake a harvest pie for the harvest home'. This is apparently another name for a quiche. If she wasn't up to a harvest pie, said the parish worker, a basket of provender would be very acceptable. Evidently the main excitement was some boys who were coming over from Uppingham to sing in the choir.

Next morning my sister-in-law's char came in panting and puffing; she wasn't going to make a harvest pie for them foreigners, she said, and what's more she didn't like the vicar.

Any significance Easter may have had for the masses has disappeared under a mass of overpriced chocolate and Easter Bunnies. And nothing can equal the flood of vulgarity which pours forth at Christmas,

'I'm toiling over a hot stove because Mummy prefers faith to works on Sunday mornings.'

burying the country under a commercial avalanche of heavenly babes, yule logs, festive robins, jolly cardinals and seasonal cheer.

The Stow-Crats have a real Christmas tree from the estate. It touches the ceiling and is decorated with candles and ancient peeling baubles. Snipe has a large mutton bone as a present, and Harry's few remaining tenants and estate servants shuffle in to collect their hams and turkeys and have a drink.

Samantha's and Gideon's parents take it in turns to go and stay with Samantha and Gideon at Christmas.

'Don't they realize you're working?' Gideon says furiously to Samantha every year. What he really minds about is not being able to drink himself stupid in front of his in-laws, and because Christmas goes on for so long he won't have a chance to see the secretary he fancies for at least ten days. Christmas staying with in-laws is invariably a nightmare: not enough to drink and Thalia breaks the crib Virgin Mary on Boxing Day. No one fights openly (the Pargeters again) but a muscle is going in both Samantha's and Mrs Upward's cheek on the last day. Gideon doesn't kick up too much because he knows Samantha's father is going to give him £500 to pay the school fees. (The middle classes often use Christmas to hand over money, so the recipient won't feel any loss of independence.) In revenge Colonel and Mrs Upward take Zacharias and Thalia to the pantomime in Bournemouth, where all over the theatre you will hear grandparents making cracks about their daughters-in-law.

'We would have had much better seats and been able to see, Thalia darling, if Mummy hadn't been so awfully vague about dates.'

Samantha would have a real Christmas tree, and she would prefer candles, but as a result of pressure from Zacharias, and worry about the fire risk, she has this year stuck to fairy lights. She insists on Thalia and Zacharias writing thank-you letters to show how good their hand-writing is. She and Gideon always get glasses as presents to make up for all the ones smashed during the year.

Mrs Nouveau-Richards has a vast silver plastic Christmas tree, groaning with tinsel. Jen Teale insists on a plastic tree too this year; she had to get last year's tree out by Boxing Day because it was moulting pine needles so badly. She hangs the Christmas cards on strings across the lounge to avoid dust. Samantha regards Christmas cards as a marvellous excuse not to dust.

Christmas cards are a great class indicator in themselves. The upper classes like simple words inside their cards like 'with best wishes for Christmas and the New Year'. If they have special cards printed, they only put their address at the bottom and write in their Christian names, or their Christian and surnames to those they know less well. The Weybridges have 'Howard and Eileen Weybridge' printed as well, and cross out the 'Weybridge' for their 'very good friends.' Mrs Nouveau-Richards has a very large card with a picture of jolly cardinals quaffing claret in front of a roaring fire, and inside a lovely poem about festive cheer, 'Hearty Xmas Greetings' and their name and address in red, loopy, spangled writing. Jison, as a member of the telly-stocracy often puts 'Yours Aye' or 'Sincerely Yours, Jison Richards' on his cards, which are usually of Santa with a red nose. Harry Stow-Crat would write 'Love', particularly if he were writing to a girl.

The spiralists have a photograph of themselves and their family on the front of their Christmas cards with a bigger and bigger house in the background, as the years go by. It is *extremely* vulgar to send your friends a roneo-ed letter bringing them boastfully up-to-date with all the doings of your family: 'Daughter Avis is now chairwoman of the Surbiton Ladies' Guild and still joint chairperson with her brother Roy of my late, beloved Hector's company, Upstarts Polishing and Machine Tool Grinding Review.'

Samantha Upward insists on buying cards to support a charity, usually painted with someone's feet. Mrs Definitely-Disgusting only sends cards to relations. She chooses one with 'To a Very Special Daughter' for Sharon, and 'To a Fine Son' for Dive, and inside underlines the bits in the poem which she thinks are applicable. Sharon and Dive club together to send a 'Dearest Nana' card to Mrs D-D's mother.

Eileen Weybridge thoroughly enjoys the festive season. Her house is a picture of yuletide holly rings, white-washed twigs, and tinsel and ribbon decorations from *Good Housekeeping*.

She has also followed to the letter an article in the *Barclaycard News Magazine* on organizing your Christmas menu, which starts off: 'With a little planning, Xmas can be a holiday for all the family', and continues with instructions about embarking on a mammoth shopping spree with your Barclaycard, getting the family 'to clean the cutlery in November', trying a 'portion of Minty Ice Cream for dinner on 3rd of December, just to test it's acceptable for Christmas night' and making kedgeree on the 5th of December to go in the freezer for breakfast on Christmas eve. Howard Weybridge is delegated to cope with the booze bill with *his* Barclaycard, and even the turkey is cooked in advance and sliced ready for re-heating. Howard brings home a festive gift box from Bentalls, and a special carrier bag full of fancy goods from the fairy grotto as a special prize for Cook.

Jen Teale also comes into her own at Christmas. Everyone comments on the daintiness of her gifts. She knows that how you wrap a parcel is so much more important than what's in it. Even boxes of chocolates are now smothered in brightly coloured gift-wrap (as she calls wrapping paper) and topped with tasteful concentric circles of coloured ribbon, just like Harrods. She also bakes all the 'Christmas Fayre' without the aid of a deep freeze, because she follows the *Woman's Own* guide for keeping bandbox fresh over the 'Festive Season'.

The Definitely-Disgustings have a real blow-out. They've contributed 50p a week all year to the Christmas Club and this year Mr Definitely-Disgusting is personally going to see that the treasurer doesn't abscond with the lot on the 22nd of December. Sharon Definitely-Disgusting trails round Woolworths with a list saying:

Nan:	Devon Violets
Mum:	Giftpack
Dad:	Condor Tobacco
Dive:	Brut
Auntie Dot:	Thomas and Sarah's brandied peaches
Marlene:	Bendy Kermit
Mr Whiskas:	Catnip Mouse
Spotty:	Bumper Xmas Choc Drops

The whole family is glued to I.T.V. over the holiday, although Mr D-D, after a surfeit of turkey and all the trimmings, snores his way like a good patriot through the Queen's speech. Spotty, having demolished the bumper Xmas Choc Drops, the Catnip mouse and a stolen turkey bone, is sick.

23 DEATH

O happy release, where is thy sting?

At last we come to Death the Leveller who lays his icy hand on Stow-Crats and Definitely-Disgustings alike. Poets over the ages have been haunted by the theme. Shakespeare wrote of golden lads and girls mingling in the dust with chimney-sweepers. Hardy described the yokels William Dewy and Tranter Reuben lying in Mellstock churchyard beside the Squire and Lady Susan. But even if we are all equal in the moment of death, the living see that our departure is celebrated in very different ways.

Once upon a time funerals were occasions for great pomp—with a long procession of carriages drawn by horses wearing floor-length black velvet, with everyone including the children in deepest black, men and boys doffing their hats along the route, and close relations going into mourning for several months. An outward and lavish display was regarded as a measure of the family's affection for the dead. But, like most fashions, it filtered down the classes, withering at the top, until today only among the working classes, who are usually much closer to their families and like any excuse for a party, does the tradition of the splendid funeral linger on.

Attitudes have changed too. In Victorian times everyone accepted and talked naturally about death. Given the rate of infant mortality, it would have been impossible even for a child to be shielded from the subject. Sex was the great taboo, with copulation never mentioned, and babies being born under gooseberry bushes. Today everyone talks about sex and birth quite naturally, it is death that has become taboo. Perhaps it is because most people no longer believe in an after-life that they cannot face up to the horror of death and so sweep everything under the carpet. In the old days a man died surrounded by his family; the Victorian deathbed was one of the great set pieces. Today, according to Geoffrey Gorer's excellent book, *Death, Grief and Mourning*, in the upper-middle and professional classes it is rare for a bereaved person to be present at death (less than one in eight).

The undertaker would pick up the body from the hospital, and none of the family would pay respects to it. In the same way, Samantha Upward or Jen Teale, even if their mother died at three o'clock in the morning, would be on to the undertaker in a flash to get the body out of the house. The Definitely-Disgustings, however, would be much more likely to be present at the death, and to visit the body if they were not. When I worked on a local paper, whenever a working-class person died I was always invited in for a cup of tea to admire the corpse lying in his coffin in the sitting room. As cremation gets more and more popular, too, the ashes tend to be left with the undertaker, and even a grave to mourn at is disappearing. According to our local undertaker, the middle classes often prefer not to watch that poignant final moment when the coffin disappears through the doors. They specify beforehand that they don't want the coffin to move, and troop out while it's still on its platform.

Fear of expressing unhappiness is also a character-istic of the upper middles—the stiff upper-middle lip again. Geoffrey Gorer said his own sister-in-law didn't even go to her husband's funeral, she was so terrified of breaking down in front of all her friends and relations and, wishing to spare the children such a de-pressing experience, took them for a picnic. Yet as a bereaved person, she found herself shunned like a leper. Only if she acted as though nothing of conse-

quence had happened was she again socially acceptable. Thus, not only death but overt suffering is taboo.
Perhaps this explains the plethora of euphemisms surrounding the subject. Howard Weybridge never 'dies',
he 'passes away', or 'passes on', or 'passes over', or 'goes
to God' or 'to his rest'. Death is even described as 'falling
asleep'. 'Flowers' become 'floral tributes'; even the undertaker prefers to call himself a 'funeral director', and
describes a burial as an 'interment'.

Harry Stow-Crat's father, Lord Egliston, would have
had a nice end to his life. He had made everything over
to Harry to avoid estate duty, and all the family have
been frantically cosseting him to keep him alive the
required five years. 'My father's great dread was going
senile,' said one aristocrat, apologising for his father
who was happily exposing himself in the orangery. 'But
now he has, he's enjoying himself enormously.' Since
his father's death would be noticed on the obituary
page, Harry might not bother to pay for an insertion
in the deaths column. If he did, it would be simple,
saying where his father had died, and where and at
what time the funeral would be held. Gideon Upward
would also put his mother's death in *The Times*, and
he might add her age (Samantha certainly would, out
of spite) and the fact that she was the widow of Colonel
Upward. Howard Weybridge would use the *Telegraph*.
Jen Teale would use the local paper and add a sentence
about 'passing peacefully away', and being the 'loving
mother of Bryan and devoted granny of Wayne and
Christine. The Definitely-Disgustings would probably
throw in 'a happy release', and 'a special auntie to
Charlene and little Terry', and a 'thank you' to the
nurses, doctors and district nurses concerned.

When a peer, a peeress in her own right or a baronet
dies it is customary for letters written to members of
his or her family to be addressed to them by the titles
by which they were previously known until after the
funeral. Consequently if a friend wrote to Harry saying

how sorry he was about the death of Lord Egliston, he would address the letter to the Hon. Harry Stow-Crat, and if *The Times* reported the funeral they would describe him in the same way. At the memorial service a fortnight later he would be called Lord Egliston.

Old Lord Egliston's funeral would be simple. Harry would wear a dark suit and a black tie, Caroline would dress soberly but not in black. Relations and friends might have to walk across the fields while the coffin was carried to the family church, which means Gucci shoes sinking into the cowpats. Although it is more upper class to be buried than cremated it is frightfully smart to *have* to be cremated because your family tomb is so full of your ancestors going back to the year dot that there is no room for you. Lord Egliston might just squeeze into the family grave. The headstone, when it was up, would bear a simple inscription: 'Henry George De Vere Stow-Crat, 5th Baron Egliston, born 12 April 1905, Died 23 April 1979'. People would send flowers picked from their own gardens with plain cards saying 'With Love' or 'In Loving Memory' in their own handwriting. Being old-fashioned like the working classes, they might also send wreaths. Afterwards, everyone would go back to lunch or tea, where, depending on the stuffiness of the family or on the intensity of the grief, a certain amount of drink would be consumed.

When very important men die, what diplomats describe as a 'working funeral' takes place, which means that heads of state from all over the world meet on neutral ground and, while pretending to admire the wreaths, the Chinese and American foreign secretaries can discuss matters of moment out of the corners of their mouths without appearing to fraternize.

The upper-middles would probably drink themselves silly at the funeral, although a few years ago this would have been frowned on. When my husband, in the early 'sixties, announced that he intended to leave £200 in his will for a booze-up for his friends, his lawyer talked him out of it, saying it was in bad taste and would upset people. The same year his grandmother died, and after the funeral, recovering from the innate vulgarity of the cremation service when the gramophone record stuck on 'Abi-abi-abi-abi-de with me', the whole family trooped home and discovered some crates of Australian burgundy under the stairs. A rip-roaring party ensued, whereupon a lower-middle busybody who lived next door came bustling over to see if anything was wrong. My father-in-law, seeing her coming up the path, uttered the immortal line:

'Who is this intruding on our grief?'

Today, however, anything goes. Samantha Upward would probably get drunk out of guilt when her mother died. She had taken her mother in when she was widowed and bedridden, but it hadn't been a success. Having lived apart for so long, it was a terrible shock when they had to live together. The upper-middles have little respect for the wisdom of age, and Samantha got very irritated when her mother gave her advice about the children or running the house, and Samantha's mother missed her friends in Bournemouth terribly. Our local undertaker also said that the better educated people are, the more matter-of-fact they are about death. They treat the undertaker like a professional and let him get on with it, not quibbling about the price. Usually only the family send flowers; everyone else is asked to send the money to charity instead. A month later everyone gets smashed out of their minds once again at the memorial service.

When Mr Nouveau-Richards dies of a heart attack, Mrs Nouveau-Richards is worried about how she should arrange things. They don't report smart funerals in *The Tatler* for her to copy. She turns up at the church in deepest black with a huge picture hat and lots of make-up. All Jison's telly-stocracy friends turn up and keep a weather eye out for photographers and television cameras. The men wear light-coloured suits and cry a lot. The girls also wear deepest black and picture hats, but cry less in case their mascara runs.

All Mr Nouveau-Richard's business colleagues send wreaths with black-edged funeral cards with 'Deepest Sympathy' printed on them. Mrs Nouveau-Richards insists on the undertakers wearing the full regalia of top hats, pinstripe trousers, and umbrellas.

After he was buried in the cemetery (Caroline Stow-Crat calls it a 'graveyard') Mrs N-R would have a splendid tomb built in strawberry roan marble, and engraved with ornate sentiments about Mr N-R 'crossing the bar to his eternal rest', and being 'the beloved father of Jason and Tracey-Diane'.

The Teale's would be very stingy and question the price of everything. Jen thinks death is 'not very naice', and would expect the undertaker to do everything. She wouldn't want the hearse outside the house. She and Bryan would drive the Volkswagen to the funeral. After all there's nothing to get upset about: Bryan's mother was 'very elderly' and had been a 'senior citizen' for a long time. There would be no 'sobbing' at the funeral; that's what the Definitely-Disgustings do. Bryan's mother would probably be cremated as it's cheaper, although if she did have a grave, Jen wouldn't want the bother of tending it, so, instead of grass, the flat bit would be sprinkled with emerald green chips which serve the same function as plastic grass. Floral tributes would be particularly tasteful, and Bryan would probably wear a black armband on his sleeve for a few weeks afterwards.

The Definitely-Disgustings really push the boat out. 'I'm going to Florrie's funeral tomorrow,' I heard one working-class Yorkshire woman saying. 'It should be a good do,' a sentiment that would never be expressed by the middle classes.

Mr Definitely-Disgusting even insured for the purpose of being buried right, but, alas, with the cost of living the policy seldom comes anywhere near covering the cost of the funeral, which means Mrs D-D is likely to be left penniless and in debt. The problem, said our local undertaker, is to stop people overspending in a fit of emotionalism. Often they get quite annoyed.

'Are you trying to tell me my missus doesn't deserve the best?' said one man.

One train driver's widow, who could ill afford it, forked out for six cars and a very expensive panelled coffin. Afterwards she came and thanked the undertaker, adding that it was worth it, 'Even if I have to go out scrubbing for the rest of my life to pay for it.'

In the old days the streets used to be sanded to deaden the sound of the horses' hooves. And even today whole streets in the North and in Wales will show solidarity by drawing every curtain from the moment the hearse leaves the house until the funeral party returns.

The working classes still send funeral cards with poems inside and pictures of lilies and purple prayer-books on the front, which are displayed on the window sill outside drawn curtains. Often the men go out specially to buy a black suit, and often as many as six cars filled with tearful relations follow the hearse. Frightful rows ensue, too, because someone who thinks he's important enough to travel in the second car only gets a seat in the third car. Invariably, according again to our local undertaker, its the 42nd cousin once removed who screams and cries the loudest because he's been on the booze since dawn.

At the funeral of a cockney gypsy who had married again after his first wife died, the first wife's family were lined up on one side of the grave, the second wife and her family on the other, each glaring across at the other. As the coffin was lowered the first wife's son shook his fist at the second wife, hissing, 'He's gone to lie with a good woman now'. Whereupon the son of the second wife nipped round the back, pushed the first wife's son into the grave and jumped on top of him. A glorious free-for-all resulted, which was only stopped by the arrival of the police.

With the floral tributes the working classes really come into their own. Once again, because of their inability to express themselves verbally, they spell it out with flowers. On the hearse are likely to be cushions and pillows with 'Mum' written across, empty chairs saying 'We'll Never Forget You, Dad', teddy bears or favourite dogs for the death of a child, bleeding hearts, harps with a broken string, all made entirely of flowers. Around the Elephant and Castle people often pay tribute to a man's profession. One East-Ender had a whole market stall full of fruit and vegetables, with all the price tickets, made entirely of different-coloured carnations, which took six men to lift onto the hearse. A landlord is often given a glass of foaming beer made entirely of white and brown chrysanthemums, while a bookie might have a floral winning post. One East-End boxer had his last fight almost to scale, with a ring, a referee and two boxers—all made of daisies. A florist told me the working classes would consider it insulting to give someone a small posy of spring flowers. If an old age pensioner comes into the shop and you steer her towards something that looks within her price range, she still insists on buying long-stemmed chrysanthemums at £1 a flower.

The party afterwards will be a terrific booze-up with crates and crates of beer and masses of stodgy food. One scrap-metal merchant even put up a marquee in his garden. Everyone gets plastered and then does song and dance acts. David Storey told me how he once went to a friend's funeral in Yorkshire. Not knowing the dead man's family, it was only after freezing beside the grave for twenty minutes that he discovered, on asking one of the mourners, that he was at the wrong funeral.

'Never mind, lad,' comforted the mourner, 'they'll all be meeting up at the Black Bull same as us afterwards'.

After the funeral Sharon and Dive would club together to buy Mr D-D a headstone, perhaps inscribed with the words 'Have a Good Sleep, Dad'. They would also put another entry in the local paper thanking everyone for their condolences and floral tributes. A year later, it would be considered very remiss if an *In Memoriam* notice didn't appear in the same paper:

> God took Dad home.
> It was his will.
> But why that way
> We wonder still.

> *Always in our thoughts, fondest love,*
> *Doris, Dive, Sharon, Auntie Edna and little Terry.*

Quite often there will be additional notices from several other members of the family. Because the working classes tend not to take part in local affairs, birth, marriage and death, or when they get caught nicking a telly, are the only times they get their names in the paper. Howard Weybridge might put an *In Memoriam* to Eileen in the *Daily Telegraph*, or even one to his elder brother who was killed at Anzio.

Finally our heroes reach the Other Side. How will they fare in the after-life? Harry Stow-Crat is thoroughly enjoying himself. He is just expressing delight at seeing Snipe and Nanny again when suddenly a beautiful angel flaps past and Harry can't decide whether to take a pot at her or ask her out to lunch. Jen Teale is speechless with admiration at the whiteness of the angels' robes and wonders whether they use a bio-wash. Mr Nouveau-Richards, having examined the burglar alarm on the Pearly Gates, is boasting to God how much better his own gates on earth were wired up against intruders, and how none of the pearls are as big as the ones he gave Mrs N-R for their silver wedding. Jison is just about to ask Jesus for an in-depth interview. Howard Weybridge is having a round of golf with the Holy Ghost, and Mr Definitely-Disgusting is having a lovely time playing golden oldies on the harp and filling in his football coupon for the match against Limbo in the afternoon.

Only Samantha Upward looked perturbed. Who would have thought, she keeps murmuring to herself disconsolately, that God would say, 'Pleased to meet you', when we arrived?

SCORE!
by Jilly Cooper

Sir Roberto Rannaldini, the most successful but detested conductor in the world, had two ambitions: to seduce his ravishing nineteen-year-old stepdaughter, Tabitha Campbell-Black, and to put his mark on musical history by making the definitive film of Verdi s darkest opera, *Don Carlos*. To achieve the latter, he enlists the help of his charismatic French godson, Tristan de Montigny, the hottest director in Europe, who is capable of coaxing magical performances out of the most wayward and wooden prima donnas.

As Rannaldini, Tristan and the entire cast, headed by Rannaldini s capricious mistress, Hermione Harefield, demand total artistic control, the recording is stormy. But nothing compares to the ructions that occur when filming begins in Rannaldini s haunted fourteenth-century abbey. To disgruntled spooks, temperamental singers and histrionic set designers is added a glamorous but bolshy French film crew determined to pull everything in sight, particularly the tempestuous Tabitha, now employed as Mistress of the Horse.

All the women — and several of the men — are determined to pull Tristan. To their disappointment, he is only interested in keeping the movie on track. But as he battles to boost the morale Rannaldini is hell bent on destroying, Tristan finds himself increasingly drawn to Tabitha — which Rannaldini will *not* tolerate. Then the news leaks out that Rannaldini is writing his memoirs, revealing dreadful secrets about everyone, and his fate is sealed.

But as Rutshire CID and the world s press pour in, doubts grow that Rannaldini is really dead. Or is it his ghost stalking the abbey cloisters in outrage that his arch-enemy, the tone-deaf Rupert Campbell-Black, has taken over as executive producer?

Terrifyingly creepy, by turns wildly funny and unashamedly romantic, *Score!* is Jilly Cooper s most thrilling novel to date. But it is also a story, like *Don Carlos*, about loneliness in high places, and heroism and passionate love triumphing against the odds.

NOW AVAILABLE FROM BANTAM PRESS

0 593 04226 3

A LIST OF OTHER JILLY COOPER TITLES
AVAILABLE FROM CORGI BOOKS
AND BANTAM PRESS

THE PRICES SHOWN BELOW WERE CORRECT AT THE TIME OF GOING TO PRESS. HOWEVER TRANSWORLD PUBLISHERS RESERVE THE RIGHT TO SHOW NEW RETAIL PRICES ON COVERS WHICH MAY DIFFER FROM THOSE PREVIOUSLY ADVERTISED IN THE TEXT OR ELSEWHERE.

* Including VAT

All Transworld titles are available by post from:

Bookpost, P.O. Box 29, Douglas, Isle of Man IM99 1BQ

Credit cards accepted. Please telephone 01624 836000, fax 01624 837033, Internet http://www.bookpost.co.uk or e-mail: bookshop@enterprise.net for details.

Free postage and packing in the UK. Overseas customers allow £1 per book (paperbacks) and £3 per book (hardbacks).